MARLENE'S MAGIC
WITH
FOOD STORAGE

- **Hundreds of Incredible Meals**
- **Vital, Useful Information**
- **Organizing and Preparing**
- **Food Storage for Today**

ACKNOWLEDGMENTS

I wish to express my appreciation to those who have aided me in this project, for their help and suggestions have proven to be of great value. My daughters, Delayne Bolick and Dennette Welling, my sisters Margaret Steinkopf and Evelyn West, and my niece Julie Steinkopf have provided endless hours in typing the manuscript, writing the foreword, editing, proofreading, illustrating and designing this book. This has involved a great deal of work and many long hours. Thank you very much.

I would like to thank my husband, Klyde L. Petersen, for his loving support. His love and prayers in my behalf have brought me great joy.

To all others, too numerous to mention, who I have worked, talked, taught and learned from over the years, thank you.

Finally, I would like to thank all of you who have been patiently awaiting the printing of this book. I sincerely hope that, in some small way, it will help you establish your own food storage program and that you will begin to share your understanding with others.

—Marlene Petersen

Printed in the United States of America
Nineteenth Printing; March 2009

TABLE OF CONTENTS

SPECIAL HELPS 3

CALCULATING YOUR FAMILY STORAGE 11

SHELF LIFE 13

NUTRITION 16

FOODS FOR BABIES 19

SPROUTING 20

COOKING TIPS ON BEANS 22

RECONSTITUTING DEHYDRATED FOODS 23

DRYING FRUITS AND VEGETABLES 24

BREAKFAST 25

SALADS 43

SOUPS 65

WHEAT ENTREES 83

MEAT ENTREES 90

RICE ENTREES 113

BEAN ENTREES 123

PASTA ENTREES 135

BREADS 143

DESSERTS 165

ESSENTIALS 211

TOFU 230

WORK SHEETS 248

ABOUT THE AUTHOR

Marlene Petersen has demonstrated a love and extraordinary talent for simple, yet tasty, as well as gourmet cooking for over 40 years.

Her love for cooking was kindled during childhood, when given the responsibility to cook daily for ten siblings. Since then Mrs. Petersen's experience has included managing and supervising others in restaurants, running a private catering service for six years, then starting her own professional catering service in 1978. Her talent continues to delight the palate of many to the present.

Mrs. Petersen is the mother of 12 children. She has managed and taught practicality in her daily cooking without foregoing excellence and taste. She has instructed many church, private and public groups on simple, practical and gourmet cooking. She has also instructed and shared her ideas with these same groups on food storage methods and use. As an author, Mrs. Petersen shares her talent for integrating dry foods and home canned products into daily cooking. She offers an excellent repertoire of cooking technique using these two food types.

WHAT THIS BOOK IS ABOUT

Great artists produce magic with palettes, brushes, canvas, and clay. Great music is created by the musician's touch to inspired notes and the wave of a baton. And the art of great food preparation begins in the kitchen of the author, Marlene Petersen.

Discover how to turn "dry" into delicious! This book combines gourmet attributes with the very basic: food storage.* The author has taken her extraordinary talent for gourmet cooking and applied it to creating tantalizing dishes from the "food storage" cupboard. Best of all, the recipes are easy to prepare. And, as you learn to cook with stored foods watch your food budget stretch! The recipes can also be easily adapted to ingredients found on the local store shelf.

As additional features, Marlene includes "starting from scratch" recipes such as homemade noodles, cottage cheese, cream cheese, sourdough starter, English muffins, tortellini shells, etc. The author shares practical tips on nutrition. Many of the recipes are low calorie and/or low fat, cholesterol free, and contain important nutritional needs. Also throughout the book are hints on how to organize and purchase food for storage based on your own individual need.

Departing from the main theme of this book, Marlene has included a section of her all time favorites for Holiday cooking!

Even if you already own cookbooks that present the concept of dry cooking, this book gives a refreshing twist. No one would ever guess these dishes came from the food storage shelves. This book will become one of your most cherished and well-worn cookbooks.

Dennette Welling
Annette Hullinger

*Dry food and home canned goods

2

SPECIAL HELPS

FOOD STORAGE AND NUTRITION

This section focuses on a good basic food storage system. It explains how to organize your food storage, what quantity to store, and which food items should be your priority in storing foods based on their nutritional value. If your only source of food was your home food storage, could you survive? The foods recommended for storage in this section provide all the essential nutrients necessary for survival.

The following charts begin with the "scratch" basic storage ending in a complete food storage system. Each step explains what can be made from the products you buy. Those foods marked with an asterisk (*) are foods that are very high in nutrients and are life sustaining.

FOOD STORAGE INVENTORY

What can I do with what I have?

STEP 1

IF I HAVE:
Basic Food Storage:
>   **Wheat
>   Powdered Milk
>   *Oil, canola or olive
>   Salt
>   Honey or Sugar
>   *Water

I CAN MAKE:

Sprouted Wheat
Cooked Cracked Wheat
Tortillas
Gluten

**Wheat has long been considered the most important "stock" item in a food storage system, not only for its shelf life but for its exceptional nutritional value. However, people who are unable or allergic to wheat can substitute with other foods such as soybeans, almonds, milk and eggs, and receive the same nutrient content.

STEP 2

IF I ADD:

    Yeast
    Baking Powder
    *Powdered Eggs
    Baking Soda

I CAN MAKE:

    Sprouted Wheat
    Cooked Cracked Wheat
    Tortillas
    Custards
    Puddings
    Pancakes
    German Pancakes
    Cookies
    Waffles
    Muffins
    English Muffins
    Crepes
    Pasta
    Breads
    Biscuits
    Crackers
    Mayonnaise
    Egg Noodles

5

STEP 3

IF I ADD:

Butter, powdered
Tomatoes
Cheese, powdered

I CAN MAKE:

Sprouted Wheat
Cooked Cracked Wheat
Tortillas
Crackers
Custards
Puddings
Pancakes
Cookies
Waffles
Muffins
English Muffins
German Pancakes
Crepes
Egg Noodles

Pasta
Breads
Biscuits
Mayonnaise
Meatless Dinners
Meatless Casseroles
Meatless Dinners
Cream Sauces

STEP 4

IF I ADD:

Unflavored Gelatin
*Canned Milk
Canned Fruits

I CAN MAKE:

Sprouted Wheat
Cracked Wheat
Tortillas
Custards
Puddings
Pancakes
Cookies
Waffles
Muffins
English Muffins
German Pancakes
Crepes
Egg Noodles
Pasta
Breads
Biscuits
Crackers
Mayonnaise

Meatless Dinners
Meatless Casseroles
Cream Sauces
Jello Salads
Whipped Cream Desserts
Baby Formula

STEP 5

IF I ADD:

Soup Base
Rice
*Legumes, soybeans
      and others
Beef Broth
Chicken Broth
*Alfalfa Seeds
*Sesame Seeds
Miso

I CAN MAKE:

Sprouted Wheat
Cracked Wheat
Tortillas
Custards
Puddings
Pancakes
Cookies
Waffles
Muffins
English Muffins
German Pancakes
Crepes
Egg Noodles
Pasta
Breads
Biscuits
Crackers
Mayonnaise

Meatless Dinner
Meatless Casseroles
Cream Sauces
Jello Salads
Whipped Cream Desserts
Baby Formula
Hearty Dinner Soups
Chili
Refried Beans
Rice Dishes
Rice Puddings
Fresh Sprouts
Gluten
Hot Broth

STEP 6

IF I ADD:

Canned Meats
Dried Potatoes

I CAN MAKE:

Sprouted Wheat	Meatless Dinners
Cracked Wheat	Meatless Casseroles
Tortillas	Cream Sauces
Custards	Jello Salads
Puddings	Whipped Cream Desserts
Pancakes	Baby Formula
Cookies	Hearty Dinner Soups
Waffles	Chili
Muffins	Rice Dishes
English Muffins	Rice Puddings
German Pancakes	Refried Beans
Crepes	Fresh Sprouts
Egg Noodles	Gluten
Pasta	Dinners
Breads	Casseroles
Biscuits	Sandwiches
Crackers	
Mayonnaise	

STEP 7

Extras

Oats, Raisins, Nuts *(almonds), Chocolate Powder,
Peanut Butter Powder, Granola, Juices,
Corn Starch, Soup Mixes, Spices and Flavorings, Lemon Powder or Juice, White Flour,
Shortening or Margarine, Cream of Tartar, Junket Rennet Tablet, Molasses, Karo Syrup, Raw
Bran, etc,.

STORAGE

Since each family's needs are different--the size of family, the amount of food they consume, and their likes and dislikes--it is difficult to apply a single food storage program to meet the needs of every family. Only you know what your family consumes and in what quantities. Keeping a well-balanced diet in mind, I've listed selected food items, giving a standard quantity of the food item, then indicating a serving size of that item and how long it would last given the standard quantity. Depending on what your family's projected average use of any food item is in a given time period, you determine from the following exactly what your family would consume in a year.

For example, the quantity given on wheat is 350 lbs. A family who projects they use 2 cups (serving size) of wheat per day would need to store 350 lbs. of wheat to last one year. If, however, you calculated your family would use only 1 cup of wheat per day, the quantity given would last your family 2 years. Continue calculating in this manner with the remaining food items you choose to store. Although it may take a little more effort on your part, the result is much more efficient, and tailored to your family's needs.

ITEM	QUANTITY	DURATION/SERVING SIZE
1 WHEAT	350 lbs	This would give you 1 lb. (2 cups) of dry wheat per day for one year.
2 POWDERED MILK	50 lbs	This would be approximately 800 glasses of milk or 2 1/2 glasses of milk per day for one year.
3 OIL	12 gallons	Approximately 1/2 cup oil per day. We cannot live without some fat in our diet.
4 SUGARS AND HONEY	100 lbs	This is approximately 200 cups or 1/2 cup per day for one year.
5 WATER	14 gallons	This is enough water for 2 weeks for one person.
6 EGGS, WHOLE POWDERED	12 #10 cans	This would give you 1 can per month. Eggs are important for baking and very nutritious. Your body utilizes egg's protein the best. They contain calcium, iron, Vitamin K, Manganese, phosphorus, magnesium, sodium, protein, and lecithin.

7	BUTTER, MARGARINE, OR SHORTENING, POWDER	1-#10 can	This would be 42 1-oz servings.
8	TOMATO POWDER	1-#10 can	This would be 42 1-oz servings.
9	CHEESE, POWDERED	1-#10 can	This would be 64 1/4-cup servings.
10	CANNED EVAPORATED MILK	150 cans	This would be 12 to 15 cans per month or 3 cans per week. Families without babies would not need as many. Canned milk has needed fat that powdered milk does not contain.
11	RICE, SOYBEANS, AND OTHER LEGUMES	100 lbs	This would give you approximately 1/2 cup dry beans per day.
12	BEEF/CHICKEN BOUILLON	1-#10 can	One can has approximately 300 teaspoons or 300 1-cup servings.
13	CANNED MEATS	120 cans	A variety of different meats would be useful. This would be 2 1/4 cans per week for one year.
14	POTATO FLAKES	1-#10 can	This would be approximately 30 1/2-cup servings.
15	VEGETABLE STEW	1-#10 can	This would be approximately 56 1/2-oz servings.
16	DEHYDRATED SWEET PEAS	1-#10 can	This would be 42 1/2-cup servings.
17	DEHYDRATED SWEET CORN	1-#10 can	This would be 35 1/2-cup servings.
18	DEHYDRATED GREEN BEANS	1-#10 can	This would be 46 1/2-cup servings.
19	DEHYDRATED CARROTS, DICED	1-#10 can	This would be approximately 75 1/2-cup servings.

20	DEHYDRATED BROCCOLI	1-#10 can	This would be 70 1/2-cup servings.
21	CHOPPED ONIONS	1-#10 can	This would be 80 1/4-cup servings
22	POPCORN	1-#10 can	This would be 150 3-cup servings (popped).
23	OATS, REGULAR	1-#10 can	This would be approximately 24 2/3-cup servings.
25	PEANUT BUTTER POWDER	1-#10 can	This would be 42 2-tablespoon servings.

SHELF LIFE

Storing food correctly means storing it at 68° or less. High temperature for prolonged periods will destroy your food storage.

Dehydrated food contains more nutrition than any other method of preserving.

NITROGEN PACKED DEHYDRATED FOODS

Beef Bouillon	5 years
Chicken Bouillon	5 years
Creamy Soup Base	5 years
Cooking Cocoa	7 years
Apple Slices	8 years
Banana Slices	8 years
Broccoli	8 years
Chopped onions	8 years
Corn, sweet	8 years
Cheese powder	3 to 5 years
Dehydrated Raisins	8 years
Diced Carrots	8 years
Egg Mix	3 to 5 years
Eggs, whole	3 to 5 years
Eggs, whites	3 to 5 years
Fruit Cocktail	8 years
Dehydrated Mushrooms	8 years
Instant Nonfat Milk	3 to 5 years

Nonfat Milk	3 to 5 years
Powdered Margarine	3 to 5 years
Peanut Butter Powder	2 years
Potato Flakes	8 years
Potato Slices	8 years
Split Peas	10 years
Sweet Peas	8 years
Tomato Powder	8 years
Vegetable Stew Mix	8 years

NITROGEN PACKED DRIED FOODS

Almonds	5 to 7 years
Brown Rice	2 years
Cereal (Nine Grain)	8 years
Cereal (Six Grain)	8 years
Cornmeal	8 years
Pearl Barley	8 years
Popcorn	8 years
Oats, Regular	8 years
Salt 15 years	
Shortening Powder	3 to 5 years
Soup Mix	8 years
White Flour	5 years
White Sugar	10 years
Wheat, whole kernel	20 years
White Rice	10 years

HOME CANNED OR CANNED PRODUCTS

Fruits	18 months to 3 years
Meats	18 months to 3 years
Evaporated Milk	18 months to 3 years
Vegetables	18 months to 3 years
Yeast	2 years frozen or 1 year shelf
Oil	1 year
Spices	3 years or longer (Chili powder, Poppy Seeds and Sesame Seeds should be kept frozen)
Baking Powder	3 years
Baking Soda	3 years

Recommended Dietary Allowances

	Age	Weight lbs.	kg.	Calories	Protein (g)	Calcium (mg)	Iron (mg)	A (mcgR.E.)	C (mg)	D (mcg)	Thiamin (mg)	Riboflavin (mgN.E.)	Niacin
Children	1-3	29	13	1300	23	800	15	400	45	10	0.7	0.8	9
	4-6	44	20	1700	30	800	10	500	45	10.0	0.9	1.0	11
	7-10	62	28	2400	34	800	10	700	45	10.0	1.2	1.4	16
Males	11-14	99	45	2700	45	1200	18	1000	50	10.0	1.4	1.6	18
	15-18	145	66	2800	56	1200	18	1000	60	10.0	1.4	1.7	18
	19-22	154	70	2900	56	800	10	1000	60	7.5	1.5	1.7	19
	23-50	154	70	2700	56	800	10	1000	60	5.0	1.0	1.6	18
	51+	154	70	2400	56	800	10	1000	60	5.0	1.2	1.4	16
Females	11-14	101	46	2200	46	1200	18	800	50	10.0	1.1	1.3	15
	15-18	120	55	2100	46	1200	18	800	60	10.0	1.1	1.3	14
	19-22	120	55	2100	44	800	18	800	60	7.5	1.1	1.3	14
	23-50	120	55	2000	44	800	18	800	60	5.0	1.0	1.2	13
	51+	120	55	1800	44	800	10	800	60	5.0	1.0	1.2	13
Pregnant					76	1200	48-78	1000	80	10.0	1.4	1.5	15
Lactating					64	1200	48-78	1200	100	10.0	1.5	1.5	18

Source: Food and Nutrition Board, National Academy of Sciences -- National Research Council

NUTRITION SECTION

A successful food storage program involves more than just storing a large amount of food. Calories alone do not sustain life. Following, the author briefly highlights the function of *some* of the essential nutrients needed to sustain life and the various sources of each.

Calcium

Calcium is important to every cell in the body (muscles, nerves, heart, bones). Calcium deficiency contributes to diseases that proceed 90% of all deaths. Sources include milk, cheese, egg yolk, apricots, figs, prunes, cranberries, gooseberries, dates, cabbage, spinach, parsnips, lettuce, onions, bran, tops of vegetables, alfalfa sprouts and yogurt.

Iron

Iron's essential function in the blood is as an oxygen carrier. It promotes vitality and energy and is necessary for the formation of red blood corpuscles. It aids in the prevention of amnesia. Sources include apples, beets, carrots, celery, mushrooms, peaches, liver, oysters, egg yolk, potato peelings, whole wheat, black strap molasses, soy beans and strawberries.

Lecithin

Lecithin is a fatty substance occurring in many foods. It is believed that Lecithin renders the cholesterol harmless. Anyone fearing hardening of the arteries or high blood pressure should get plenty of Lecithin. It is found in largest quantities in egg yolks and soy beans.

Manganese

Manganese is important in controlling the nerves in the body. It coordinates thought and action and it improves memory. Sources include egg yolk, almonds, walnuts, watercress, mint and parsley.

Magnesium

Magnesium prevents and relieves constipation. It relaxes nerves, refreshes the system and promotes new cells in the body. Sources include grapefruit, oranges, figs, apples, cashew nuts, celery, chives, dates, grapes, soy beans, corn, wheat, goat's milk, egg yolk.

Proteins

Sometimes referred to as the "age vitamin." All parts of your body are dependent upon protein in some way for survival. Protein deficiency can cause kidney disease, liver disease, peptic ulcers, poor wound healing, lack of resistance to infection, fatigue, irritability, low blood sugar and in severe deficiencies, mental retardation. Proteins cannot be stored in the body for long. Every body needs a continuous daily supply of protein to maintain health. Primary sources include meat, fish, fowl, milk, eggs. Other protein sources do not supply all needed amino acids but can be substituted supplementing amino acids in other foods. For example, soybeans have a high protein content. Supplementing the soybeans with peas would give the needed protein plus amino acids found in meats.

Vitamin C

Vitamin C in large doses can lower blood cholesterol. Vitamin C also helps in calcium absorption.

Vitamin K

Vitamin K is concerned with the clotting factor and has been known to rebuild teeth. Sources include leafy vegetables, liver, egg yolk, yogurt and alfalfa sprouts.

Vitamin A

Vitamin A is essential for proper growth of children. Throughout life it is needed for healthy skin, normal eyesight, germ-resistant linings of nose, throat, and lungs.

green and yellow vegetables	carrots	broccoli	carrots
	dandelion	parsley	milk
cantaloupe	egg yolk	spinach	
tomato	sweet potato	beets	
alfalfa sprouts	tops of vegetables	squash	

Vitamin E helps all of the other vitamins work in your body.

sunflower seeds	wheat germ, raw	pecan halves	almonds
peanut butter	hazelnuts	alfalfa sprouts	salmon

Fats

Everyone needs a moderate amount daily--one to two tbsp.--to supply energy and to provide the fat soluble vitamins A, D, E, and K and essential fatty acid, lanolic acid!

Pregnant mothers who do not have enough protein and fats in their diets may produce retarded or slow babies; children from ages 1 to 6 may also suffer if they do not get enough fat.

Beans and Other Legumes

Legumes are the richest source of protein in the vegetable kingdom. The protein content of beans ranges from 20 to 25 percent, except soybeans, which may contain as much as 40 percent protein. Beans are an excellent source of Iron, Niacin, Phosphorous, Potassium, Vitamin B1 and B2. A good amount of Calcium is also present in beans. When sprouted, beans lose some of their starch and gain more nutrients. (See SPROUTING section.)

Dried peas are 22 percent protein and contain all eight of the essential amino acids. When sprouted they have a flavor similar to fresh peas. (See SPROUTING section.)

Lentils

Lentils contain substantial amounts of Vitamin B, Iron and Phosphorous and small amounts of Vitamins C and E, which are increased when sprouted. (See SPROUTING section.)

Soybeans

Soybeans are an excellent meat substitute because they contain up to 40 percent protein. They are rich in Vitamin B and contain many minerals. Lecithin is an important product extracted from soybeans which has been used to reduce blood cholesterol.

Peas

Dried peas are 22 percent protein and contain all eight of the essential amino acids. When sprouted they have a flavor similar to fresh peas. (See SPROUTING section.)

Rice

Whole brown rice is an excellent source of niacin and contains an appreciable amount of Vitamin E. Rice has a small amount of Vitamin C which is markedly increased when the grains are sprouted. The protein content of rice is only about 7 percent, but it contains all eight of the essential amino acids.

Sesame Seeds

100 grams of whole sesame seeds contains 1125 milligrams of calcium, whereas two glasses of cows milk contains only 500 milligrams. Sesame seeds are 18 percent

protein and provide a well balanced source of essential amino acids. They are good suppliers of Vitamin B1, Niacin and small amounts of Vitamin E. The abundance of Calcium and Lecithin makes sesame a valuable aid in preventing cholesterol from collecting in the blood.

Wheat

Hard wheat contains more protein than any other cereal except oats. The wheat grains have a high content of Thiamine and Niacin. Wheat contains little fat and is rich in Vitamin E. Although wheat contains little Vitamin C, it is increased 600 percent during early sprouting. Vitamin E and Niacin are also increased during sprouting. (See SPROUTING section.)

Alfalfa Sprouts

Sprouting almost any edible grain or seed increases nutritional value as noted in the following examples. (For more information on sprouting, see SPROUTING section which follows.) However, alfalfa is king of sprouts. Alfalfa sprouts provide a good source of Vitamins A, B, C, D, E, G, K and U. They contain vital cell building amino acids. Alfalfa sprouts are also a rich source of minerals such as Phosphorus, Chlorine, Iron, Silicone, Aluminum, Calcium, Magnesium, Sulfur, Sodium and Potassium. Because of the especially high chlorophyll content of alfalfa it contributes to the healing process and sweetens the breath. Alfalfa sprouts contain 35 percent protein which is higher than most meats.

Almonds

Almonds are superior to other nuts in that their protein content is 18%. They are rich in Calcium and Potassium. When sprouted they are crisp and crunchy. (See SPROUTING section.)

FOODS FOR BABIES

ALMOND MILK 221
BABY FORMULA 224
BREAD PUDDING 167
GRAHAM CRACKER 160
RICE PUDDING 165
TOFU (section) 230
WHOLE WHEAT CEREAL 224

SPROUTING

Sprouting is one of the fastest ways of improving the nutritional value of foods. During sprouting, the starch is changed to simple sugar. This is the reason why so many sprouts may be eaten raw. Any seed can be sprouted. Use them in place of lettuce or in combination with it, in salads, sandwiches, soups, main dishes and breads.

There are several methods of sprouting, but the most simple and inexpensive is the jar method. Use a quart jar, covering the amount of seeds needed with a generous amount of lukewarm water, let soak 8 to 12 hours or overnight. Cover jar with plastic screen or cheese cloth lid, then drain (you may save water for plants or cooking). Rinse with lukewarm water until water is clear. Lay jar on side and place in dark warm cupboard. Rinse two or three times daily. Rinse mung beans or garbanzos more often, and in warmer water. Be sure to drain well.

On the fifth day, place only the alfalfa in the light of the kitchen (not in the sun) to gain vitamin A and chlorophyll. When seeds are finished, give a final rinse, cover airtight and refrigerate, ready to use and enjoy.

For larger amounts, make a wooden tray with strong plastic screen across the bottom. Metal, glass, or plastic trays act as radiators and draw the heat from the sprouts and dispel it into the room. This will retard the growth of the sprouts.

For almonds and oats, use the paper towel method. Place a wire rack inside a glass tray or stainless steel pan. (Rack makes it possible for air to circulate around seeds.) Soak a two-layer thickness of paper towels in water. Squeeze out excess water. Spread the damp towels over the rack, leaving room at two ends for air to circulate. Scatter pre-soaked seed evenly over the surface of the towels. Cover loosely with another double thickness of moist towels. Do not cover with towel when sprouting oats. Slip container into a plastic bag, leaving the end open for air. Place in the cupboard. To water the seeds, remove the top layer of towels; sprinkle seeds with water and re-soak the top layer of towels, squeezing out excess moisture each time. Water only enough to provide a moist atmosphere.

Some sprouts should be harvested before the first leaves are fully developed. Sunflower seeds, wheat and other grains are best when the root is only as long as the seed. Alfalfa sprouts however, should be between 2 and 2 1/2 inches with 2 green leaves. To prevent further growth, store sprouts in the refrigerator.

Alfalfa sprouts in sprouting tray
Place 1/3 cup seed in bowl and soak overnight or for 8 hours. Drain and place into sprouting tray. Set lid on top and place on sink or cupboard. Rinse and drain 4 times per day. On the fifth day leave lid off. Store in the refrigerator in a covered container.

Amounts to sprout:	Time needed for sprouting:
Alfalfa 1 to 2 Tbsp	4 to 5 days
Beans 1/8 to 1/4 C	3 to 4 days
Lentils 3/4 C	3 to 4 days
Wheat, Oats, or Rye 1/4 C	3 to 4 days
Radishes 2 or 3 Tbsp	3 days

Buy seeds for sprouting from your health food store. Never use seeds for sprouting that have been treated for planting. Discard any broken seeds.

QUICK ALFALFA PICKUP　　　EXCELLENT!　　　LOW FAT

In a blender, liquify 1 cup of alfalfa sprouts with 2 cups pineapple or orange juice and 1 banana. Sweeten to taste. You can add 2 tablespoons of chopped, sprouted cooked soybeans or almonds, or you may use any nut butter.

You can replace the nuts in any recipe with chopped, sprouted soybeans. This will also add Vitamin C, etc.

Chopped or whole sprouts may be added to meat loaves, casseroles, soups, stews, and all types of salads. Always add them just before serving to ensure crunchy goodness and to prevent vitamin loss.

A new and delightful taste treat is chopped sprouted soybeans added to peanut butter for making sandwiches. Chopped, sprouted soybeans added to pancakes are extra good.

Try them in cookies, or cake recipes and also add them to your breakfast cereals. Your children will think they are nuts. Add the sprouts of mung, lentil, or soybean to your favorite bean recipe. You may also add them to your split pea recipes and to all pasta dishes. Try sprouts sauteed with onions or peppers. Also try with tomatoes.

SPROUTING DRY BEANS

Wash and sort beans; place in large bowl with 6 cups of water per pound of beans. Let stand overnight, or at least 12 hours. Drain and rinse, then put beans into a sprouting container.

To sprout in a quart jar, measure 1 cup of soaked beans and cover with a piece of nylon net secured with a rubber band or jar ring, or use a commercial sprouting lid.

In a sprouting tray or strainer cover with a layer that is 2 or 3 beans thick.

Cover and place in a warm area like the kitchen sink, rinsing and draining at least 2 times a day with warm water. The rinsing and draining is the most important of the sprouting process.

Within 2 days most fresh seeds will have sprouted as long as the seed. Older seeds may take as long as 5 days. Be sure to rinse and drain thoroughly, as older seeds easily become slimy.

SOAKING DRY BEANS

Dry beans, whole peas, and split peas need soaking before cooking. Lentils do not.
• Overnight soak: Wash and sort beans; place in large sauce pan with 6 cups of water per pound of beans. Let stand overnight.
• Quick soak: Follow above instructions, but bring beans and water to a boil and cook 2 minutes. Remove from heat, cover, and let stand 1 hour.
IMPORTANT: Cook Soybeans 5 to 7 hours.

FLATULENCE FREEING AGENTS FOR BEANS

EPAZOPTE - Purchase at a Mexican food specialty store. (Tie in a cheese cloth bad and cook with the beans.)
KOMBU - Purchase at health food stores. (It is a sea weed product and contains complete minerals.) Kombu will cook completely with beans and give added flavor.

COOKING TIPS

If a recipe calls for lemon juice, vinegar or tomatoes, wait until the beans are almost tender before adding them, as the acid in these items slows the softening process.

At high altitudes or in hard water areas, increase both the soaking time and cooking time.

Gently simmer beans to prevent them from bursting, causing floating skins which must then be skimmed off of soups or stews.

Two to three teaspoons of oil or butter added during cooking reduces foaming and boil-overs

RECONSTITUTING DEHYDRATED FOODS

Nonfat Powdered Milk   2 cups nonfat powdered milk to 1 gallon water
                             1/2 cup nonfat powdered milk to 1 quart water

Mix with a wire whip or in a blender with cold water. Let stand several hours or refrigerate before drinking.

Powdered Whole Eggs   1 Tablespoon egg powder to 1-1/2 Tablespoons water equals
                            1 egg

Make a paste with egg powder and a few drops of water. Blend until smooth then add remaining water.

Butter, Margarine, and Shortening Powder
                            1 cup powder to 1/4 cup water

Combine butter powder and water and stir into a smooth paste. Makes 1 cup

Dehydrated Fruits   1/3 cup dehydrated fruit to 1 cup water

Add water to dehydrated fruit and let set overnight or for several hours. Makes 1 cup.

Dehydrated Vegetables   1/3 cup dehydrated vegetables to 1 cup water.

Add water to dehydrated vegetables and let set overnight or for several hours. Makes 1 cup.

The recipes in this book measure the ingredients in their reconstituted state unless otherwise mentioned. For example, 1 C dehydrated butter, reconstituted would be 1 cup of the butter powder reconstituted in 1/4 cup of water.

DRYING FRUITS AND VEGETABLES

Vegetables and fruits should be placed on a frame made of 1 x 4 inch material. A fine mesh screen wire on top and bottom of a lower section and screen on top only of an upper section. These two sections are connected by hinges. This arrangement keeps bugs off the food being dried.

Allow fruits and vegetables to dry in hot sun for 2 to 3 days then transfer to a cloth bag to hang and air in sunshine, being bought in at night. No dips or preservatives need be used. Peeled apples and unpeeled pears may be sliced 1/4 inch thin and laid flat on the screen. To reconstitute the dried fruit, cover with warm water and let stand for a few hours. Vegetables may be soaked before cooking or adding to soups or stews. For longer storage these keep well in the freezer.

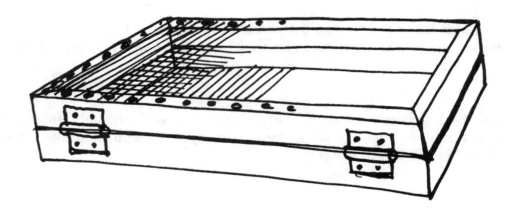

NOTE: Fruit Leather recipe on page 216.

BREAKFAST

CRACKED WHEAT CEREAL

1 C cracked wheat
*4 C boiling water
1 tsp salt (optional)

Add wheat gradually to boiling water so that the water continues to boil. Cover pan and turn flame down until wheat barely simmers. Then gently simmer 25 to 35 minutes. Stirring is necessary.

COOKED WHOLE WHEAT

1 C whole wheat
1 tsp salt
2 C boiling water

Bring water to boil, add wheat gradually. Turn heat down and simmer for 3 to 6 hours. If made the night before, it is very good mixed with cracked wheat cereal. Add more water if necessary.

EZEKIEL PANCAKES AND WAFFLES

2 cups Ezekiel flour (see pg. 229)
2 cups milk
2 eggs
2 teaspoons baking powder
1 teaspoon salt
1/4 cup oil, melted shortening, butter, or
    margarine.

Beat together and cook as usual.

PACKAGE CEREAL

3 C nonfat reconstituted milk or 3 C
   buttermilk
2 Tbsp honey
1/2 tsp molasses (optional)
4 C whole wheat flour
1 tsp soda
1/2 to 7/8 C packed brown sugar
1 tsp salt

Mix first 3 ingredients until dissolved. Combine and mix dry ingredients together. Combine milk mixture with flour mixture. Beat until smooth. Spread 1/4 inch thick on at least two cookie sheets. Bake at 350° for 45 minutes or until crisp, and golden. If center is not crisp remove edges as they become brown to prevent burnt edges. Let cool, then grind in a food grinder with coarse blade. Store in air tight container. Makes 6 cups cereal.

GRAPE NUTS

6 C whole wheat flour
1 1/2 C brown sugar
1 tsp salt
2 C buttermilk
1 tsp soda

Mix and press or roll onto 2 cookie sheets and bake at 300° for 1 hour, or until dry. Grind with a meat grinder to the size of grape nuts and put in oven at 400° until golden brown, about 8 minutes. After grinding, the crumbs may be sifted from the cereal. Use the crumbs in place of crackers to make a crust.

HOMEMADE COLD CEREAL

3 C milk
2 Tbsp honey
4 C whole wheat flour or 3 C whole wheat
   flour and 1 C oatmeal
1 tsp soda
1 C (not packed) brown sugar
1 tsp salt

Mix milk and honey together. Add wheat flour, soda, brown sugar, and salt and mix thoroughly. Beat until smooth. Spread 1/8 to 1/4 inch thick on 2 or 3 greased cookie sheets. Bake at 350° for 35 to 45 minutes until golden crisp. Remove edges if cereal starts to brown to much. Cool thoroughly, then break up into flakes or grind with a coarse blade. Store in an air tight container. Makes up to 6 cups cold cereal.

Note: TOFU APPLE SAUCE GRANOLA see Tofu Section

BRAN FLAKES

2 C bran
2 C whole wheat flour
1/2 C nonfat powdered milk
3 Tbsp brewer's yeast (optional)
1 tsp salt
1/4 C oil
1 Tbsp molasses
1 C water

Combine dry ingredients. Make a well in the center and add oil, molasses and water. Mix well. Divide into three parts and roll out as thin as possible on greased cookie sheets. Bake at 350° for 15 to 20 minutes, or until lightly browned and crisp. If dough is not completely dry, turn oven off and let it remain longer. Break into small pieces. Store in an airtight container. Makes 1 lb cereal.

EXCELLENT!

GRANOLA

6 C oats
1 C nonfat powdered milk
1 C coconut
1 C whole wheat flour
2 C oat bran or wheat germ
1 C chopped almonds or
1 C peanut butter
1 C sesame seeds
1 C pumpkin seeds
1 C sunflower seeds
2 tsp cinnamon
1 C salad oil
1 C honey
1 C raisins

Stir all dry ingredients in a large bowl. Mix salad oil and honey together and add to mixture in bowl. Mix well. Pour into large pans and bake at 250° for 1 hour, stirring every 15 minutes. Be sure it is light brown and done. Add raisins while granola is still warm.

EXCELLENT!

GRANOLA VARIETY

6 C rolled oats
1 C shredded coconut
1 C wheat germ
1 C chopped nuts
1 C hulled sunflower seeds
1/2 C sesame seeds
1/2 C bran
1/2 C oil
1/2 C honey
1/2 C brown sugar
1/2 C water
2 Tbsp vanilla

In a large bowl, mix oats, coconut, wheat germ, nuts, sunflower seeds, sesame seeds, and bran. Warm oil, honey, sugar, water, and vanilla over low heat, then combine with dry ingredients. Spread on cookie sheets and bake at 350° for 20 to 30 minutes, stirring often. Cool and place in an air tight container. Raisins, currants, or dates may be added as desired.

WHEAT PUDDING
(Can be used to introduce children to wheat cereal)

6 C water
1 1/2 C wheat flour (coarse grind)
1/2 C sugar
1/2 C nonfat milk, reconstituted
3 eggs, separated

Bring 4 of the 6 cups of water to a rolling boil. In blender, whirl wheat flour with remaining 2 cups of cold water. Pour this wheat mixture into the boiling water, beating with a wire whisk. Cook 10 minutes on low heat, stirring continually so as not to burn.

In blender, whirl milk, egg yolks and sugar. Add to cooked wheat, stirring continually.

Beat egg whites until very stiff. Beat 1 cup of the hot wheat mixture into the egg whites, then add remaining wheat mixture. Serve in dishes topped with strawberry or raspberry jam and whipped cream. Can also be topped with a scoop of ice cream.

WHOLE WHEAT BUTTERMILK PANCAKES

3 C whole wheat flour
3 tsp baking powder
1/3 C oil
3 eggs,* reconstituted, or 3 fresh eggs
3 C buttermilk or powdered milk

Mix all ingredients together with a wire whip. If dough is too thick, add 1/2 C water.

(Buttermilk makes a lighter pancake.)

*Dehydrated eggs, to reconstitute mix 1 Tbsp water with 1 Tbsp whole egg powder. Beat in a blender to get rid of the lumps.

HONEY SYRUP

1 C honey
1 cube margarine or butter
1/2 tsp cinnamon

Heat honey and margarine in a saucepan over low heat, until melted. Add cinnamon. Stir well.

GERMAN PANCAKES

5 eggs
2 1/2 C milk
1 C flour <u>or</u> 1 C whole wheat flour
Pinch of salt

Whirl all ingredients in a blender or beat well by hand. Pour small amounts into a greased frying pan. Fry like a crepe.

POPOVERS

4 eggs
2 C powdered milk, reconstituted
2 C flour
1 tsp salt

Heat oven to 450°. Grease 12 deep custard cups. (5 oz.) With hand beater beat eggs slightly. Add milk, flour, and salt. Beat just until smooth. Pour into individual cups and place in oven. Bake at 450° for 20 minutes, then reduce temperature to 350° and bake for an additional 20 minutes. Do not open oven while baking. Remove from cups immediately.

WAFFLES

3 eggs
2 C buttermilk
1 C flour <u>or</u> 1 C whole wheat flour
2 tsp baking powder
1 tsp baking soda
1/4 C oil
1/2 tsp salt

Separate eggs. Beat egg yolks with buttermilk. Add oil, then stir in flour which has been mixed with baking soda and baking powder. Fold in stiffly-beaten egg whites.

Heat waffle iron. Pour 1/2 cup batter into center of waffle iron. Bake about 5 minutes or until golden brown. Makes 8 waffles.

NOTE: German pancakes are good served with strawberry and whipping cream, apple sauce and whipping cream or Honey Syrup.

PFANNKÜCHEN

(German oven pancake)

EXCELLENT!

1/2 C flour
3/4 C fresh eggs or 4 eggs reconstituted in
3/4 C water
1/2 C powdered milk, reconstituted
5 tsp margarine melted or 5 tsp oil
2 C sliced fruit, such as bananas, peaches, strawberries, or berries
2 Tbsp sour cream
Brown sugar

Preheat oven to 450°. Gradually add flour to eggs. Stir in milk and melted margarine or oil. Lightly oil or spray with non stick spray a 9 inch or 10 inch oven proof skillet (round cake pan works also). Pour batter into skillet and place in oven. Bake for 20 minutes. Do not open oven while baking. Pancake will form a well in center and sides puff up. Remove from oven and place on a large plate. Spoon fruit in center of pancake. Top with sour cream and brown sugar. Serve immediately. Makes 2 servings.

Note: A pfannküchen is wonderful for brunches or late night snacks.

QUICHE LORRAINE

10 inch pie pastry shell
4 thin slices of ham or 12 slices of bacon
1 C grated swiss cheese
5 eggs
1 1/4 C nonfat powdered milk reconstituted
1 1/4 C canned milk
1/4 tsp salt
1/8 tsp red pepper
1/2 tsp Season All
Dash of nutmeg

Cut ham into small pieces (should be about 3/4 cup) and heat in fry pan for a few minutes. Sprinkle into pastry shell. If using bacon, cook bacon until crisp, then crumble into small pieces. Sprinkle cheese on ham. Beat eggs and add remaining ingredients. Mix well. Pour over cheese and ham or bacon. Bake at 375° for 40 minutes. Serves 8 to 10.

ENGLISH MUFFINS

EXCELLENT!

4 C flour
1 tsp salt
1 Tbsp dry yeast
1/2 C warm milk or 1/2 C reconstituted
    nonfat milk
Sugar
1 C warm water
1/4 C butter, softened
Corn meal

Sift flour and salt together. Combine yeast with warm milk and set aside for 5 minutes. Mix in water and sugar. Work in 2 cups flour mixture and let stand 1 1/2 hours.

Beat in softened butter and remaining flour. Place dough on board which has been covered lightly with corn meal. Cover and let rise.

Roll out dough 1/2 inch thick on the cornmeal covered board. Cut in 4 1/2 inch circles (use a tuna fish can). Let stand 20 min.

Heat a lightly-oiled electric fry pan or hot griddle. Place muffins in fry pan and cover with lid. Fry for 5 to 7 minutes.
Turn and fry second side for another 5 to 7 minutes.

LOW FAT

EXCELLENT!

SUPER-HEALTHY CARROT BRAN MUFFINS

1 1/2 C All Bran or raw bran
1 C boiling water
1/2 C oil
1 1/2 C brown sugar
1/4 C honey
3 whole eggs, reconstituted
1 pt buttermilk
2 1/2 C whole wheat flour
3 1/2 tsp baking soda
1 1/2 C oatmeal
1 1/3 C shredded carrots or reconstituted
    carrots
3/4 C raisins
1 tsp salt

Note: When using raw bran use 1/2 C
    more boiling water.

Pour boiling water over All Bran and set aside for 10 minutes. Beat oil, sugar and honey until well blended. Add eggs, one at a time, beating well after each addition. Stir in buttermilk and soaked bran cereal. Mix all dry ingredients together in separate bowl. Add dry ingredient mixture to egg mixture. Mix well. Stir in oatmeal, carrots, and raisins. Let stand 1 hour or overnight in refrigerator.

Heat oven to 350°. Fill greased muffin cups 2/3 to 3/4 full with batter. Bake 25-35 min. Makes 36.

BLUEBERRY PUMPKIN MUFFINS

1 2/3 C flour
1 tsp baking soda
1/2 tsp baking powder
1/2 tsp salt
1 tsp cinnamon
1/2 tsp allspice
1 C canned pumpkin
1/4 C evaporated milk
1/3 C shortening
1 C packed brown sugar
1 egg
1 C blueberries
1 Tbsp flour

Combine first 6 ingredients. Combine pumpkin and milk until blended. Cream shortening and sugar in a large mixing bowl. Add egg. Beat until mixture is fluffy. Add flour mixture alternately with pumpkin mixture, beating well after each addition. Combine blueberries and flour. Gently stir into batter. Fill 18 paper-lined muffin tins 3/4 full. Sprinkle Streusel (below) over top. Bake at 350° for 40 minutes. Makes 18.

STREUSEL

2 Tbsp flour
2 Tbsp sugar
1/4 tsp cinnamon
1 Tbsp butter

Combine flour, sugar and cinnamon together. Cut in butter until crumbly.

APPLE BANANA MUFFINS

2 C whole wheat flour
1 1/2 C oatmeal
1 tsp salt
5 tsp baking powder
1/2 tsp baking soda
1 1/2 tsp cinnamon
1/2 tsp cloves
1/2 tsp allspice
1/2 tsp nutmeg
1 C nonfat milk, reconstituted or 1 C
    buttermilk
1/2 C honey
1/2 C mashed banana
1/2 C applesauce
2 eggs

Stir dry ingredients together in a large bowl. In a separate bowl, combine wet ingredients and beat at high speed for one minute. Combine the two mixtures together and beat just until moistened. Grease muffin tins. Fill each 3/4 full. Bake at 400° about 10 to 12 minutes.

MAPLE BRAN MUFFINS

3/4 C natural wheat bran
1/2 C milk
1/2 C maple syrup
1 egg, lightly beaten
1/4 C oil
1 1/4 C whole wheat flour
3 tsp baking powder
1/2 tsp salt
1/3 C chopped walnuts

Combine bran, milk and maple syrup. Mix in egg and oil. Combine remaining ingredients. Add bran mixture, stirring until moistened. Divide batter into 12 greased muffin cups. Bake at 400° for 18 to 20 minutes. Glaze while still warm.

GLAZE

1 Tbsp butter
1/2 C powdered sugar
1 Tbsp maple syrup

Combine ingredients, stirring to blend and spread over warm muffins.

OATMEAL APPLE MUFFINS

1 egg
3/4 C nonfat milk, reconstituted
1 C raisins
1 chopped apple
1/2 C oil
1 C flour
1 C quick oats
1/3 C sugar
3 tsp baking powder
1 tsp salt
1 tsp nutmeg
2 tsp cinnamon

Beat egg. Stir in remaining ingredients, mixing just until moistened. Fill 12 greased muffin cups about 3/4 full. Bake at 400° for 15 to 20 minutes.

POPPY SEED MUFFINS

3/4 C sugar
1/4 C soften butter or margarine
1/2 tsp grated orange peel
2 egg
1 C flour
1 C whole wheat flour
2 1/2 tsp baking powder
1/2 tsp salt
1/4 tsp nutmeg
1 C milk
1/2 C chopped pecans
1/2 C golden raisins
5 Tbsp poppy seeds

Cream the sugar, butter or margarine, and orange peel together. Add eggs, one at a time, beating well after each addition. Combine flours, baking powder, salt and nutmeg. Add to creamed mixture alternately with milk, beating well after each addition. Fold in raisins, nuts, and poppy seeds. Spoon batter into greased muffin cups to about 3/4 full. Bake at 400° for 20 minutes. 12 Muffins.

CRANBERRY ORANGE MUFFINS

1 egg, beaten
1 C milk
1/4 C vegetable oil
16 oz whole cranberry sauce
1 tsp grated orange peel
1 1/2 tsp orange extract
1 C flour
1 C whole wheat flour
1/3 C sugar
1 Tbsp baking powder
1 tsp salt

Heat oven to 400°. Grease 12 muffin cups. Mix egg, milk, oil, cranberries, orange peel, and orange extract. Add remaining ingredients all at once. Stir just until flour is moistened. Batter will be lumpy. Fill muffin cups about 3/4 full. Sprinkle tops with sugar. Bake until golden brown, about 20 minutes. Remove from pan immediately. Makes 12.

HONEY CRUMB CAKE

2 Tbsp sugar
3 Tbsp warm water
1 1/2 Tbsp active dry yeast
1/2 C milk
2 Tbsp butter
3 1/4 C flour, (1/2 wheat flour can be used)
1/4 tsp salt
3/4 C sliced almonds
3 Tbsp raisins
1 egg, beaten

Filling and Topping:
4 Tbsp butter
4 Tbsp sugar
1/3 C honey
1/2 tsp cinnamon
1 C chopped almonds

To make yeast dough, stir a pinch of sugar into water and sprinkle in yeast. Let stand 5 minutes. Boil milk in a small saucepan. Stir in remaining sugar and butter. Cool. Sift flour into a large bowl. Add salt, almonds, and raisins. Combine yeast, egg and milk mixture. Add to flour. On a floured surface, knead dough until smooth. Cover and let rise in a warm place for 20 minutes. Grease a 9 inch springform pan. Roll out dough to a 12x14 inch rectangle.

To make filling and topping, spread half of butter over dough. Sprinkle with half of the sugar and cinnamon. Roll up from shorter end. Cut into 1 inch slices. Heat remaining butter, honey, remaining sugar, and almonds in small saucepan over low heat. Pour dissolved honey mixture into pan. Form balls from dough slices. Arrange in pan. Let rise in a warm place for 35 minutes. Preheat oven to 375°. Bake for 30 minutes or until golden brown.

YOGURT BREAKFAST CAKE

1/2 C margarine or butter
1 1/2 C brown sugar
2 C whole wheat flour (ground fine)
1/4 C white flour
1 egg or 1 powdered egg, reconstituted
1 C sour milk or yogurt
1 tsp baking soda
1/4 tsp cloves
1/4 tsp cinnamon
1/2 tsp salt

Preheat oven to 350°. With pastry blender, cut brown sugar and flour into margarine or butter until mixture resembles crumbs. Set aside one cup of mixture. To remaining crumbs, add remaining ingredients and beat thoroughly. Spoon into greased 9x15 pan. Sprinkle reserved crumbs on top. Bake for 30 minutes or until cake springs back when touched lightly.

EXCELLENT!

HAM STRATA

8 slices white bread, crust removed
1 C ham, sliced and chopped
4 slices sharp Cheddar cheese
2 C milk
4 eggs
1 tsp minced dry onions
dash of pepper
1/2 tsp salt
1/4 tsp dry mustard

Layer bread on greased 9x13 pan. Spread ham and cheese on top. Mix remaining ingredients in a blender and pour over bread. Set in the refrigerator overnight then bake at 325° for 1 hour.

CREPE BATTER

2 1/2 C nonfat milk, reconstituted
1 C flour
Pinch of salt
2 whole eggs, reconstituted
1 Tbsp melted butter or oil
Oil or butter for frying

Sift flour with salt into bowl. Make a well in the center of the flour and add eggs. Pour in half of the milk slowly, stirring constantly. Stir in melted butter or oil. Beat well or until smooth.

Add remaining milk, cover and let stand at room temperature for at least 30 min before using. The batter will thicken as it stands. If it is too thick, add a little more milk.

Heat crepe or omelet pan over moderate heat. Add a few drops of oil or butter. Turn pan so it is well coated. Add 2 or 3 tablespoons butter, immediately rolling it around clockwise to coat base of pan evenly. Cook over fairly high heat until crepe is light brown. Turn quickly.

Cooked crepes can be frozen. Place waxed paper between each crepe. Wrap and freeze.

NOTE: See ENTREES for chicken filling for crepes.

WHOLE WHEAT CREPE BATTER

2 C nonfat milk, reconstituted
1 C whole wheat flour, finely ground
Pinch of salt
2 whole eggs, reconstituted
1 Tbsp melted butter or oil
Oil or butter for frying

Sift flour with salt into bowl. Make a well in the center of the flour, and add eggs. Pour in half of the milk slowly, stirring constantly. Stir in melted butter or oil. Beat well or until smooth.

Add remaining milk, cover and let stand at room temperature for at least 30 min before using. The batter will thicken as it stands. If it is too thick, add a little more milk.

Heat crepe or omelet pan over moderate heat. Add a few drops of oil or butter. Turn pan so it is coated. Add 2 or 3 tablespoons butter, immediately rolling it around clockwise to coat base of pan evenly. Cook over fairly high heat until crepe is light brown. Turn quickly.

Cooked crepes can be frozen. Place waxed paper between each crepe. Wrap and freeze.

NOTE: See ENTREES for chicken filling for Crepes on pg. 99.

APPLE FILLING FOR CREPES

6 large apples
2 tbsp flour
1/2 C each brown and white sugar
3/4 tsp cinnamon
1/4 tsp nutmeg
1/8 tsp each salt and ginger
1 tbsp lemon
3 tbsp butter or margarine

Cook apples adding enough water not to burn. Cook until firm. Add rest of ingredients except flour. Mix small amount of water with flour to make a paste, add and cook until thick. Cool and fill crepes. Top with whipping cream.

BASIC CREPES

3 eggs
1/2 C milk
1/2 C water
3 Tbsp butter, melted
3/4 C flour
1/2 tsp salt

Blender Method: Combine all ingredients in blender container. Blend about 1 minute. Scrape down sides of blender, if necessary. Blend until smooth, about 30 additional seconds.

Mixer or Whisk Method: Combine eggs, milk, water, and butter in mixing bowl. Beat until combined. Add flour and salt. Beat until smooth.

Refrigerate batter 1 hour.
Bake following directions above.

VARIATIONS:
PARMESAN CHEESE CREPES: Add 1/4 C grated Parmesan cheese to batter. Stir batter frequently to keep cheese distributed.

HERBED CREPES: Add 1/2 tsp dried dill weed to batter. Stir batter frequently to keep dill distributed.

WHOLE WHEAT CREPES: Substitute whole wheat flour for white flour. Stir batter frequently to keep flour distributed.

CORNMEAL CREPES: Reduce flour to 1/4 C and add 1/2 C cornmeal. Add 1/4 tsp cayenne pepper. Stir batter frequently to keep cornmeal distributed.

NOTE: The exact number of crepes you can bake from this or any other batter depends on a variety of things - the batter itself, the size and type of crepe pan you use, and your skill in pouring or dipping the batter. This batter will make about 2 cups or 12 crepes in a 10 inch crepe pan.

SALMON SOUFFLE CREPES

12 Crepes
4 eggs
1/2 C dairy sour cream
1 16-oz can salmon, drained and flaked
1/2 C fine dry bread crumbs
1/4 C finely chopped celery
1/4 C finely chopped onion
2 Tbsp chopped parsley or parsley flakes
1 tsp seasoned salt
1/2 tsp pepper
1 C mayonnaise
1 Tbsp prepared mustard
1 tsp dried dill weed

Separate one egg and set aside egg white. Beat yolk together with 3 remaining whole eggs and sour cream. Mix in salmon, bread crumbs, celery, onion, lemon juice, parsley, salt, and pepper. Spoon 1/4 C salmon filling down center of each crepe and roll up. Arrange crepes, seam-side down, in buttered 9x13 baking dish. Bake at 375° for 30 minutes. While crepes are baking, stir together mayonnaise, mustard and dill. Beat the reserved egg white until stiff but not dry, just until white no longer slips when bowl is tilted. Gently fold mayonnaise mixture into egg white. Spoon mayonnaise mixture over crepes and return to oven for 5 minutes or until top is lightly browned. Serve immediately. Serves 6.

BASIC QUICHE

1 9-inch baked pie shell
1/2 to 1 C shredded cheese
1/2 to 1 C chopped, cooked, and drained
    meat, seafood, poultry, or vegetable
6 eggs
1 C half and half or milk
1/2 tsp herb or other seasoning
1/2 tsp salt

Sprinkle cheese and meat into pie shell. Beat together remaining ingredients until well blended. Pour over cheese and meat.

Bake at 375° for 30 to 40 minutes, or until knife inserted near center comes out clean. Let stand 5 minutes before serving.

QUICK QUICHE COMBINATIONS

Swiss cheese with: corned beef, onion, dry mustard; chicken or turkey, green onions with tops, poultry seasoning; ham, caraway seed or dry mustard; potatoes, pimento, dill weed

Cheddar cheese with: tuna, tarragon, or dry mustard; green beans, toasted slivered almonds, garlic powder; carrots, walnuts, marjoram or nutmeg; ground beef, mushrooms, onion salt; peas, onion, rosemary.

Muenster or brick cheese with: spinach, bacon, onion; broccoli, oregano; cauliflower, dry mustard; shrimp, dill weed; pork sausage, onion.

QUICK AND EASY BRAN MUFFINS

1/4 C oil
1 egg, beaten
2 Tbsp molasses
1 C milk
1 C bran
1/2 C whole grain flour
1/2 tsp salt
2 tsp baking powder
1/2 C raisins
Sunflower seeds, optional

Combine ingredients in a bowl and mix. Pour into oiled and floured muffin pans or lined muffins tins. Bake at 400° for 20 minutes. Makes 8 muffins.

LOW FAT

EXCELLENT!

PINEAPPLE JUICE DRINK

1/2 C alfalfa sprouts*
1 C unsweetened pineapple juice, cold
1 Tbsp honey
1 ripe banana, sliced

Put all ingredients in a blender and whirl at high speed for 10 seconds.

ALFALFA OMELET

6 egg whites, stiffly beaten
6 egg yolks, lightly beaten
1/4 C evaporated milk
1/2 tsp salt
1/3 C grated cheese
1 C alfalfa sprouts*
1 1/2 Tbsp butter

Mix egg yolks, milk, salt, and cheese. Fold egg whites and sprouts into egg yolk mixture. Melt butter in a very large frying pan. Pour all of egg mixture into pan. Cover and cook on low heat until firm. Fold omelet over and with a pancake turner, gently lift out onto a hot plate. Serves 4.

BREAKFAST RICE

2 C brown rice sprouts*
3/4 C milk
1 C raisins
1/4 tsp cinnamon
1 Tbsp butter
Honey

Put rice, raisins, cinnamon, and milk into a saucepan. Cover and cook over low heat until done, about 30 minutes. Stir in butter and pour into individual bowls. Top with warm honey. Sprinkle with nuts, (optional).

BREAKFAST TREAT

1 ripe banana
2 Tbsp honey
3 apples, grated
3 Tbsp lemon juice
1 C sunflower seed sprouts*
1 C wheat sprouts*
1/2 C light cream
1/2 C wheat germ
Chopped almonds

In a large bowl, mash and whip banana with honey. Grate apples into the bowl and add lemon juice. Mix well and fold in the sprouts, wheat germ, and light cream. Serve in bowls topped with chopped almonds.

CHIVE-CORN MUFFIN

1 C yellow cornmeal
1/4 C flour
2 1/2 tsp baking powder
1/2 tsp sugar
Salt
1 C nonfat powdered milk, reconstituted
2 Tbsp freeze-dried chives or fresh
1 Tbsp butter or margarine, melted

Heat oven to 400°. Grease 12 muffin cups. In a medium bowl, combine cornmeal, flour, baking powder, salt, and sugar. Set aside. In small bowl, combine milk, egg, chives, and butter. Pour all at once into the cornmeal mixture. Stir with a fork only until blended. Spoon 2 tablespoons batter into each muffin cup. Bake until lightly golden, about 20 minutes. Make 12.

SUNDAY BREAKFAST

2 C rye sprouts
1 C sunflower seed sprouts*
3 ripe bananas, thinly sliced
1/2 C raisins
1/4 C pine nuts (optional)
1/2 C yogurt
1 Tbsp honey
2 apples, grated
Chopped almonds

In a bowl, combine sprouts, bananas, raisins, and pine nuts. In a small bowl, whip yogurt and honey until well blended, then stir in grated apples. Spoon sprout and banana mixture into bowls; top with yogurt mixture and sprinkle with nuts. Serves 4.

* See SPROUTING section in the front of the book for detailed information on sprouting seeds.

SALADS

GERMAN POTATO SALAD

EXCELLENT!

8 C cooked and diced potatoes
1/2 C chopped parsley
1/2 C green onion, chopped fine
1 Tbsp prepared mustard
1 1/2 C diced dill pickle
1 1/2 C mayonnaise
1 1/2 tsp summer savory*
1 tsp salt
1/4 C pickle juice

* important spice, easy to grow in your garden

Place potatoes in a large mixing bowl. Add all the remaining ingredients and mix well.

AVOCADO SALMON SALAD

1 1/2 C can salmon, flaked
1/4 C celery, thinly sliced
1/4 C green onions, thinly sliced
1/4 C almonds toasted and slivered
2 avocados

Combine ingredients. Cut avocadoes in half and arrange on salad greens. Spoon salmon mixture on avocadoes. Garnish with more almonds.

TABOULI SALAD

LOW FAT

1 C uncooked bulgur
2 C boiling water
2 tomatoes, finely diced
1 bunch green onions with tops, sliced
3 Tbsp chopped fresh mint <u>or</u> 2 tsp dried
    mint
1 C finely chopped parsley
3 Tbsp olive oil
1/2 C lemon juice
salt and pepper to taste

Three to four hours before serving, place uncooked bulgur in a large bowl. Pour boiling water over bulgur and let soak for 1 hour. Stir occasionally. Drain well.

Return bulgur to bowl and stir in the remaining ingredients. Chill for 2 hours.

SOYBEAN SALAD

LOW FAT

2 C uncooked soybeans
1/2 C each, chopped onions, celery, carrots,
    red cabbage, cucumber, mushrooms, and
    green pepper
1/4 C vinegar
3 Tbsp olive oil
1 tsp soy sauce
1/4 tsp pepper
1 tsp dill weed
salt to taste

Soak soybeans overnight (or sprout for 3 days). In a large saucepan cook beans in enough water to cover, for 5 hours or until tender. Add more water, if necessary. Drain soybeans. If sprouting, you may have to skim the top of the water to remove soybean shells.

Combine all ingredients and chill for one hour or more.

COLE SLAW

EXCELLENT!

1 head green cabbage, finely shredded or
    chopped
3 carrots, grated
2 apples, cubed
1 large can crushed pineapple
1 C raisins
1 C miniature marshmallows
1/2 C honey
1 C mayonnaise
salt to taste

Mix all ingredients together and serve.

CRUNCHY SALMON SALAD

1/2 C mayonnaise
1/4 tsp salt
1/8 tsp pepper
2 Tbsp lemon juice
1 Tbsp grated onion
1/2 C light cream
1-1 lb can salmon, drained and flaked
1/4 C chopped sweet pickles
1/2 C sliced celery
2 C crushed potato chips
lettuce leaves

Blend together mayonnaise, salt, pepper, lemon juice, and grated onions. Stir in cream. Fold in drained salmon, pickles, and celery. Chill. Just before serving mix in potato chips and put on lettuce leaves. Serves 4 to 6.

EXCELLENT!

DOUBLE DECKER SALMON LOAF

Cheese Layer
1/2 Tbsp unflavored gelatin
2 Tbsp cold milk
1/4 C hot milk
3 C cottage cheese
1/4 tsp onion, chopped
1/4 tsp salt

Salmon Layer
1/2 Tbsp unflavored gelatin
2 Tbsp cold water
2 C salmon, flaked
1 C mayonnaise
1/2 C celery, finely chopped
1 Tbsp lemon juice

Soften gelatin in cold milk and dissolve in hot milk; combine with remaining ingredients. Chill until mixture begins to thicken. Pour into a 1 1/2 quart mold which has been oiled. Refrigerate until firm.

Soften gelatin in cold water, then dissolve over hot water. Combine salmon, mayonnaise, celery, and lemon juice. Add gelatine to salmon mixture. Pour over cheese layer, chill until set.

To serve; unmold on a large platter and garnish with watercress and tomato slices.

SALMON LOUIS DRESSING

1/2 C mayonnaise
2 Tbsp whipped cream
2 Tbsp chili sauce
2 Tbsp green pepper, chopped
2 Tbsp green onion, chopped
1 Tbsp ripe olives, chopped
2 hard cooked egg whites, chopped
1/2 tsp lemon juice
Salt and Pepper

Combine ingredients and serve over above salad.

MACARONI SALMON SALAD

2 C macaroni, cooked and cooled
1 C cucumber, diced
1 1/2 lb can salmon
1 Tbsp onion, grated
1 Tbsp parsley, minced
3/4 C mayonnaise
1/2 tsp salt
1/4 tsp pepper

Combine ingredients. Toss together lightly and serve on salad greens. Garnish with French Fried onion rings.

WHEAT, RICE, AND TUNA SALAD

3 C cooked rice
1 C whole wheat, cooked
1 7-oz can tuna
3 Tbsp capers
1 red bell pepper, chopped
1 Tbsp lemon juice
Salt and white pepper to taste
Grated peel of 1/2 lemon
1 to 1 1/2 C mayonnaise
1/3 C minced green onions

Drain tuna and flake with fork. In medium bowl, combine rice, wheat, red pepper, tuna, and onions.

In small bowl, beat together capers, lemon juice, salt and pepper, grated lemon peel, and mayonnaise. Stir dressing into salad. Cover and let stand a few minutes. Serve with parsley sprigs. Serves 4.

WHOLE MEAL SALAD

3 eggs, hard cooked
1 sweet pickle, diced
2 stalks celery, diced
6 radishes, sliced
1 cucumber, diced
1/2 to 1 C salad dressing, thousand island or
    french (optional)
2 C cooked whole wheat
1 large carrot shredded
1/4 C green pepper, chopped
1 C diced ham or other meat, or 1 can tuna
    or shrimp
Sprouts
4 green onions, chopped

Mix all ingredients together and serve on a bed of lettuce with tomato.

SUMMER TUNA MOLD

1 pkg unflavored gelatin
1/2 C cold water
1 1/4 C heated tomato juice
1 8-oz pkg crumbled cream cheese
1 C mayonnaise
1/3 C chopped green pepper
1/3 C chopped onion
1/3 C drained pickle relish
6 1/2-oz tuna, drained and flaked

Dissolve gelatin in 1/2 cold water, add heated tomato juice. Stir until gelatin is well dissolved. Cool, then add cream cheese. Beat until smooth then add mayonnaise. Chill till partly set then add the remaining ingredients.

COPPER PENNIES

5 C peeled, thinly sliced, cooked carrots
    (cook 12 to 15 minutes)
1 C vinegar
1 C sugar
1 onion, thinly sliced
1 green pepper, diced
1 can tomato soup
1 C oil
1 Tbsp dry mustard
4 C whole raw mushroom (optional)
Salt and pepper

Mix together and refrigerate 24 hours before serving.

CRAB SALAD IN ASPIC RINGS

1 8-oz can tomato sauce
1 C hot water
2 whole cloves
1/2 tsp dill seeds
1/2 tsp onion salt
1 Tbsp unflavored gelatine
1/4 C cold water
1 Tbsp lemon juice
1 Tbsp horseradish
1 tsp sugar
1 7 1/2-oz can crab, chilled
1/2 C sliced celery
6 pitted ripe olives, sliced
French dressing
Lettuce and mayonnaise

Simmer first 5 ingredients together 5 minutes. Soften gelatine in cold water; strain hot mixture over it; stir till dissolved. Blend in next 3 ingredients. Pour into 4 or 5 individual ring molds; chill firm. Drain crab and mix with celery and olives. Season lightly with French dressing. Unmold rings on lettuce. Fill with crab mixture and top with mayonnaise.

PEAR-ADISE SALMON SALAD

1 can Bartlett pears
1/4 C French dressing
1 pkg lemon flavored gelatin
1/4 C vinegar or lemon juice
1 tsp each, salt and dry
    mustard
1 lb canned salmon, flaked with liquid
1 C finely diced celery
1 tsp finely chopped onion
1/2 C heavy cream, whipped

Drain pears, reserve liquid. Marinate drained pears in French dressing. Meanwhile, dissolve gelatin in 1 1/2 cups hot pear syrup and water. Add vinegar, mustard and salt. Thicken until syrupy. Add salmon, celery, onion, and whipped cream. Fold into salmon mixture, Pour into greased mold. Chill until firm. Unmold and surround with pears garnished with seasoned dairy sour cream.

BEANS AND CASHEW SALAD

1 bag fresh spinach
1 C chopped broccoli or 1 C dehydrated
    broccoli, reconstituted
1 or 2 C cooked navy or pinto beans
1/2 C Italian dressing
1/4 C toasted cashew bits
1/2 C bacon, cooked and chopped, or bacon
    T.V.P.

Cook broccoli until tender but not soft. Drain and cool. When cooled, combine with beans and Italian dressing. Chill. Wash and dry spinach, discarding stems. Tear into bite-sized pieces. Add spinach and cashews to bean mixture. Sprinkle bacon on top. Toss prior to serving. Serves 4 to 6.

ANCHOVY AND BEAN SALAD

1 small can anchovy fillets
2 C cooked baby lima beans
Dressing below

Cut anchovies into small pieces and add to dressing. Mix with baby lima beans and serve.

Dressing:
1/2 tsp grated onion
2 tsp white wine vinegar
2 Tbsp oil
2 Tbsp heavy cream or can evaporated milk
1 Tbsp chopped parsley

Whisk all ingredients together.

EXCELLENT!

TUNA, BANANA, PINEAPPLE SALAD

3 ripe bananas
1 C drained pineapple, diced
1/4 C celery
1/4 tsp salt
3/4 C salad dressing
2 Tbsp lemon juice
1 7-oz can tuna, drained and flaked
Lettuce

Peel and dice bananas and combine with diced pineapple. In separate bowl, celery, salt, salad dressing and lemon juice. Fold in fruit. Add tuna. Serve on lettuce. Serves 6-8.

SHRIMP, RICE, AND WHEAT SALAD

3/4 C cooked rice
1/4 C cooked whole wheat
1 can shrimp, drained and rinsed
3/4 tsp salt
3/4 C chopped raw cauliflower
1 Tbsp chopped stuffed green olives
1/4 C diced green pepper
1/4 C lemon juice
2 Tbsp French dressing
2 Tbsp sour cream
1/3 C mayonnaise
1 Tbsp chopped green onion
Pepper to taste
Lettuce leaves

Lightly toss together the cooked rice, wheat, shrimp, salt, cauliflower, stuffed olives, and green pepper. Blend together lemon juice, French dressing, mayonnaise, sour cream, onions, and pepper. Pour dressing mixture over salad and toss. Serve in lettuce cups. Serves 4.

BEAN AND CHEESE SALAD

1 C dried red kidney beans or pinto beans, soaked overnight
1 bouquet garni, made from 1 bay leaf, stalk of celery, 4 or 5 parsley stalks.
Salt
1 medium onion, finely chopped
2 tomatoes, peeled, seeded, and cut into strips
2 oz white cheese cut into strips (Gouda, Edam, or Jack)
2 tsp chopped parsley
Black pepper, freshly ground
1/2 C vinaigrette dressing

Drain beans; cover with cold water and add bouquet garni. Bring to a boil and reduce heat. Simmer for 1 hour or until beans are tender. Do not overcook. Cool beans slightly in the liquid, then drain.

Cook onions in boiling salted water for 3 to 4 minutes, or until just tender. Drain. Mix beans with onions, tomatoes, cheese, parsley and seasonings to taste. Spoon over vinaigrette dressing. Cover and chill at least 2 to 3 hours so flavors blend.

SPAM AND BEAN SALAD

4 C cooked beans (can be mixture)*
3/4 C diced green pepper
3/4 C thinly sliced celery
1/2 C chopped onions or 1/2 C reconstituted dried chopped onions
2 Tbsp chopped parsley
2/3 C vegetable oil
1/2 C wine vinegar
1 1/2 tsp sugar
3/4 tsp salt
1/2 tsp garlic powder
Freshly ground pepper to taste
1 C slivered spam
Tomato wedges (optional)

Toss beans with green pepper, celery, onion, and parsley. Combine oil, vinegar, sugar, salt, garlic powder and pepper. Pour over beans. Toss to combine. Cover and refrigerate several hours. Add ham at serving time. Garnish with tomato wedges. Serves 6 to 8.

* Do not overcook beans, and drain immediately after cooking.

MARINATED RAW MUSHROOMS

1 lb mushrooms
3/4 C olive oil
1/2 C tarragon vinegar
1/2 tsp salt
Freshly ground black pepper
2 tsp minced parsley
6 chopped anchovies
2 or 3 cloves garlic, mince

Wash and slice, or leave whole, the mushrooms. Set aside.
Mix all other ingredients together; add to mushrooms and marinate 6 hours before serving.

MARINATED BEAN SALAD

5 to 6 C cooked mixed beans
8 oz Cheddar cheese cut into cubes
1/4 tsp garlic, crushed
1 Tbsp sugar
1/2 C bottled Italian dressing (Low Fat)
1 or 2 cans shrimp, drained
1 jar marinated artichoke hearts (optional)
Lettuce leaves

Combine all ingredients. Marinate in refrigerator about 1 hour. Mound on lettuce leaves. Serves 6.

COMPLETE PROTEIN BEAN AND CORN SALAD

2 C dehydrated green beans, reconstituted
   and cooked
2 C pinto beans, cooked
2 C dehydrated corn, reconstituted and
   cooked
1 C lima beans, cooked
2 C diced fresh tomatoes
1/2 C thinly sliced or chopped onions
Mexicali dressing

Combine all ingredients carefully. Stir to distribute ingredients. Refrigerate overnight. Serves 10 to 12.

Note: Do not overcook beans for salad. Always drain immediately and cool.

MEXICALI DRESSING

1/2 C oil
3 Tbsp lime juice
3 Tbsp white vinegar
1 tsp sugar
1 tsp garlic salt
1/2 tsp crushed oregano
1/8 tsp bottled hot pepper sauce

Combine all ingredients and mix well.

MACARONI SALAD

1 lb macaroni
12 green onions, including tips
4 hard boiled eggs
1 C diced celery
12 strips bacon, crumbled, or Bacon T.V.P.
1 4-oz jar pimento
1 C chopped dill pickles
1 1/2 C mayonnaise
1 Tbsp horseradish sauce
2 tsp prepared mustard
1 Tbsp dill pickle juice
Salt and pepper

Cook macaroni in boiling water. Rinse and drain. Cool. Turn into a large bowl and add green onions, eggs, bacon, celery, pickles, and pimento. Combine mayonnaise, horseradish sauce, pickle juice, and mustard. Blend well. Stir into pasta mixture.

EXCELLENT!

MACARONI SHRIMP SALAD

1 pkg alphabet noodles
1 C mayonnaise
1/2 C green onion, chopped
Salt
1 C shrimp
1 C sour cream
1 small jar green stuffed olives, finely chopped
Garlic powder

Boil and drain alphabet noodles. Add remaining ingredients. (You may want to vary amounts according to your taste). Chill.

LOW FAT

EXCELLENT!

TOMATO SHRIMP SALAD

2 3-oz pkg. lemon jello
2 C tomato juice
3/4 C cold tomato juice
Juice of one fresh lemon
2 Tbsp chopped green pepper
1 C diced celery
1 small can drained divined shrimp
3/4 tsp salt
Dash freshly ground pepper
1 green onion, chopped fine
1 tsp horseradish

Heat 2 C tomato juice to boiling and add to jello. Stir until dissolved. Stir in cold tomato juice. Add lemon juice. Add and mix together all remaining ingredients. Cut the white off ends of whole hard cooked eggs and divide into thirds. Place in bottom of mold. Pour into gelatin mixture. When serving, pass mayonnaise.

CREAMY BROWN RICE SALAD

EXCELLENT!

3 C cooked brown rice
1/2 C chopped green onions
3 C shrimp or chicken
1 C chopped celery
1 C chopped green pepper
1 8-oz can water chestnuts
Salt and pepper to taste
3/4 C mayonnaise
1/4 C lemon juice
1 tsp grated lemon peel
1/4 tsp minced garlic
1 Tbsp prepared mustard
1 Tbsp horseradish
2 Tbsp chopped parsley
1/2 C sliced almonds

In a mixing bowl, combine the first 7 ingredients. In a separate bowl, mix mayonnaise, lemon juice, grated lemon peel, garlic, mustard, horseradish, and parsley together. Add two mixtures together and mix until well moistened. Sprinkle top of salad with sliced almonds.

LOW FAT

WHEAT BERRY AND MUSHROOM SALAD

3 C cooked wheat or rye
Vinaigrette dressing (below)
1/4 lb mushrooms, thinly sliced
1 C chopped green onion
1 green pepper, seeded and
  sliced into rings

In a salad bowl, mix together cooked wheat or rye, dressing, mushrooms, and olives. Cover and refrigerate at least 1 hour or overnight. Stir in green onion.

To serve, garnish with the green pepper rings. Serves about 6.

VINAIGRETTE DRESSING

1/4 C each salad oil and white
  wine vinegar
1 clove garlic, minced
1 Tbsp Dijon mustard
1 1/2 tsp oregano leaves
1/4 tsp salt
1/8 tsp pepper

In a small bowl, combine all the ingredients.

WHEAT BERRY AND APPLE SALAD

3 C cooked wheat or rye
1 C chopped celery
Caraway dressing (below)
2 small red-skin apples, cored and diced
1/4 lb Swiss cheese, cut into
    julienne strips
1/4 C finely chopped parsley

In a salad bowl, combine cooked wheat or rye, celery, and dressing. Cover and chill at least 1 hour or overnight. Stir in apples.

To serve, garnish with Swiss cheese strips and parsley. Serves 6.

CARAWAY DRESSING

1/2 C mayonnaise
1 Tbsp each prepared mustard and white
    wine vinegar
1 tsp caraway seed

In a small bowl, mix all ingredients together.

PEARLS O' BARLEY SALAD

3 C water
1/2 C pearl barley
1/2 tsp salt
1/2 C cubed Swiss cheese
1/2 medium cucumber, cut into
    matchstick pieces
1/3 C sliced celery
1/3 C sliced green onions
1/4 C finely chopped parsley
1/4 C sliced pimento-stuffed green olives
1/4 C Italian salad dressing
1/4 tsp dried oregano leaves, crushed
1/8 to 1/4 tsp ground red pepper
Fresh spinach leaves, rinsed and trimmed
2 to 3 Tbsp dry roasted sunflower kernels
Tomato wedges (optional)

Bring water to a boil; stir in barley; cover, and simmer for 50 to 60 minutes, or until tender. Drain.

In a large bowl, combine barley with remaining ingredients, except spinach leaves, sunflower kernels and tomato wedges. Marinated several hours or overnight. Serve on spinach leaves. Sprinkle with sunflower kernels. Garnish with tomato wedges.

GRACE AND CHEESE MOLD

First layer
1 C lemon juice
3 envelopes unflavored gelatine
4 tsp hot water
2 C black or red grapes, cut into halves and
    seeded
1/2 C (or more) sugar
4-1/2 C cold water

Cheese layer:
1-1/2 C cream cheese
1 C cottage cheese (strained)
1-1/3 C sour cream
3 envelopes unflavored gelatine
4 Tbsp hot water
4 tsp grated orange rind
4 Tbsp frozen concentrated orange juice
1 or 2 Tbsp sugar

First layer
Oil a bundt pan and set aside.
Dissolve the gelatine in hot water. Add sugar; stir well. Add lemon juice and 4-1/2 cups water. Pour 1/4 of lemon juice mixture into bundt pan; chill until barely set. Layer grape halves right side up, on top of set gelatine; carefully pour enough lemon mixture to surround and cover grapes; chill until almost set. Pour remaining lemon mixture over. Chill.

Cheese layer
Mix together cheeses and sour cream. Dissolve gelatine in hot water; add to cheese mixture. Mix well. Add orange rind, orange juice and sugar.
When first layer is almost set, spoon cheese mixture over and chill.
Note: Great made day before!

CURRY CHICKEN SALAD

2 C chopped chicken (fresh or canned)
1/2 C celery chopped
1 C red seedless grapes
1 tsp curry powder
1 tsp dry mustard pepper to taste
1 C or more of mayonnaise
1/2 C toasted slivered almonds

Mix all ingredients together. Let chill in refrigerator. Serve on lettuce or alfalfa sprouts.

TOMATO BULGUR SALAD

1/2 C bulgur
1/2 C boiling water
1 14-oz can stewed tomatoes
1/2 C snipped parsley
1/4 C snipped fresh mint (optional)
1/4 C currants or raisins
1/4 C olive oil
1/4 C lemon juice
1 clove garlic, minced
1 tsp curry powder
1/4 tsp cumin
1/4 tsp ground cinnamon
1/4 C peanuts, chopped

In a colander, rinse bulgur with cold water; drain well. In a bowl, pour boiling water over bulgur; stir. Let stand 15 minutes; drain well. Drain tomatoes, reserving 1/4 cup juices. Cut tomatoes into large pieces. In a large bowl stir together drained tomatoes, parsley, mint, and currants. Toss bulgur with tomato mixture. For dressing, in blender container combine reserved tomato juice, oil, lemon juice, garlic, curry powder, cumin, and cinnamon. Cover; blend till smooth. Pour dressing over bulgur mixture; toss. Refrigerate 4 to 24 hours. (Liquid is absorbed during chilling.) To serve, spoon salad onto plates. Top with chopped peanuts. Serves 6.

BING CHERRY AND PINEAPPLE MOLD

2 qt jars Bing cherries and juice, pitted
6 envelopes unflavored gelatin
1 tsp almond flavoring
1 20-oz can crushed pineapple
1 8-oz cream cheese
1 C whipping cream*
1/2 C sugar

*Can use canned milk whipped

Drain cherries in a medium saucepan reserving juice. Add 3 envelopes unflavored gelatin to juice and dissolve. Heat until gelatin is well dissolved. Set aside to cool. Meanwhile, cut cherries in half and pit. Use only 1 1/2 jars cherries and save remaining 1/2 for use later. In a Bundt pan, place cherries and cherry juice. Put into freezer just until barely set. Beat cream cheese and sugar until smooth. Add crushed pineapple with its juice. Put the remaining 3 envelopes unflavored gelatin in 1/2 C water. Place in the microwave for 1 to 2 minutes to dissolve. Add to pineapple mixture. In a separate bowl, whip the cream. Add slowly to cream cheese mixture. Pour this mixture over the set cherry layer and return to the refrigerator. Let set for several hours or overnight. Unmold just before serving.

FROZEN BING CHERRY SALAD

1 qt jar Bing cherries, pitted
1-16 oz can pineapple tidbits
8 oz cream cheese
1 C sour cream
4 Tbsp sugar
1/8 tsp salt
1 tsp lemon peel
3/4 tsp ginger
1/4 tsp mace
1 tsp vanilla
2 C miniature marshmallows

Drain and pit cherries. Drain pineapple. Beat cream cheese until fluffy. Add sour cream and remaining ingredients, except drained fruit. Mix carefully. Stir in cherries, pineapple, and marshmallows. Pour into a 2 quart mold. Freeze. When ready to serve, remove from mold and place on lettuce.

CRANBERRY FROZEN SALAD

1 12-oz pkg raw cranberries
1 small pkg miniature marshmallows
1 C sugar
1 20-oz can pineapple
1 pint whipping cream

Wash and grind raw cranberries in food processor. Add marshmallows, sugar, and pineapple. Set aside for 1 hour. Whip the cream and add to above mixture. Pour into Bundt pan or 9x13 pan and freeze. Take from freezer 1 to 2 hours before serving.

APRICOT FRUIT COCKTAIL JELLO SALAD

1 C dehydrated fruit medley or 1 qt jar
   canned fruit cocktail
5 envelopes unflavored gelatin
1 C cold water
3 C boiling water
1 qt apricots
3/4 C sugar
3 Tbsp frozen orange juice concentrate

In a one quart bowl, soak fruit medley in 3 cups warm water for 1 to 2 hours.

In an eight cup measuring pitcher dissolve gelatin in cold water. Set aside for 10 minutes or until thickened. Next, add boiling water and stir until dissolved. Add sugar and stir to dissolve. Whirl apricots in blender and add to gelatin mixture. Add frozen orange juice concentrate. Mix well. Pour into a Bundt pan or jello mold. Put drained fruit medley in. Place in refrigerator to gel. (Sliced bananas, fresh peaches, frozen berries, or other canned fruits can be added for variety).

PINEAPPLE PECAN JELLO SALAD

EXCELLENT!

5 pkgs unflavored gelatin
1 C cold water
3 C boiling water
1 C sugar
8 ice cubes
1 C buttermilk
8 oz frozen orange juice concentrate
1 can crushed pineapple (20 oz)
1/2 C chopped pecans
1 pint whipping cream, whipped

Dissolve unflavored gelatin in cold water. Let set for 5 minutes. Pour boiling water over gelatin and stir until dissolved. Add sugar, mixing well. Add orange juice, buttermilk, and ice cubes, stirring until cooled. Then fold in whipped cream, pineapple and pecans. Pour into a mold and set.

NECTARINE CREAM MOLD

EXCELLENT!

10 medium nectarines, chopped
Pinch of allspice
1 C powdered sugar
2 tsp Brandy flavoring
2 envelopes unflavored gelatin
8 Tbsp hot water
2 C whipping cream or chilled canned milk whipped

Mix together the nectarines, a pinch of allspice, powdered sugar, and Brandy flavoring. Dissolve gelatin in the hot water and strain into the nectarine mixture. Stir well. Whip the cream until it is thick and fold into the nectarine mixture. Spoon into a greased Bundt pan. Chill for 2 hours or until set. Unmold to serve.

WEDDING COCONUT LEMON MOUSSE

EXCELLENT!

5 envelopes unflavored gelatin (or 1/4 C)
1 C cold water
3 C boiling water
2 C sugar
1 1/4 C lemon juice (bottled)
2 tsp finely grated lemon rind
1 12-oz can evaporated milk, chilled
1/2 C flaked coconut

Dissolve gelatin in cold water and let stand for 4 minutes. Add boiling water and stir well until dissolved. Add the sugar, lemon juice, and lemon rind. Refrigerate until almost set. Whip evaporated milk with an electric mixer, in a beater then add almost set gelatin mixture, beating well. Mix in coconut. Quickly pour into a Bundt pan. Set in refrigerator until well set or overnight. Decorate with mint leaves and red cherries.

ALL-AMERICAN MOUSSE

1 pint strawberries, hulled and divided <u>or</u>
   1 pint frozen strawberries
2 Tbsp plus 1 C sugar
1 15-oz can blueberries in heavy syrup,
   drained
6 envelopes unflavored gelatin
3 8-oz containers vanilla low-fat yogurt
1 3/4 C heavy cream
1/3 tsp almond flavoring
1/2 pint blueberries for garnish

Spray a 10 cup metal mold with non-stick cooking spray; set aside. Place mixing bowl and beaters in freezer. In food processor, blend 1/2 pint strawberries and 2 Tbsp sugar for 30 seconds, scraping sides. Remove puree to large bowl; set aside. In a 2 cup glass measure, sprinkle gelatin over 1 1/2 C cold water. Let stand 3 minutes. Meanwhile, in another bowl, whisk 1 cup sugar into yogurt.

In microwave, cook the softened gelatin for 1 to 2 minutes, or until gelatin is dissolved. Meanwhile, with mixer at high-speed, beat cream until stiff peaks form. Remove 1/2 cup whipped cream for garnish; chill. Gradually whisk gelatin into yogurt mixture until well-blended. With whisk, gently fold whipped cream into yogurt mixture until blended.

Whisk 1 cup yogurt mixture into strawberry puree; immediately pour into mold. Whisk 4 cups yogurt mixture into blueberry puree; set aside. Whisk flavoring into remaining yogurt mixture; spoon into mold and smooth. Chill for 30 minutes. Cut remaining strawberries in half, chill. To unmold, immerse mold in warm water for 5 to 10 seconds. Fill center of mousse with reserved strawberries, fresh blueberries and cream. Serves 16.

APPLESAUCE MOUSSE

2 C canned applesauce
3 egg whites
1 Tbsp lemon juice
1 tsp vanilla
1/2 C sugar
1 C whipping cream
Strawberry sauce

Combine first five ingredients in a large bowl of electric mixer. Beat at high speed until light and fluffy. In a separate bowl, whip the cream, then fold into the applesauce mixture. Freeze until firm in an 8 or 9 inch square pan. Top with strawberry sauce.

STRAWBERRY SAUCE

1 qt fresh strawberries, sliced
Sugar to taste

Mix sliced strawberries and sugar together. Chill until syrup firms. Or thaw 2 pkgs frozen strawberries in their pouches and serve with their syrup.

SWEET FRENCH DRESSING

1 C oil
1/2 C lemon juice
1/2 C catsup
1/3 C sugar
3/4 tsp pepper
1 tsp dry mustard
1 tsp salt
1 Tbsp dried chopped onions

Put all ingredients, except oil, in a blender and mix well. Turn blender to high speed and pour oil very slowly into mixture, making sure it mixes well. Dressing should thicken as oil is added.

EXCELLENT!

ORANGE DRESSING

1/4 C cider vinegar
2 tsp orange rind
1/2 C frozen orange juice concentrate
Juice from 1 large lemon
1/4 C sugar
1/2 tsp dry mustard
1/2 tsp salt
1 C salad oil

Put all ingredients, except oil, in a blender and mix well. Turn blender to high speed and pour oil very slowly into mixture, making sure it mixes well. Dressing should thicken as oil is added.

RANCH STYLE SALAD DRESSING

1 C mayonnaise
1 C buttermilk
1/2 tsp onion salt
1/4 tsp garlic salt
1/4 tsp M.S.G.
1/8 tsp celery salt
1/4 tsp black pepper
1/4 tsp marjoram
1/8 tsp savory
1/2 tsp parsley flakes

Combine all ingredients. Mix well. Refrigerate 30 minutes before serving.

EXCELLENT!

GERMAN SALAD DRESSING

1 C cider vinegar
1 C sugar or honey
1 Tbsp salt
1 Tbsp dried chopped onions
1 tsp garlic powder
1/2 Tbsp thyme leaves
1 tsp rosemary leaves
1 tsp sweet basil leaves
1 Tbsp capers, with juice
1/2 tsp whole dill weed
1/4 C fresh lemon juice
1/2 C fresh orange juice
Salad oil

Crush dried onions with a mallet and mix with remaining ingredients, except oil, in a quart jar. Shake well or until sugar and salt are dissolved. Fill quart jar with salad oil and shake well again.

This dressing is good on fruit or vegetable salads.

EXCELLENT!

POPPY SEED DRESSING

3/4 C sugar
1 tsp dry mustard
1 tsp salt
1/3 C cider vinegar
1 C salad oil
1 Tbsp dried chopped onions
1 tsp poppy seed
1 tsp toasted sesame seed

Whirl sugar, mustard, salt, and vinegar in a blender. Slowly pour in oil. Add chopped onions and whirl only a couple of times. Stir in poppy seed and sesame seed. Makes 1 1/2 cups of dressing.

Note: This dressing is ideal to serve over all kinds of fruit.

SIMPLE YOGURT DRESSING*

LOW FAT

3/4 C yogurt
1/4 tsp salt
1/2 tsp celery seeds

Mix and chill. Good on sprouts and slaw.

COOKED YOGURT DRESSING*

LOW FAT

1/2 C yogurt
1 egg
2 tsp honey
1 Tbsp vinegar
1/2 tsp salt
1/2 tsp celery seeds

Mix well in top of double boiler, and cook gently just until creamy.

BLUE CHEESE YOGURT DRESSING*

LOW FAT

1 1/2 C yogurt
1/2 C mayonnaise
2 Tbsp chopped green onion
1 Tbsp lemon juice
1/2 tsp salt
4 Tbsp crumbled Blue cheese

Combine all ingredients except blue cheese. Mix well. Fold in blue cheese.

BLUE CHEESE DRESSING

1/3 lb Blue cheese
1/3 C grated onions **or** dried onions
5 C mayonnaise
1/2 C buttermilk
1/4 C milk
2 Tbsp lemon juice
1/8 C oil
1/8 C vinegar
1/4 tsp salt
White pepper
1/2 tsp garlic
Tabasco sauce

Crumble blue cheese. Whip and mix all ingredients together.

* Low fat dressings

LEMON-AVOCADO DRESSING

1/2 C lemon juice
1/2 C oil
1 Tbsp honey
Pinch of salt
1/2 avocado
2 Tbsp chopped onion

In a blender, combine and blend together all ingredients.

LOW FAT

CRUNCHY SALAD

2 large tomatoes
1 C alfalfa sprouts*
1 C wheat sprouts*
1 C mung bean sprouts*
1 C sunflower seed sprouts*
3 T olive oil
2 Tbsp lemon juice or vinegar
Salt and pepper to taste

Mix tomatoes and sprouts in a large bowl. Drizzle oil over top and toss until sprouts are evenly coated. Add lemon juice and seasonings. Toss lightly. Serves 4 to 6.

LOW FAT

BEAN SPROUT SALAD

1 head butter lettuce
1 cucumber, thinly sliced
3 tomatoes, sliced
2 C bean sprouts* or pea sprouts*
6 radishes, sliced
Sour Cream Dressing (below)
Ripe olives

Place lettuce leaves on a salad plate, then place a layer of beans sprouts. Place alternate layers of sliced cucumbers, radishes, and tomatoes over bean or pea sprouts. Top with Sour Cream Dressing. Garnish with ripe olives.

Sour Cream Dressing:
1/2 C sour cream
1 1/2 Tbsp chopped chives
1 Tbsp lemon juice or vinegar
1/4 tsp salt

Mix all ingredients together and serve.

SESAME SALAD

1 C watercress
1 C torn lettuce
1 C sunflower seed sprouts*
1 C alfalfa sprouts*
Sesame Dressing (below)

Mix all ingredients in a large bowl and toss with Sesame Dressing.

Sesame Dressing:
1/4 C ground sesame seeds
1/4 C water
1/4 tsp kelp
2 Tbsp lemon juice
1/4 small garlic clove

Blend all ingredients together in a blender until smooth. Makes about 1/2 cup.

LOW FAT COTTAGE CHEESE SALAD

1 C low fat cottage cheese
1/2 C plain yogurt
1/4 C finely chopped radish
1 Tbsp minced onion
1/4 C finely chopped celery
2/3 C wheat sprouts*
Salt
Alfalfa sprouts*

Mix cottage cheese and yogurt. Add all remaining ingredients except alfalfa sprouts. Chill. Serve on a bed of alfalfa sprouts. Serves 2.

* See SPROUTING section at the front of the book for detail information on sprouting seeds.

NOTE: Tofu Egg Salad (See Tofu Section)

SOUPS

NOTE: Many of the recipes in this section call for a commercial creamy soup base but if you do not have one, this recipe is a good substitute.

CREAMY SOUP BASE MIX

4 C powdered milk
4 C white flour
4 C dehydrated margarine or butter
1 tsp salt
1/2 C instant chicken bouillon
1/2 tsp white pepper

Mix all ingredients well and store in an air tight container.

When ready to use, mix 1/2 cup creamy soup base with 1 cup of water. Whirl in a blender. Cook to boiling. It can also be used as a sauce for creamed vegetables, creamed potatoes, or creamed meats.

NOTE: All recipes calling for bacon and ham can be substituted with can spam or bacon TVP.

EXCELLENT!

TACO BEEF SOUP

1 lb ground beef
1/2 C dried chopped onions, reconstituted
6 C water
1 qt jar canned tomatoes
2 C kidney beans soaked overnight
1 8-oz can tomato sauce
2 Tbsp taco mix
2 avocadoes (optional)
Grated cheese
Corn chips
Sour cream

Brown ground beef in 1 Tbsp. oil. Add onions and saute lightly. Add beans and water. Cook 2 hours or until almost done. Add tomatoes and tomato sauce and taco mix. Cook another 30 minutes.

Top soup with chopped avocadoes, grated cheese, corn chips, and sour cream.

CURRIED CREAM OF CORN SOUP

2 cans creamed corn (4 cups)
1 Tbsp dried chopped onion
1 tsp chicken bouillon
4 C water
1/4 C dehydrated creamy soup base
1/4 C nonfat powdered milk
3/4 tsp curry powder
1/4 tsp salt
Dash of pepper

In a 4-quart pot, boil water, onions and chicken bouillon for 5 min. Add creamed corn. Cook 1 min. Mix the soup base and powdered milk in a blender with 1 cup of water. Blend until smooth and add to corn mixture. Stir in spices and heat until steaming. Serves 6.

BOSTON CLAM CHOWDER

1/4 lb bacon, chopped
1 C dehydrated potato slices, reconstituted
1/2 C chopped celery or 1/2 C vegetable
    stew, reconstituted
6 C water
2 cans chopped clams
1/2 C nonfat milk
1/2 C dehydrated creamy soup base
2 Tbsp onions, reconstituted
Salt and pepper to taste
1/2 tsp sugar

Cook bacon in a saucepan. Drain fat except for 1 or 2 Tbsp. Add reconstituted potatoes, onions and celery or vegetable stew. Saute lightly. Add water and cook until vegetables are tender. Whisk in powdered milk and soup base. Add clams with juice, sugar and salt and pepper to taste. If soup is not thick enough, thicken with 2 Tbsp cornstarch mixed with water.

ELEGANT CREAMY CLAM CHOWDER

EXCELLENT!

6 slices bacon, diced
1/4 C onions, reconstituted*
1 C vegetable stew mix, reconstituted*
2 cloves garlic, minced
2 potatoes, peeled and chopped or 1 C
    dehydrated sliced potatoes,
    reconstituted*
1 or 2 cans chopped clams
1 bay leaf
1/2 tsp liquid hot pepper
1/4 tsp white pepper
1 1/2 tsp Worcestershire sauce
1/4 tsp thyme
1 12-oz can evaporated milk
**1 C dehydrated creamy soup base
8 C water

In an 8-quart pan, cook bacon over medium heat until lightly browned. Remove. Drain and set aside. Discard all but 3 Tbsp bacon drippings. Saute drained onions and garlic for 2 or 3 min. Add drained vegetable stew and potatoes. Cook 2 or 3 minutes longer. Add water and simmer until done, about 1 hour. Add all seasonings. Whirl milk and creamy soup base in a blender until mixed. Add to the vegetables and simmer another 15 minutes. Add clams and juice. Heat thoroughly. Add more water if desired. Serves 10.

*To reconstitute onions, vegetable stew mix, and potatoes, place each in a separate container and add three times as much water. Soak 2 or 3 hours. Drain, saving the water for use in the recipe.

**To substitute creamy soup base add 1/2 C flour mixed to a paste with a little water. Add 1 tsp salt.

SAUERKRAUT AND RIB SOUP

3 lbs country-style pork ribs
3 Tbsp white wine vinegar
2 Tbsp salad oil
1/4 C dried chopped onion, reconstituted
1 tsp caraway seeds
2 bay leaves
1 can or 1-lb 12-oz jar of sauerkraut, rinsed
    and drained
2 C shredded green cabbage
1 can or jar of tomatoes
1/2 C pearl barley
4 tsp beef bouillon, diluted in 8 C water

In a 6- to 8- quart pan over high heat, cook ribs, turning often, until well browned. Lift out and set aside.

Add vinegar to drippings in pan, scraping pan to loosen browned bits. Then add oil, onions, caraway seeds, and bay leaves. Cook, stirring, until onion is soft, about 10 minutes. Break tomatoes into smaller pieces and add with their liquid. Add sauerkraut, cabbage, and barley. Return ribs to pot then add beef bouillon. Bring to a full boil over high heat. Reduce heat, cover and simmer until meat pulls easily from the bones, about 2 1/2 to 3 hours. Skim fat from soup and discard. Serves 6.

SAUERKRAUT SOUP

EXCELLENT!

1 small pork shoulder blade roast
1/8 tsp black pepper
2 bay leaves
1/4 C dried mushrooms
1 large can sauerkraut
1 head cabbage, sliced
2 Tbsp sugar
1 qt jar tomatoes or 1/4 C dehydrated tomato
    powder in 1 qt water
1 large Kielbasa smoked sausage, sliced
1 8-oz pkg egg noodles
Sour cream for topping

In large kettle put pork, pepper, bay leaf, mushrooms, sauerkraut, and sliced cabbage. Cover with water and bring to a boil. Cook for 2 hours. Remove pork and cut into cubes. Return to kettle and add remaining ingredients. Boil 1 more hour. When serving, top with sour cream.

MINESTRONE

LOW FAT

1 C baby lima beans
7 C water
1/4 C dried chopped onion
1 C dehydrated vegetable stew
1/8 tsp garlic powder
1/4 c olive oil
1/4 tsp crushed red pepper
1/2 lb fresh spinach
2 tsp beef bouillon
1/8 tsp rubbed sage
1/4 tsp ground thyme
2 tsp salt
1/4 tsp coarsely ground pepper
2 C canned tomatoes
1 small zucchini, thinly sliced
1 C elbow macaroni
Grated Parmesan cheese

Soak beans overnight in enough water to cover. Drain. Add 7 cups water. Cover and simmer for 3 hours or until tender. Add remaining ingredients. Cook over low heat for 1 hour or until done. Sprinkle with Parmesan cheese and serve. Makes 3 quarts.

This is a thick soup. If you prefer, add a little water to thin.

SOYBEAN MINESTRONE

2 C soybeans
1 Tbsp dehydrated chopped onion
1/3 C dehydrated mushrooms reconstituted
1/2 C dehydrated carrots reconstituted
3 Tbsp olive oil
1/2 C brown rice
1/2 C each chopped bell pepper and celery
1 qt jar whole tomatoes
5 C water
3 tsp beef bouillon
1/2 tsp each, dry rosemary, oregano leaves,
    and dry basil
1/4 tsp each thyme leaves and summer
    savory
1/8 tsp ground red pepper (or cayenne)
1 C sliced zucchini (optional)
1/2 C chopped parsley
Grated Parmesan cheese

Soak 2 cups soybeans overnight. Rinse; cover with water and cook 5 hours.

Soak carrots, mushrooms, and onions 2 hours or overnight. Drain. Set aside.

Heat oil in a 4- or 5-quart pan over medium heat, add rice, onions, mushroom, carrots, bell peppers and celery. Cook, stirring often. Add tomatoes and their liquid. Add soybeans, water and beef bouillon and all spices. Bring to a boil over high heat, reduce and simmer for 40 minutes. Add additional water if needed. Add zucchini and simmer 8 or 10 more minutes. Add parsley and sprinkle each individual serving with Parmesan cheese.

LIMA BEAN SOUP

2 C baby lima beans, soaked overnight and
    drained
1 Tbsp oil
1/2 lbs sliced bacon, diced
1/2 C dried chopped onion, reconstituted
1 qt whole tomatoes
1/2 tsp paprika
3 whole cloves
1/2 tsp allspice
2 qt water
Salt and pepper
1 small head cabbage, shredded
2 Tbsp chopped parsley

In a kettle, fry the bacon (not too brown). Drain fat except for 1-2 tbsp. Saute onions. Add drained lima beans, tomatoes, spices and water. Bring to a boil. Cover and simmer about 2 hours or until beans are almost tender. Season to taste with salt and pepper. Add shredded cabbage and cook 20 minutes longer. Sprinkle individual servings with chopped parsley.

CREAM OF CAULIFLOWER SOUP

1 medium to small head of cauliflower
2 tsp chicken bouillon
1 Tbsp dried chopped onion
6 C water
1/2 C dehydrated potato flakes
1/2 C nonfat powdered milk
1/2 C dehydrated creamy soup base
Ground nutmeg, white pepper
Salt to taste

Slice cauliflower into 3-quart pot. Add bouillon, onions and 3 C water. Cover and simmer until vegetables are tender (15 to 20 min.). Add potato flakes and stir. Remove from heat and blend cauliflower mixture in food processor or blender until smooth and creamy. Return to pot. Blend remaining 3 C water, powdered milk, and soup base in blender and add mixture to the cauliflower mixture in pot. Stir and season. Serves 6.

FRENCH ONION SOUP

1/2 C dried chopped onions
4 Tbsp dehydrated butter powder,
　　reconstituted
4 C hot water
2 Tbsp beef bouillon
1/2 bay leaf
1/4 tsp black pepper
1/4 tsp ground marjoram
Herb croutons
Grated Parmesan cheese

Saute onions in butter but do not brown. Add hot water, beef bouillon, bay leaf, pepper and marjoram. Simmer for 30 minutes. Serve with croutons and Parmesan cheese.

EXCELLENT!

LENTIL SOUP

1 1/3 C lentils
7 C water
1 tsp salt
1/4 tsp coarsely ground pepper
1 Tbsp celery flakes
1 tsp basil leaves
1/4 C dehydrated dried chopped onions
1 tsp marjoram leaves
1/4 C dehydrated carrots or 1 C sliced
　　carrots
1 can or jar of whole tomatoes (optional)
Ham bone or 1/2 lb Kielbasa sausage

Rinse lentils and place in large kettle with water, seasonings, carrots, tomatoes, and meat. Cover and bring to boil. Boil gently for 2 hours. If you prefer a thinner soup add more water.

TURKEY SOUP

Turkey or chicken carcass (with at least 1 C
    of meat remaining)
1/4 C dehydrated vegetable stew
1/4 C dehydrated dried chopped onions
6 peppercorns
5 whole cloves
Dash of nutmeg or mace
1 bay leaf
1 Tbsp chicken bouillon
1 C white rice

Remove meat from carcass. For full flavor you should have about 1 cup of meat, more is better. Crack bones and put in a large saucepan along with any skin. Add vegetable stew, onions, peppercorns, cloves, nutmeg, and bay leaf. Add enough water to cover bones. Heat to boiling; reduce heat. Cover and simmer for 2 hours.

When cool, remove bones and strain, saving the broth. Skim fat, if desired. Add to chicken bouillon, turkey or chicken meat, rice, and salt, if needed. Simmer 20 to 25 minutes. Serves 6-8.

Note: Can use canned turkey.

SPINACH SOUP

1 10-oz package fresh spinach or 10-oz
    frozen spinach or 1/2 C dehydrated
    spinach
1/4 C dehydrated creamy soup base
1/2 C nonfat powdered milk
4 C water
1/4 tsp salt
1/4 tsp nutmeg
1/2 tsp white pepper
1 Tbsp dried chopped onions
1 tsp chicken bouillon

Wash and drain spinach, or thaw frozen spinach. Put milk and soup base in blender with 1 cup water. Add spinach a little at a time, blending until smooth after each addition. Place remaining water and spices in a saucepan. Heat. Stir in spinach mixture. Add onions and chicken base. Cook, stirring constantly, over medium heat until it comes to a boil. Reduce heat and simmer 10 minutes or until done. Makes 6 cups.

Note: Add more water when using dehydrated spinach.

CORN CHOWDER

3 slices bacon
1 stalk celery, chopped
3 C water
1/4 C dehydrated creamy soup base
1/3 C nonfat powdered milk
4 C dehydrated reconstituted sweet corn* or
    1 17-oz can creamed corn and 1 12-oz
    can corn
2 Tbsp dried chopped onion
1 tsp Season-All
1/8 tsp white pepper
1/8 tsp basil leaves

Fry bacon in large saucepan over medium heat until crisp. Drain on absorbent paper. Saute celery in remaining bacon fat for 3 minutes. Remove from heat. In a blender or food processor, blend water, powdered milk, and soup base. Add to celery. Place crisp bacon, and remaining ingredients in saucepan and return to heat. Cook over medium heat until mixture comes to a boil. Cook 1 minute. Serve topped with crumbled bacon.

*When using reconstituted corn, cook corn in 3 cups of water until tender, then blend in blender until creamed.

CREAMY CARROT SOUP

LOW FAT

1/2 C dehydrated carrots
3 C water
1 Tbsp dried chopped onions
1/4 C white rice
2 Tbsp dehydrated tomato powder
2 Tbsp chicken bouillon
4 C boiling water
1/2 C evaporated milk
Salt and pepper to taste

Soak carrots in water over night or 2 hours. Cook carrots in water for 1 hour. Place in a blender and blend well. Set aside.

Add onions, rice, tomato powder, and chicken bouillon to the boiling water. Cook until rice is done, about 20 minutes. Add the blended carrots and evaporated milk. Simmer 1 minute. Salt and pepper to taste. Serves 4.

BROCCOLI SOUP

8 C water
1/2 C dehydrated broccoli, soaked
overnight or 8 hrs in 1 1/2 C water
1 C dehydrated potatoes, soaked overnight
1 C creamy soup base
1/2 C cheese blend
2 tsp chicken base

Bring water, broccoli, and potatoes to a boil. Boil for 30 minutes or until tender. Whip in remaining ingredients and simmer for 4 minutes.

CURRIED CARROT BISQUE

1 C dehydrated carrots or fresh
3 C water
1/4 C butter or margarine
2 cloves garlic, minced or pressed
2 Tbsp dried chopped onions
1 tsp ground coriander
3/4 tsp curry powder
1/4 tsp ground ginger
1/8 tsp ground allspice
3 Tbsp flour
2 C water
2 Tbsp chicken bouillon
1 C non-fat powdered milk
5 C water
Salt to taste

Soak carrots in water overnight for 2 hours. Set aside.

In a 5- or 6-quart pan, melt butter over medium heat. Add garlic, onions, coriander, curry powder, ginger, and allspice. Saute for 3 minutes, stirring consistently. Stir in flour and mix until vegetables are coated. Gradually stir in water. Add soaked carrots with liquid and chicken bouillon. Bring to a boil and simmer for 1 hour or until carrots are very tender. Meanwhile, reconstitute milk in the 5 cups of water. Remove carrots from heat and whirl small portions at a time in a food processor or blender, alternating with milk, until smooth. Return to heat and warm until steaming (do not boil). Serves 8-10.

BROCCOLI BUTTERMILK SOUP

1 C dehydrated broccoli, soaked in 2 C
    water for 1 hour
1 Tbsp beef bouillon
1 C water
2 tsp dried chopped onion
1 bay leaf
1 tsp dry basil
1/2 tsp sugar
1 clove garlic
1 3/4 C buttermilk
Salt and pepper to taste

In a 3-quart pan, combine broccoli, beef bouillon, onion, bay leaf, basil, garlic, and sugar. Bring to a boil over high heat. Reduce heat and cover. Simmer until broccoli is tender, about 1 hour. Remove and discard bay leaf. Whirl mixture a small portion at a time in a food processor or blender. Return to pan. With a wire whisk, whip in buttermilk. Heat and season with salt and pepper. Serves 4-6.

CREAM OF SOYBEAN SOUP

1 C soybeans
3 C water
6 medium leeks
3 Tbsp butter
1 Tbsp dried chopped onion
1 C sliced celery
1/4 C dehydrated carrots, reconstituted and diced
1 medium turnip or parsnip, diced
2 Tbsp beef bouillon
2 C water
1/8 tsp thyme leaves
1 can evaporated milk
Dash of salt and pepper
3 Tbsp finely chopped parsley
Lemon wedges

Wash soybeans, drain and place in large bowl with 3 cups water. Cover and let sit 6 hours or overnight.

Trim ends and discard tops of leeks, leaving about 3 inches of greens. Discard tough outer leaves. Split leeks in half lengthwise; rinse well, then thinly slice crosswise.

In a 4- or 5-quart pan, melt butter over medium heat. Add leeks, onions, celery and carrots. Cook, stirring occasionally, until onion is soft, about 10 minutes. Add turnip or parsnip, soybeans and their soaking liquid, beef bouillon, water, and thyme. Bring to a boil over high heat, reduce heat. Cover and simmer until beans are tender, about 5 hours.

Whirl bean mixture a portion at a time in a blender until smooth. Return to pan, blend in milk. Heat, stirring occasionally. Season with salt and pepper. Sprinkle with parsley and serve with lemon slices. Serves 6-8.

MULLIGATAWNY

1/4 C butter
1 3-lb chicken, cut into pieces
2 Tbsp dried chopped onion
3 quarts boiling water
1/4 C dehydrated vegetable stew
1 Tbsp curry powder
1/4 tsp MSG
1 tsp turmeric
3 Tbsp chicken bouillon
1/8 tsp mace
1/2 tsp parsley flakes
1/4 tsp black pepper
6 Tbsp flour

Melt butter in large saucepan or Dutch oven. Add chicken pieces and onions. Cover and simmer over low heat 20 min. Add remaining ingredients except for flour. Simmer 40 min. or until chicken is tender. Remove chicken and strain stock. Return stock to saucepan. Remove chicken from bones. Chop meat and add to stock. Simmer 15 min. Make a thin smooth paste by mixing the flour with equal amounts of water. Then stir into soup, cook until thickened. Makes 3 quarts.

CHILI CORN CHOWDER

4 slices bacon
1/4 C dried chopped onion, reconstituted
1/2 C dehydrated potato slices
1 C water
2 C dehydrated sweet corn, reconstituted
1 can diced green chiles
1-2 oz. jar sliced pimentos, drained
1 can evaporated milk
Salt and pepper

In a 4- to 5-quart pan, cook bacon over medium heat until crisp. Remove from pan, drain and crumble. Set aside. Discard all but 2 tablespoons dripping from pan. Add onions to drippings and cook, stirring occasionally until onions are soft. Stir in potatoes, corn, and water. Bring to a boil over high heat. Reduce heat, cover and simmer until potatoes and corn are tender. Whirl mixture in a blender until corn is creamed but still chunky. Stir in chiles, pimentos and milk. Heat, stirring occasionally. Add more water if desired. Season to taste with salt and pepper. Serves 6.

RUSSIAN SALMON SOUP

1 Tbsp butter
1/4 C dried chopped onions, reconstituted
1/4 C dehydrated carrots, reconstituted
1 tsp paprika
1 tsp chicken bouillon, diluted in 3 C water
1 can stewed tomatoes
2 Tbsp each, drained capers, sliced pimento-
    stuffed olives
1 Tbsp wine vinegar
1 tsp sugar
1 can pink salmon (about 1 lb)
Sour cream (optional)

In a 3- to 4-quart pan, melt butter over medium heat. Add onions and carrots. Cook, stirring occasionally, about 10 minutes. Stir in paprika, bouillon, tomatoes, capers, olives, vinegar, and sugar. Bring to boil over high heat. Reduce heat and simmer until carrots and onions are tender, about 20 to 30 minutes.

Drain salmon liquid into soup. Remove bones and skin from salmon and break into chunks. Add to soup. Simmer, uncovered, until steaming. Spoon sour cream on individual servings. Serves 4.

CHICKEN AND BARLEY SOUP

1 Tbsp butter or margarine
1/4 C dried chopped onion, reconstituted
1 clove garlic
1/4 C dehydrated carrots, reconstituted
3 tsp chicken bouillon, diluted in 6 C water
1/4 C pearl barley
1/8 tsp anise seed
2 med oranges
1 large can cooked turkey or chicken
    (about 2 C)

In a 3- to 4-quart pan, melt butter over medium heat. Add onions, garlic, and carrots. Cook, stirring occasionally, about 10 minutes. Add bouillon, barley, and anise seeds. Bring to a boil over high heat. Reduce heat and simmer until barley is tender, about 30 or 40 minutes.

Grate 1/4 tsp peel from one of the oranges and set aside. Cut remaining peel and white membrane from orange. Discard. Cut segments free. Add grated orange peel, orange segments, and chicken with liquid to barley mixture. Cover and heat until steaming. Serves 4 to 6.

CREAMY POTATO BISQUE

6 Tbsp butter or margarine
1/4 C dried chopped onions, reconstituted
1 C chopped celery, including some leaves
2 C dehydrated potato slices, reconstituted
1/4 C finely chopped parsley
1/2 tsp salt
1/4 tsp pepper
2 tsp chicken bouillon, dissolved in 4 C
 water
1 C nonfat powdered milk, dissolved in 4 C
 water
1 Tbsp corn starch
1/4 C water
Finely chopped parsley

In a 5- to 6-quart pan, melt 6 Tbsp butter. Add onions and celery. Cook, stirring occasionally, about 15 minutes. Add potatoes and 1/4 C parsley, the salt, pepper, and bouillon. Bring to boil over high heat. Reduce heat, cover and simmer until potatoes are tender, about 30 minutes. Whirl in blender. Return to pan. Stir in milk and heat until it comes to a boil. Stir in corn starch. Continue cooking until thickened. Season to taste. Sprinkle with parsley just before serving. Serves 6 to 8.

OYSTER STEW

6 slices bacon, diced
1 clove garlic, minced or pressed
3 1/2 C boiling water
1 Tbsp chicken bouillon
2-10 oz jars or cans of oysters
4 C evaporated milk
1/4 C Parmesan cheese
1/4 C chopped parsley
2 Tbsp butter or margarine
Dill weed

In a 3 to 4 quart pan, cook bacon over medium heat until crisp. Remove from pan, drain and set aside. Discard all but 1 tsp. of fat drippings. Add garlic to drippings and cook, stirring, for 1 minute. Pour in boiling water and chicken bouillon, then add oysters and their liquid. Bring to a simmer over medium high heat. Add evaporated milk. Heat until steaming. Add remaining ingredients. Serves 8.

VEGETARIAN CHOWDER

1 lb white beans, lima, small white, or great
    northern
1 C dried chopped onion, reconstituted
1 1/2 C chopped celery
1/8 tsp pepper
3 C nonfat powder milk, reconstituted
2 C whole tomatoes
2 C dehydrated sweet corn, reconstituted
1/4 C butter or dehydrated butter,
    reconstituted
1/4 C flour
1/2 tsp salt
1/4 lb Monterey Jack cheese or 1 C
    dehydrated cheese powder

Soak beans overnight. Drain. Cook beans in 6 to 8 cups of hot water with 1 1/2 tsp salt. Cook until tender. Do not drain. Meanwhile saute onions and celery briefly in butter in a 1 1/2 quart saucepan. Blend in flour, salt, and pepper. Stir in milk that has been whirled in blender with 1 cup powdered cheese. Bring to boil. Add beans and liquid along with remaining ingredients. For added zip, add a few dashes of bottled hot sauce. Serves 12.

SHRIMP AND CORN CHOWDER

1 C dehydrated sweet corn, soaked in 1 C
    water
3 Tbsp butter or margarine
1/3 C dried chopped onions, reconstituted
1/4 C dehydrated carrots, finely chopped,
    reconstituted
1/4 C chopped green pepper
1 tsp chicken bouillon, diluted in 2 C water
1 can (about 2 C) Italian-style tomatoes
1/4 tsp ground ginger
1-6 oz. can shrimp
Salt and pepper

In a 3- to 4-quart pan, melt butter over medium heat; add onions, carrots, and pepper. Cook, stirring until onions are tender. Whirl corn and liquid in a blender until chunky. Add bouillon, corn mixture, tomatoes, and ginger to cooked onions, and bring to a boil. Simmer until vegetables are tender. Stir in shrimp. Season to taste with salt and pepper. Serves 4.

See Tofu section for Tofu Soups

HAM AND BABY LIMA BEAN SOUP

2 C baby lima beans
Ham bone with some meat on it or ham
    hocks
1/2 C dehydrated sliced carrots, reconstituted
2 C chopped celery
1 green pepper
1/3 C dried chopped onion, reconstituted
1 qt jar whole tomatoes
Salt
Pepper

Wash and soak baby lima beans overnight and/or sprout for 3 days.

In a kettle cover beans with clean water, about 6 cups. Place ham bone in and cook for at least 2 hours. Remove bone and skim fat from beans. Cut meat from the bone and chop into small cubes. Return meat to beans and add remaining ingredients. Cook at least 1 more hour or until done. Season to taste with salt and pepper.

MIXED BEAN SOUP WITH KIELBASA SAUSAGE

3 C beans, a variety of beans should be use
    i.e. baby lima, soy, pinto, white, and
    small red beans.
Ham bone or ham hocks
1/2 C dried chopped onions
2 qts tomatoes or 1 C dehydrated tomato
    powder reconstituted in 2 qts water
1/2 C rice
1 C dehydrated vegetable stew, reconstituted
1 large Kielbasa sausage, thinly sliced
Salt and pepper to taste

Wash and soak beans overnight. Drain and cover with water. Cook 3 to 5 hours with ham bone and onions. During the last half hour, add tomatoes, rice, vegetable stew and Kielbasa sausage. Season with salt and pepper.

This soup tastes even better as leftovers.

HEARTY SPLIT PEA SOUP

2 C chopped celery
4 C split green peas
16 C water, approx.
1/2 C dried chopped onion, reconstituted
1 C dehydrated carrots, reconstituted
Ham bone or ham hocks
2 bay leaves
1 tsp thyme leaves
1/4 C chopped parsley
Salt and pepper

Rinse peas well. Drain. In an 8- to 10-quart pan, combine all ingredients except salt and pepper. Bring to a boil over high heat. Reduce heat, cover and simmer about 2 1/2 to 3 hours. Add water if needed. Season to taste with salt and pepper. Serves 10.

GREEN BEAN AND SAUSAGE SOUP

4 slices bacon cut into 1/2 inch pieces
1/2 C dried chopped onions, reconstituted
3 tsp chicken bouillon
6 C water
1 C dehydrated potato slices, reconstituted
1/2 C dehydrated carrots, reconstituted
1/4 C chopped parsley
1 tsp dill weed
1/2 tsp marjoram leaves
1/4 tsp white pepper
2 C dehydrated green beans, reconstituted
1 lb Kielbasa sausage, thinly sliced

In a 5- to 6-quart pan, cook bacon over medium heat until crisp. Remove from pan and set aside. Discard all but 1 Tbsp of drippings. Add dried chopped onions. Cook, stirring until soft but not brown. Dissolve bouillon in water and add to onions. Stir in remaining ingredients except bacon. Bring to a boil over high heat. Reduce heat, cover and simmer for 1 hour or until vegetables are tender. Skim fat from soup. Add bacon. Serves 6-8.

CROCK POT LENTIL SOUP

1 lb lentils, sprouted or dried
2 1/2 quarts water
1 1/2 Tbsp dehydrated chicken bouillon
1 1/2 C diced potatoes
1 medium onion, chopped
1 C sliced carrots
1 C sliced celery
1 lb Polish sausage or 2 C diced ham
Salt
Chopped parsley

Put all ingredients, except salt and chopped parsley, in a crock pot. Cook for 8 hours on high, or until vegetables are tender. Top with chopped parsley and add salt as needed.

NETHERLANDS BEAN AND VEGETABLE SOUP

1 medium onion, chopped
2 Tbsp salad oil
1/2 C flour
1 1/2 quarts beef broth
3 C cooked or 2 16-oz cans Northern beans, drained
1 medium celery root, peeled and cut into 1/2 inch cubes
2 medium carrots, thinly sliced
3/4 lb Brussels sprouts, trimmed and cut in half
1/2 C whipping cream

In an 8-quart kettle, cook onion in oil, stirring, over medium-high heat until onion is limp, about 5 minutes. Stir in flour, then remove from heat. Gradually blend in broth; add beans, celery root, and carrots. Cover and bring to a boil; reduce heat and simmer until vegetables are tender when pierced, about 10 minutes. Stir in Brussels sprouts and cream and cook, uncovered, just until sprouts are tender, about 10 minutes. Serves 8.

GUADALAJARA BEAN SOUP

EXCELLENT!

3-4 lbs pork shoulder
1 Tbsp oil
1 C dried chopped onions, reconstituted
2 clove garlic, minced
2 tsp chili powder
1 tsp oregano leaves
1 tsp cumin
7 C water
2 C dried kidney beans
3 tsp beef bouillon
3 C water
4 C sliced carrots or 1 C dehydrated carrots,
    reconstituted
1 C corn, reconstituted or 1 can corn
Salt and pepper

Soak beans overnight. Cut meat into one-inch cubes. Brown in oil. Set aside. Saute onion and garlic in meat drippings. Stir in chili powder, oregano, and cumin. Add 7 cups water plus dried beans. Cook 2 hours, skimming fat, then add remaining ingredients. Simmer 30 minutes.

LOW FAT

SOYBEAN AND VEGETABLE SOUP

4 C water
1 C fresh peas or pea sprouts*
1 C finely chopped celery
1/2 C grated carrots
1/2 C diced turnips
1 onion finely chopped
2 C coarsely ground soybean sprouts*
1 tsp salt
2 tsp powdered chicken bouillon
Minced parsley

Put all ingredients, except salt and parsley, in a saucepan. Cover and cook for 20 minutes. Add salt and garnish with parsley. Serves 4 to 6.

LOW FAT

CREAM OF SOYBEAN SOUP

3 C soybean sprouts*
1/2 C water
3 C milk
1 tsp chicken bouillon
Alfalfa sprouts*, chopped

Put soybean sprouts and water in a saucepan and cook over low heat for 15 minutes or until tender. Whirl beans in blender or food chopper until smooth. Heat milk with bouillon in saucepan and add soybean puree. Salt to taste. Serve topped with alfalfa sprouts.

* See SPROUTING section in front of book for details on sprouting seeds.

LENTIL AND BROWN RICE SOUP

5 C chicken broth, or more
3 C water, or more
1-1/2 C lentils, rinsed
1 C brown rice
1 Can (35 oz) tomatoes
3 carrots, sliced
1 large onion, chopped
1 large stalk celery, chopped
3 large cloves garlic, chopped
1/2 tsp basil
1/2 tsp oregano
1/2 tsp thyme
1 bay leaf
1/2 C parsley
2 Tbsp vinegar
Salt and pepper

In large, heavy pan or Dutch oven, combine broth, water, lentils, rice, tomatoes, carrots, onion, celery, garlic, basil, oregano, thyme and bay leaf. Bring to a boil; reduce heat, cover pan and simmer, stirring occasionally, for about 1 hr. or until lentils and rice are both tender. Remove and discard bay leaf. Stir in parsley, vinegar, salt and pepper. If necessary, thin soup with additional hot broth or water.

ENTREES

BULGUR WHEAT

Whole kernel wheat
Water

Place wheat in a medium saucepan with enough water to cover wheat about 2 inches. Bring to boil. Turn off heat and let rest 1 to 2 hours.

Add more water if needed, and bring to boil again. Turn off heat and let rest again for another 1 to 2 hours.

Drain (save water for soups, other cooking or for watering plants). Dry wheat in oven at 200°. When dry, it can be cracked in a blender or grain mill or stored whole in a container on the shelf.

Bulgur wheat takes on a new flavor from the regular wheat.

SUGGESTIONS FOR PREPARING

1. Reconstitute 1 cup Bulgur wheat in 2 cups of water. Saute onion,green peppers and beef bouillon. Add wheat and saute until brown. Serve with Cream of Mushroom or Cream of Chicken soup on top. Optional: add canned chicken, pimento, almonds or tuna.
2. Melt butter, add onion and celery. Cook until tender. Blend in flour. Stir in chicken broth and milk. Cook over low heat, stirring constantly, until thickened. Add seasonings, wheat, turkey, ham and cheese. Pour into buttered two-quart casserole. Sprinkle almonds over top. Bake for 35 to 40 minutes at 350°. Serves 6 to 8.

SPANISH WHEAT

4 to 6 C cooked cracked wheat
1/4 C dried chopped onions, reconstituted
2 Tbsp olive oil
1 quart jar tomatoes
1 small can tomato sauce
1 clove garlic, chopped
1/2 C chopped green pepper
1 or 2 tsp chili powder
1/2 tsp cumin
1 tsp salt
1 tsp Worcestershire sauce
1 lb ground beef, cooked and browned
   (optional)
3/4 C grated Cheddar cheese

Put olive oil in large fry pan and saute drained onions, garlic, and green pepper for about 5 minutes or until done but not browned. Add tomatoes, tomato sauce and spices. Cook 10 minutes add. Pour over cooked cracked wheat and continue cooking for another 10 minutes. Serve topped with grated cheese. Serves 6 to 8.

Note: If you want added flavor, bake in oven for 25 minutes.

LOW FAT

EXCELLENT!

RICE AND WHEAT PILAF

3 Tbsp butter or olive oil
1 large green pepper, chopped
2 C rice, uncooked
2 1/2 tsp chicken bouillon powder, diluted in
   3 3/4 C boiling water
1/8 C chopped dried onion reconstituted, or
   1 fresh onion, chopped
2 C chopped celery
2 C whole wheat cooked

In a medium saucepan, melt butter; saute onions, green pepper, and chopped celery, saute until limp. Add the rest of the ingredients, and bring to a boil. Cover for 20 minutes and simmer.

Delicious Suggestion: Serve with Chicken Filling for Crepes (pg. 99).

HAMBURGER AND WHEAT CASSEROLE

2 C whole wheat
4 C water
2 lbs hamburger or ground turkey
1/4 C dried chopped onions, reconstituted
1/2 C chopped green pepper
1 tsp chili powder
1 tsp garlic powder
1 clove garlic, chopped
1 tsp cumin or oregano
1 qt tomatoes
2 C tomato sauce
1 small can chopped olives
1 1/2 C grated Monterey Jack cheese

Cook whole wheat in water for one and one half hours. Drain off any liquid.

Brown hamburger with drained onions and chopped green pepper. Add to drained wheat along with spices. Add tomatoes, sauce, and olives and simmer for 30 minutes. Place in a casserole dish and top with cheese. Bake at 350° for 25 to 30 minutes or until cheese is melted. Serves 8.

WHOLE WHEAT CHEESE BAKE

5 slices bacon cut into cubes
4 Tbsp flour
3 C tomato juice or 3 C reconstituted tomato
   paste
1 tsp salt
1/8 C dried chopped onions, reconstituted
3/4 C dehydrated cheese powder
3 C cooked whole wheat or cracked wheat
1/4 C buttered bread crumbs

Fry bacon until crisp. Remove from fat. Set aside. Save 4 Tbsp bacon fat and discard the rest. Saute onions in fat. Stir in flour and mix well. Add tomato juice and salt. Cook until thickened. Whip in cheese powder. Add cooked bacon. Pour mixture over cooked wheat and mix well. Place in a greased baking dish and top with buttered bread crumbs. Bake at 350° for 45 minutes.

CHICKEN CASSEROLE

2 C cooked whole wheat
1 4-oz can pimentos, chopped
1 1/2 C diced, cooked chicken
1/4 to 1/2 C canned mushrooms
1/2 C blanched almonds
1 3/4 C chicken broth
1 1/2 Tbsp flour

Combine wheat and pimentos. Place 1/3 of wheat mixture in greased casserole. Alternate layers of chicken, mushrooms and almonds. Pour over chicken broth seasoned with salt and pepper and blended with flour. Bake in oven at 350° for 1 hour. Serves 6 to 8.

SHRIMP JAMBALAYA

2 Tbsp butter or margarine
1/2 C chopped onion
1 green pepper, chopped
1 Tbsp flour
1 clove garlic, minced fine
1 C canned tomatoes
1/2 C water
1/2 tsp salt
1/4 tsp red pepper
1/4 tsp thyme
1 Tbsp Worcestershire sauce
2 C cooked whole wheat
1 can shrimp
1 C tomato juice
3/4 C grated nippy cheese
2 Tbsp parsley

Melt butter or margarine in saucepan, add onions, and green pepper, and cook until tender. Stir in flour and blend thoroughly. Add garlic, tomatoes, water, salt, red pepper, thyme, Worcestershire sauce, stirring occasionally. Add wheat, shrimp, and parsley over the top. Place in a 350° oven for 15 minutes. Serves 6 to 8.

TURKEY AND HAM CASSEROLE

1/4 C butter or margarine
1/4 C finely chopped onion
1/2 C chopped celery
1/4 C flour
2 C chicken broth or 1 tsp dehydrated
    chicken bouillon, in 2 C hot water
1 C milk
1 tsp salt
1/8 tsp pepper
1 tsp Accent
1/2 tsp poultry seasoning
3 C cooked whole wheat
2 C cubed turkey or chicken
1 C cubed cooked ham
1 C grated Cheddar cheese
1/2 C slivered, toasted almonds

Melt butter, add onion and celery. Cook until tender. Blend in flour. Stir in chicken broth and milk. Cook over low heat, stirring constantly, until thickened. Add seasonings, wheat, turkey, ham, and cheese. Pour into buttered two-quart casserole dish. Sprinkle almonds over top. Bake for 35 to 40 minutes at 350. Serves 6 to 8.

CROCK POT CRACKED WHEAT AND LENTILS

LOW FAT

1 C lentils, washed well
1 C coarse cracked wheat
4 C tomato juice or vegetable cocktail juice
1 lb ground beef (lean)
1 C chopped celery
1 medium onion or 1/8 C chopped
    dried onion, reconstituted
1 1/2 tsp salt
1 tsp chili powder
1/4 tsp pepper
1/4 tsp oregano
2 C whole canned tomatoes
1 Tbsp sugar

EXCELLENT!

LOW FAT

Place cracked wheat and lentils in crock pot. Add tomato juice and cook on high for 5 to 6 hours, or until grains are tender. Brown meat and onion in a skillet and cook. Add to crock pot with the remaining ingredients. Cook an additional 1 or 2 hour. Add more juice or water if desired.

GROUND TURKEY AND HAMBURGER MIXTURE
(large batch to freeze)

12 lbs ground turkey burger or lean
    hamburger
8 C cooked cracked wheat cereal, cooled
4 eggs
3 onions, chopped fine
1/4 C soy sauce
2 Tbsp ground coriander
1 tsp garlic powder
1 tsp nutmeg
4 tsp allspice
2 tsp salt
1 tsp pepper

In a large bowl, mix all ingredients very well. Meat can be frozen before or after baking it. Use in the following ways.

For meatballs: On a cookie sheet shape meat into meat balls (a small ice cream scoop may be used). Bake at 350° for 20 minutes.

For hamburger patties: Form meat into patties and place on a large baking pan. Bake at 350° for 30 minutes.

For meat loaf: Place meat in loaf pans and bake at 350° for 1 hour.

Divide into individual meal servings and place in freezer for later use in such meals as Sweet and Sour Meatballs, Spaghetti and Meatballs, and Barbecue Meat loaf.

EXCELLENT!

CRACKED WHEAT CHILI

2 onions, chopped fine
1 C celery, chopped
1 green pepper, chopped
2 Tbsp olive oil
1 can tomato sauce
1 qt jar canned tomatoes
1 Tbsp chili powder
1/2 Tbsp cumin
Salt to taste
1 lb ground meat, browned and
    drained (optional)
1 Tbsp sugar
6 C cracked wheat, cooked

Saute onion, celery, and green pepper in olive oil until limp but not browned. Add tomatoes and tomato sauce, spices, and sugar. Add meat if desired. Cook for 20 minutes to blend flavors together. Add cracked wheat and cook 1/2 hour, stirring occasionally. Top with grated cheese.

WHEAT AND RICE CASSEROLE

3 C cooked whole wheat
3 C cooked rice*
1 lb ground beef, browned or ham
1 onion, chopped
1 stalk celery, chopped
1 green pepper, chopped
2 carrots, chopped
Bean sprouts (optional)
Mushrooms (optional)
Garlic salt and white pepper to taste

Place all ingredients in a large skillet with 1/4 cup butter and soy sauce to taste and saute until hot.

* To cook rice: start in cold salted water. After it boils, simmer only 10 minutes. Rice will be firmer than usual.

BOSTON BAKED WHEAT

4 C cooked wheat
1 C catsup
1 C water
1/2 C mild molasses
1 onion, chopped
3/4 tsp prepared mustard
3 slices bacon, cut up and fried (optional)
Salt to taste

Mix all ingredients together and place in a baking dish. Bake at 325° for 30 minutes.

SPANISH MILLET LOAF

1 C millet
2 C water
Dash salt
1 C whole wheat bread crumbs
1 small can green chiles
2 C canned tomatoes
1 egg, beaten
2 Tbsp vegetable bouillon*
2 Tbsp olive oil
1 tsp chili powder

Add millet to 2 cups of water with salt in a sauce pan. Simmer gently for 10 min with lid on. Turn off heat; leave lid on; let stand 10 min.
Add remaining ingredients to the cooked millet. Pour into greased loaf pan. Bake at 350° for 45 minutes. Remove from oven; top with grated cheese. After cheese is melted, slice and serve.

*Bouillon can be purchased at Health Food Stores.

GROUND BEEF CRACKED WHEAT CASSEROLE

1 lb hamburger
1/2 onion
1 tsp salt
1 tsp poultry seasoning
2 C boiling water
3/4 C cracked wheat, uncooked
1 can tomato soup
Dash of pepper

Pour boiling water over cracked wheat. Brown onions and meat in a fry pan, using a little more fat if necessary. Add salt and pepper. Add soaked wheat. Add soup and poultry seasoning and mix thoroughly. Place in a greased casserole dish and bake at 325° for 1 hour to 1 hour and 20 minutes.

WHEAT SPROUT PATTIES

2 C wheat sprouts*
1 egg, slightly beaten
2 Tbsp minced onion
2 Tbsp minced green pepper
2 Tbsp chopped mushrooms
Butter or oil
Celery salt

Grind sprouts; add egg and vegetables. Mix well. In a skillet, heat butter, spoon sprout mixture in and press with the back of a spoon to form patties no more than 1/2 inch thick. Cook for 2 minutes on each side over medium heat until lightly browned. Sprinkle with celery salt. Serves 4.

* See SPROUTING section in the front of the book for detailed information on sprouting seeds.

WHITE BEANS AND CHICKEN CHILI

EXCELLENT!

1 lb Great Northern beans
6 C chicken broth
2 cloves garlic
2 to 3 tsp cumin
2 tsp oregano
2 7-oz cans chiles, chopped
Pinch Cayenne pepper
2 med. onions, chopped
3 or 4 C cooked chicken, chopped
2 Tbsp oil
Sour cream
Jack cheese

Wash, then soak beans overnight covered with water. Drain. In frying pan, saute onions and garlic briefly. In a crock pot or large kettle, place the beans with all other ingredients except chicken, sour cream, and Jack cheese. Cook until done, about 4-5 hours. Then add the cooked (or canned chicken. Heat thoroughly. Serve with sour cream and Jack cheese.

CHICKEN ENCHILADAS

EXCELLENT!

15 medium flour tortillas (Fajita size - 7-8 inches across)
4 - 5 chicken breasts (depending on size) cooked and cut bite size
20 oz cream of chicken soup (2 cans)
2 8-oz cans Ortega green chiles, diced
1 pint sour cream
1 lb grated Jack cheese
1 lb grated medium Cheddar cheese
1 small can sliced black olives
1 medium sized onion, grated
chopped green onion (for garnish) optional

Combine soup, chiles, onions, sour cream and olives with some of the cheese (save enough to spread on top). Reserve 2 1/2 cups of this mixture for the top. To the remaining sauce add the chicken. Place 2-3 heaping Tablespoons of the chicken mixture on the tortillas and roll. Place in 2 9x13 inch greased baking dishes. Cover with the reserved sauce, and sprinkle with remaining cheese and chopped green onion tops. Sprinkle with paprika and refrigerate overnight. May be frozen. Bake at 350° for approx. 45 min. or until heated through.

KULEBIAKU
(Russian dish made of layered eggs, spinach, salmon, and rice.)

Quick Puff Pastry:
2 C flour <u>or</u> 1 1/2 C flour and 1/2 C wheat
    pastry flour
1/4 tsp salt
3/4 C cold butter
2/3 C cold water

#1

#2

#3

Combine flour and salt in a medium bowl. Cut butter into about 60 pieces. Drop into flour and toss lightly to break butter pieces apart and coat with flour. Add cold water all at once and mix quickly. Mixture will be lumpy. Turn onto a lightly-floured surface and knead 10 times to form a rough ball. Shape into a rectangle and flatten slightly.

The following process of rolling out, folding, and turning the dough is called a turn. Adding flour to work surface as necessary, roll out dough away from you and towards you, not sideways. Making a 15x6 inch rectangle and keeping dough as uniformly thick as possible, fold into thirds like a letter. Give dough a quarter turn so the long opening is to your right. Repeat the turn twice for a total of 3 turns. If butter begins to break through dough, sprinkle that spot generously with flour. If dough becomes difficult to roll, wrap in plastic and refrigerate 10 minutes. If dough has streaks after the third turn, give 1 more turn. Makes 2 cups.

IMPORTANT:
If you do not want to make this dough, you can buy Puff Pastry sheets in the grocery store.

#4

KULEBIAKU (continued)

Filling:
1 can pink or red salmon
Few drops liquid smoke
    seasoning
1 9-oz pkg frozen creamed
    spinach
3 hard boiled eggs

Rice Layer:
1 Tbsp butter
1/2 C chopped onion
1/2 C rice
1 C chicken broth
1/4 tsp salt
2 Tbsp chopped parsley
1/2 C canned mushrooms

Egg Glaze:
1 egg
1/4 tsp salt

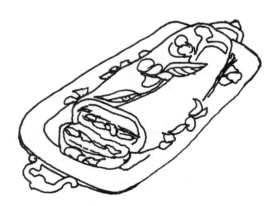

Prepare dough for pastry. Flake salmon, discard bones. Add a few drops of liquid smoke and set aside. Prepare rice layer; cook all ingredients together for 20 minutes. Let cool and set aside. Coarsely chop eggs, set aside. On a lightly-floured surface, roll out dough to a 14 inch square. Place chopped eggs in center of square in a 9x4 inch strip. Place salmon layer on top of eggs shaping a rectangle with neat straight sides. Arrange creamed spinach evenly over salmon. Top with rice layer, keeping sides straight and patting layers down. Filling will lie 3 to 4 inch high. Cut a 4x2 inch rectangle from each corner of the square for decorations. Refrigerate scraps. Prepare Egg Glaze.

Beat egg with salt until think, making a smooth liquid.

Brush a 2-inch wide strip at edge of one long side of dough with glaze. Fold unglazed long side over filling. Fold side with glazed edge to overlap unglazed side. Dough should fit snugly around filling. Brush short ends with glaze. Tuck in excess dough and fold ends up. Place an ungreased baking sheet next to loaf. Gently roll loaf onto baking sheet seam side down. Make small hole in center top. Brush top generously with glaze. Using scraps, cut decorations. Press on top of loaf and brush with glaze. Refrigerate for 30 min, then bake at 400° for 40 minutes. Serve with Dill Sauce (pg. 93).

COOK'S TIP: This recipe is also excellent using chicken and broccoli in place of the salmon and spinach.

Also, to make either recipe more creamy, simply saute 1/4 cup chopped green onion in 1 tablespoon of butter. Add 8 oz. softened cream cheese and heat but do not let boil. Add your choice of either the salmon or chicken and continue as directed in above recipe.

CREAMY DILL SAUCE

EXCELLENT!

2 Tbsp butter
1/4 C sliced green onions
2 Tbsp flour
1 tsp dried dill weed
1/2 tsp salt
3/4 C milk or 3/4 C nonfat
    powdered milk,
    reconstituted
1/2 C dairy sour cream

Melt butter in a small saucepan over medium heat. Add green onions. Saute for 5 minutes, stirring occasionally. Add flour, dill weed, and salt. Mix well, add milk, stir constantly over medium heat until mixture thickens and comes to a boil. Remove from heat, stir in sour cream. Keep warm over very low heat (do not boil).

SHRIMP AND CRAB CASSEROLE

2 onions, chopped
3 Tbsp vegetable oil
4 bay leaves
1 tsp thyme
Pinch of tarragon
1 pint heavy cream, half and half, or 1 can
    evaporated milk
1 6-oz can tomato paste
1/4 C lemon juice
2 cans shrimp, or 1 can shrimp and 1 can
    crab
Salt
Pepper

Saute onions in vegetable oil until golden brown, Lower heat. Add bay leaves, thyme, and tarragon. Blend in heavy cream, tomato paste, and lemon juice. Add shrimp, salt and pepper. Simmer 20 minutes, stirring. Serve with rice. (If sauce is too thick, add a little water.)

EXCELLENT!

SALMON LOG
(Christmas or holidays)

1 C canned salmon
1 8-oz cream cheese
1 Tbsp lemon juice
2 tsp chopped green onions
1 tsp horseradish
1/4 tsp liquid smoke
1/2 C chopped almonds

Mix all ingredients together well. Shape into 2 or 3 logs. Roll each log in nuts. Chill.

Note: Creamy dill sauce is wonderful served over any fish.

SALMON PIE WITH DILL SAUCE

1 double-crust wheat pastry
2 dehydrated whole eggs, reconstituted
1/2 C nonfat powdered milk, reconstituted
1/2 tsp salt
1/4 tsp pepper
1/4 tsp dried dill weed
1 16-oz can salmon
2 slices whole wheat bread
3/4 C thinly sliced celery
1/2 C sliced ripe olives
1/2 C sliced green onions or 1/8 C dried chopped onions, reconstituted

Prepare dough for pastry.

In small bowl, combine egg, milk, salt, pepper, and dill until smooth, set aside. Drain salmon and flake with fork. Tear bread into 1/2-inch pieces. In a large bowl, place salmon, bread pieces, celery, olives and onions. Add egg mixture. Stir gently to mix. Preheat oven to 375°.

Roll out wheat dough to fit a 9-inch pie pan. Spoon salmon mixture into unbaked pie shell. Roll out remaining dough. Cut into slits. Place slits over filling. Flute edges. Glaze with beaten egg if desired. Cover edges with foil. Bake for 25 minutes and remove foil. Continue baking for 25 to 30 more minutes. Let stand for 5 or 10 minutes before serving.

Prepare Creamy Dill Sauce (pg. 93) and serve with pie. Serves 8.

TUNA OR SALMON PATTIES

1 C chopped onion
1 16-oz can salmon, drained or 2 7-oz cans tuna
1 C cooked rice
1 tsp instant chicken bouillon
1 4-oz can mushrooms
1 tsp salt
1 tsp dill
1 tsp parsley
2 eggs, beaten
2 C whole wheat bread crumbs

Mix all ingredients together except bread crumbs. Form into patties. Coat with bread crumbs. Place carefully in greased skillet and cook until golden brown. Serve with Tartar Sauce (pg. 95).

TARTAR SAUCE

1 C mayonnaise
1/2 onion, chopped fine
1 large dill pickle, diced
1 Tbsp lemon juice
Salt to taste
1/2 tsp Worcestershire sauce

Mix all ingredients together.

TUNA AND BROCCOLI

2 7-oz cans tuna, drained
3 C chopped broccoli
5 Tbsp margarine
4 Tbsp flour
1 tsp salt
1 tsp basil
1 quart milk
1 1/4 to 1 1/2 C chicken broth
1 C mushrooms (optional)
1 large onion (optional)

Saute broccoli and onion. Melt margarine, stir in flour, salt, and basil. Remove from heat and stir in milk and broth. until thick. Stir in mushrooms, onions, and broccoli. Simmer 15 minutes. Remove from heat and stir in tuna. Serve.

TUNA CASSEROLE

1 12-oz pkg egg noodles
1/2 C chopped onions
1/2 C diced green onions
1 4-oz can mushrooms
2 cans cream of mushroom soup
1 Can drained tuna
1/2 C milk
1 C frozen or canned peas
2 C grated Cheddar cheese
2 C crushed potato chips

Cook noodles according to package directions, leaving them slightly under cooked. Combine all other ingredients except cheese and potato chips. Place in casserole dish and top with grated cheese and crushed potato chips. Bake at 350° for 45 minutes.

CRAB AND ARTICHOKE CASSEROLE

6 oz macaroni
Boiling salted water
3 Tbsp butter or margarine
3 Tbsp flour
1/4 C nonfat powdered milk,
    reconstituted to 1 C
1 tsp instant chicken bouillon
    reconstituted in 1/2 C water
1/2 C shredded Swiss cheese
2 tsp Worcestershire sauce
2 pkgs (9 oz) frozen artichoke hearts
1 to 2 cans crab meat
2 to 3 Tbsp Parmesan cheese

Cook pasta in large kettle. Drain.

Melt butter in small pan over medium heat. Blend in flour and cook, stirring, until bubbly. Remove pan from heat. Whip in milk. Return to heat and cook, stirring, until smooth and thick. Slowly blend in chicken bouillon, Swiss cheese, and Worcestershire. Cook until cheese melts.

Spoon a thin layer of sauce into a 2 1/2 quart casserole dish. Divide the artichokes, crab meat, and pasta in half. Layer first half in even layers over sauce.   Repeat with second half and end with sauce. Sprinkle Parmesan cheese over top. Bake uncovered at 350° for 35 minutes. Serves 6.

EXCELLENT!

CRAB AND SHRIMP OVER ENGLISH MUFFINS

1 tsp salt
1/2 tsp white pepper
1/2 tsp cayenne
1/4 tsp sweet basil
1/8 tsp thyme leaves
1/8 tsp oregano
4 Tbsp butter
1/4 C chopped onions
1/2 C chopped green onions
1 Tbsp flour
1 can evaporated milk
1 can crab
1 can shrimp
6 toasted English muffins

Combine the seasonings in a bowl; mix and set aside.   Melt the butter in a 2-quart saucepan over high heat. Add the onions and saute until they start getting tender, about 2 or 3 minutes, stirring occasionally. Add the seasoning mix and cook about 1 minute.   Add the green onions and flour, stirring until flour is completely blended into the butter. Then stir in the evaporated milk and bring to a boil, stirring frequently. Reduce heat and simmer until sauce has slightly thickened (about a minute). Add canned crab and shrimp, heat through. Remove from heat and serve over muffins immediately.

PASTRIES

Pastry Crust:
1 C margarine
1 C cottage cheese
2 C flour
Dash of salt

Mix ingredients together to form a ball. Roll on a floured board. Cut into 2 to 3 inch circles.

Place an even amount of one of the following fillings in the center of each circle. Brush edges with an egg yolk and milk mixture. Fold over to make a half-moon shape and seal by pressing edges with a fork. Brush tops with egg yolk and milk mixture to glaze. Place on a greased baking sheet and bake at 375° for 20 minutes or until golden brown.

CHICKEN OR TURKEY FILLING

3 Tbsp butter
1/2 small onion, finely chopped or 1/2 C
    dried chopped onion, reconstituted
1 4-oz can mushrooms
2 Tbsp flour
Salt
Pepper
1/4 tsp nutmeg
1 tsp oregano leaf
1/4 tsp tabasco sauce
1/2 C canned evaporated milk
1 C canned or fresh diced chicken or turkey
1/2 C diced ham or canned Spam

Melt 2 Tbsp butter in a saucepan; add onions and fry until tender but not brown. Add drained mushrooms, and cook for 3 to 4 minutes. Remove vegetables from pan with slotted spoon and set aside. Add remaining butter to the pan, melt. Stir in flour, salt, and pepper to taste, nutmeg, oregano, and tabasco. Cook, stirring, for 1 minute. Remove from heat and gradually stir in evaporated milk. Return to heat; cook until thickened. Remove from heat, stir the cooked vegetables into sauce and add chicken and Spam. Cool and stuff in pastries.

CRAB AND SHRIMP FILLING

1 can crab meat
1 can shrimp
1/4 C butter
1/4 C dried chopped onions, reconstituted
1 4-oz can mushrooms
1/4 C flour
1/2 tsp salt
1/4 tsp marjoram leaf
1/2 C chicken broth
1 C evaporated milk
1 Tbsp lemon juice
1 Tbsp chopped parsley

Rinse seafood, drain. Melt butter in a medium saucepan over medium heat. Add onions and mushrooms. Saute until onion is tender, stirring occasionally. Stir in flour, salt and marjoram. Add broth and evaporated milk all at once. Stir until mixture thickens. Stir and boil for 1 minute. Stir in lemon juice, parsley, and seafood. Cool and stuff in pastries.

CORNED BEEF TURNOVERS

1 C canned corned beef
1/4 C finely chopped onion
1 8-oz can sauerkraut, drained
1 tsp caraway seeds
1 egg, beaten
1/4 tsp salt
1 C shredded Swiss cheese

Combine corned beef and onion in small bowl. Combine sauerkraut and caraway seeds in another bowl.

Using the pastry dough recipe on pg. 97, roll out an 18x12 inch rectangle. Cut into six 6-inch squares. Beat egg and salt together until smooth and lightly brush around edges of each square, making a 3/4 inch border. Place about 3 Tbsp corned beef mixture slightly off center on each square. Spread to inside edge of glazed border. Top with about 2 Tbsp sauerkraut mixture and about 2 1/2 Tbsp cheese. Fold half of square over filling, matching opposite points and making a triangle. Firmly press edges together with fork. Make two 1-inch slits on top of each turnover. Place on an ungreased baking sheet. Lightly brush turnovers with egg glaze. Sprinkle with 1 tsp caraway seeds. Bake about 20 minutes or until golden brown -- 375° to 400°.

Note: Puff Pastry can also be used.

CHICKEN FILLING FOR CREPES, NOODLES, OR RICE

1 frying chicken or can chicken or turkey
1/2 cube butter
1 onion, chopped, or 1/4 C chopped
    onions, reconstituted
2 Tbsp capers
4 tsp chicken bouillon
6 C boiling water
1 C evaporated milk
1 C creamy soup base
1/4 C mushrooms, reconstituted
    (optional)
1/3 C broccoli, reconstituted (optional)
1/4 tsp white pepper
2 Tbsp lemon juice
Salt to taste
1/2 C Parmesan cheese

Boil chicken, bone and let cool.

Saute onions for 3 to 4 minutes in butter*. Add capers and saute another minute. Dissolve chicken bouillon in the boiling water and add to onion mixture. Simmer 10 minutes. In a blender, whirl creamy soup base in evaporated milk and pour into boiling chicken broth. Cook to thicken. Add pepper, lemon juice, salt, and Parmesan cheese. Mix the cooled chicken into sauce and serve rolled in crepes, or on top of noodles or rice.

*To substitute creamy soup base use 1/2 C flour. Add this to butter mixture.

CROCK POT CHICKEN

LOW FAT

1 chicken, cut up and skinned
2 stalks celery, sliced
1 8-oz can water chestnuts
1 4-oz can mushrooms, drained
1 onion, chopped
1 C chicken broth
1 Tbsp cornstarch
1/4 C water

Place all ingredients except cornstarch and water in crock pot. Cook on low for about 8 hours. Remove large pieces of chicken from pot; set aside. Make a paste using cornstarch and water. Thicken the sauce with the cornstarch paste. Bring to a boil and stir briefly. Remove bones from chicken and return to pot. Reheat and serve over Rice and Wheat Pilaf (pg. 84).

CORNED BEEF CASSEROLE

1 6-oz pkg egg noodles or elbow
    macaroni, cooked
1 12-oz can corned beef
1/4 C reconstituted chopped onions
3/4 C creamy soup base diluted in 2 C
    water
2 tsp beef bouillon
Grated Swiss or Cheddar cheese

Make a cream sauce by mixing creamy soup base, water, and beef bouillon together. Mix well. Add onions, corned beef, and noodles. Place in a 2 quart buttered casserole dish. Sprinkle with cheese. Bake at 350° for 45 minutes.

CHICKEN POT PIE

1 recipe Mock Puff Pastry (recipe below)
1 Tbsp butter
1/   1/3 C dehydrated mushrooms,
    reconstituted
4 green onions
2 Tbsp flour
1 tsp dehydrated chicken bouillon
    dissolved in 1 C boiling water
1 tsp Worcestershire sauce
1/3 C dehydrated sweet peas,
    reconstituted
1/3 C dehydrated sliced carrots,
    reconstituted
1 Tbsp chopped pimento
1 dehydrated whole egg, reconstituted
1/4 C evaporated milk
1 1/2 C diced cooked chicken or canned
    chicken or turkey
Salt
Pepper

Prepare dough for Mock Puff Pastry. Wrap and refrigerate.

In large skillet, melt butter. Add mushrooms and green onions and saute about 4 minutes or until onions are soft. Sprinkle with flour. Stir until blended. Stir in bouillon, Worcestershire sauce, peas, carrots and pimentos. In a small bowl, combine egg and evaporated milk. Stir into mushroom mixture. Add chicken or turkey. Cook over low heat until heated through. Season with salt and pepper. Pour into a casserole dish.

On a lightly floured board, roll out chilled dough. Make a 1/8-inch thick rectangle. Place dough over filling in casserole dish and seal dough to edge. Cut vent holes into the top of pastry. Brush with milk. Bake 20 to 30 minutes or until pastry is crisp and golden. Makes one small casserole.

MOCK PUFF PASTRY

1 1/2 C flour
1/2 tsp salt
1/2 C plus 2 Tbsp butter, chilled
1 egg, slightly beaten
2 tsp lemon juice
3 to 4 Tbsp iced water

Mix flour and salt. With pastry blender, cut butter into flour until mixture is in pea-sized pieces. In small bowl, beat egg and lemon juice and 3 Tbsp water. Sprinkle egg mixture over flour mixture. Stir with fork until dough holds together, forming a ball. Add more water if necessary. Roll out and use.

HAM AND POTATO CASSEROLE

3 large boiled potatoes or 3 C reconstituted
    potato slices
Ham slices or 1 can Spam, chopped
2 small onions or 1/4 C reconstituted
    chopped onions
2 dill pickles, sliced thin
1/2 C sour cream
3 Tbsp butter
2 Tbsp flour
1 C beef bouillon reconstituted
1 tsp Worcestershire sauce
3 drops tabasco sauce
Sharp Cheddar cheese, grated

If using reconstituted potatoes, pre-cook them. Arrange ham, potatoes, pickles, and chopped onions in layers in a casserole dish. Melt butter and add flour, stirring constantly. Cook 3 minutes. Add beef bouillon, sour cream, Worcestershire sauce, and tabasco sauce. Stir well. Cook until thick. Pour into casserole dish and sprinkle top with Cheddar cheese. Bake at 350° for 30 minutes, or until potatoes are well done.

EXCELLENT!

LOW FAT

SWEET AND SOUR VEGETABLES WITH TOFU

2 Tbsp cornstarch
1/2 C vinegar
1/2 C brown sugar
2 Tbsp low sodium soy sauce
1/4 tsp ginger
1 16-oz crushed pineapple with juice
1 Tbsp oil
1-2 clove garlic, crushed
1 onion, chopped
1 large green pepper, sliced
6 large mushrooms, sliced
1 8-oz can sliced water chestnuts, drained
1 pkg frozen pea pods, thawed
12 oz firm tofu, cubed

Prepare sauce by making a paste of cornstarch and vinegar. Cook over medium heat, adding brown sugar, soy sauce, ginger, and pineapple. Simmer until thick, and set aside.

Heat oil and garlic in fry pan. Stir in vegetables, except tomatoes, and cook until done. Gently stir in cubed tofu, and sauce. Add the quartered tomatoes. Heat until warmed through. Serve over rice!

Note: To substitute frozen pea pods use mixed frozen vegetables such as broccoli, cauliflower and carrots.

TAMALE PIE

1 lb hamburger
1/4 C chopped onions, reconstituted
2 tsp oil
1 can tomato soup
1 tsp salt
1 to 2 tsp chili powder
1/3 C sweet corn, reconstituted
1 C black olives

Topping:
1/3 C whole wheat flour
1/2 tsp salt
2 tsp baking powder
1/2 C cornmeal
1 reconstituted egg
2 Tbsp oil
1/4 C nonfat milk diluted in 3/4 C water

Brown hamburger and onions in oil. Add remaining ingredients and cook over low heat while mixing the topping.

For topping: Sift together all dry ingredients. Combine egg, oil, and milk and add to dry ingredients. Stir just until blended.

Place hamburger mixture in 2-quart casserole dish. Cover with topping. Bake at 400° for 25 minutes.

DELUXE TAMALE PIE

2 Tbsp vegetable oil
1/4 C dried chopped onions, reconstituted
1 C chopped green peppers
1 lb extra-lean ground beef
1 large can or 1 qt jar of tomatoes
2 Tbsp dehydrated tomato powder,
    reconstituted
3/4 C dehydrated sweet corn,
    reconstituted
1 C sliced stuffed green olives or black
    olives
2 tsp cumin
2 tsp unsweetened cocoa powder
1 1/2 tsp salt
1/2 tsp allspice
2 tsp chili blend
1/4 to 1 tsp hot pepper sauce
1 Tbsp yellow cornmeal
Tamale topping (recipe follows)

In large skillet, heat oil. Add onions and green pepper and saute until tender. Add beef; cook until crumbly and no longer pink. Add tomatoes, tomato paste, corn, olives, cumin, cocoa, salt, allspice, chili blend, pepper sauce, and cornmeal. Simmer for 30 minutes, stirring frequently. Spoon into a shallow 2 1/2 quart casserole dish.

Preheat oven to 400°. Prepare tamale topping. Spoon topping in large spoonfuls around edge of casserole. Bake uncovered 10 minutes. Reduce heat to 350° and continue baking for 30 minutes or until cornmeal topping is cooked through and lightly browned. Serves 8.

TAMALE TOPPING

1 C flour
1 C yellow cornmeal
3 Tbsp sugar
2 tsp baking powder
3 Tbsp dehydrated butter, reconstituted
3/4 C nonfat powdered milk,
  reconstituted
1 dehydrated whole egg, reconstituted
1/2 C dehydrated cheese powder
1 4-oz can diced green chiles

In large bowl, mix flour, cornmeal, sugar, and baking powder. Add butter, milk, and egg. Stir until dry ingredients are just moistened. Quickly stir in cheese and chiles. Spoon on top of casserole.

TAMALE PIE CASSEROLE

1 C dried chopped onions, reconstituted
2 Tbsp oil
1 lb ground beef
2 Tbsp each chili powder, and sugar
2 tsp salt, divided
1/2 tsp oregano, crushed
3 1/2 C drained cooked pinto or red
  beans
1 minced clove garlic
1/4 tsp cumin
1 29-oz can tomatoes
1 6-oz can tomato paste or 1 C dehydrated
  tomatoes, reconstituted
1 2 1/4-oz can sliced ripe
  olives
5 C water, divided
1 C cornmeal
1/2 C shredded Cheddar cheese

Saute onions in oil until tender. Add ground beef and brown, breaking apart with fork. Add chili powder, sugar, 1 tsp salt, oregano, beans, garlic, cumin, tomatoes, tomato paste, olives and 1/2 cup water. Simmer for 1 hour. Combine cornmeal with 1/2 cup water. Bring remaining 4 cups water to a boil. Add 1 tsp salt and cornmeal. Cook 10 minutes or until thickened.

Spread half of corn meal mixture in bottom of deep 3-quart baking dish. Add bean mixture. Spread remaining cornmeal mixture over beans. Bake at 350° for 20 to 30 minutes. Sprinkle with cheese. Bake for 5 minutes longer. Serves 8.

MACARONI AND SAUSAGE BAKE

1 1/2 lbs mild sausage or spicy Italian
    sausage
6 oz macaroni
Boiled salted water
1/2 C dehydrated cheese reconstituted to
    1 C
1 tsp Italian spice
1/2 tsp salt
1/2 tsp pepper
Dash of cayenne pepper
1/2 C dehydrated sweet peas,
    reconstituted
1/2 C evaporated milk

Cook reconstituted peas for 1/2 hour in their liquid.

Remove and discard sausage casings. Crumble sausage into wide frying pan and cook over medium heat until browned, about 6 minutes. Drain and set aside.

Cook macaroni in boiling salted water until done. Drain. Turn into large bowl. Add sausage, cheese, Italian spice, salt, pepper, cayenne pepper, drained peas, and milk. Toss lightly to blend ingredients. Turn into 2 1/2-quart baking dish. Bake covered at 350° for 20 minutes or until bubbly. Serves 6.

MEAT TURNOVERS

Crust:
1 C margarine
1 C cottage cheese
2 C flour
Dash of salt

Mix until forms a ball. Roll on floured board. Cut into softball-size circles, about 12.

Filling:
1 lb ground beef or 1 can beef in gravy
1 pkg onion soup mix

Fill circles with about 1 tablespoon of filling. Seal edges with fork. Bake at 375° for 30 minutes. Don't overbake. Serve with brown gravy.

CHICKEN SAUCE

1 frying chicken
1/2 cube butter
1 onion chopped or 1/4 C chopped onions
    reconstituted
2 Tbsp capers
4 tsp chicken bouillon
6 C boiling water
1 C evaporated milk
1 C creamy soup base
1/4 C mushrooms, reconstituted
    (optional)
1/3 C broccoli, reconstituted (optional)
1/4 tsp white pepper
2 Tbsp lemon juice
Salt to taste
1/2 C Parmesan cheese

Boil chicken, bone and let cool.

Saute onions for 3 to 4 minutes in butter. Add capers and saute another minute. Dissolve chicken bouillon in the boiling water. Simmer 10 minutes. Whirl creamy soup base in evaporated milk and pour into boiling chicken broth. Cook to thicken. Add pepper, lemon juice, salt, and Parmesan cheese. Mix the cooled chicken into sauce and serve over egg noodles.

EXCELLENT!

LOW FAT

ERWIN'S SALMON LOAF

2 1-lb cans salmon, with juice
1 Tbsp Dijon mustard
1/4 C lemon juice
2 C cracker crumbs
1 large onion, chopped
1/2 tsp lemon pepper
2 eggs, beaten
1 tsp dill
skim milk to moisten, as needed

Mix all ingredients together and place in a loaf pan. Cover with foil (optional). Bake at 350° for 30 to 45 minutes. Remove foil and return to oven for 15 more minutes to brown.

SPAM CASSEROLE

1 can Spam, grated
1/2 lb sharp cheese, grated
1 can mushroom soup
1 onion, chopped
2 eggs
6 slices dry bread
1 1/2 C milk

Place all ingredients, except the milk in a casserole dish. Heat oven to 325°. Pour milk over ingredients and let stand 15 minutes. Bake for 45 minutes.

KAREN'S IMPOSSIBLE SALMON PIE

1 C dairy sour cream
1/2 tsp dried dill weed
1 can (7 3/4-oz) salmon, drained and flaked
1/2 tsp dried dill weed
1 1/2 C milk
3/4 C buttermilk baking mix
3 eggs
1/2 tsp salt
1/4 tsp pepper
1 tsp lemon juice

Mix sour cream and 1/2 tsp dried dill weed. Cover and refrigerate.

Heat oven to 400°. Lightly grease a 9 or 10 inch pie plate. Sprinkle salmon and 1/2 tsp dill weed in pie plate. Beat milk, baking mix, eggs, salt, pepper, and lemon juice until smooth, 15 seconds in a blender on high speed or 1 minute with a hand beater. Pour into pie plate. Bake until golden brown and a knife inserted comes out clean, about 35 minute. Let stand for 5 minutes before cutting. Serve with sour cream mixture.

SALMON MOUNTAIN STRATA

LOW FAT

1 1-lb can salmon
1/2 C chopped onion
1/2 C chopped celery
4 eggs
2 C milk
1 1/2 tsp salt, divided
1/4 tsp dried dill weed
1/8 tsp pepper
4 medium potatoes (6 C sliced)

In large bowl combine salmon, onion, celery, eggs, milk, 1/2 tsp salt, dill, and pepper. Mix well. Pare and cut potatoes into thin slices. Place half of the potatoes in a greased 1 1/2 quart baking dish. Sprinkle with 1/4 tsp salt and spread half of the salmon mixture over potatoes. Repeat with remaining potatoes, salt and salmon. Bake uncovered at 350° for 1 hour and 15 minutes, or until potatoes are tender when pierced with a fork. Let stand 5 minutes and serve with Dill Sauce (pg. 93) or Tarter Sauce (pg. 95). Serves 8.

POTATO FINGERS

1/4 C butter or margarine
1/2 C chopped onion
1/4 C chopped red pepper
1/4 C grated Parmesan cheese
1/2 tsp salt
1/2 tsp garlic powder
1 large potato or more
1 medium green pepper, cut in rings

In a medium skillet melt butter, add onion and red pepper, cook until vegetables are tender. Stir in cheese, salt and garlic powder. Pare potato, cut into 1/2 inch thick, lengthwise strips; add to skillet, toss to mix well. Turn into greased 1 quart baking dish. Arrange pepper rings on top. Bake covered at 350° for 30 to 40 minutes or until potatoes are tender when pierced with a fork. Serves 6.

CRAB A LA KING

3 Tbsp butter or margarine
3 Tbsp flour
1/4 tsp salt
1/8 tsp mace
1 1/4 C milk
1 7 1/2-oz can crab, undrained
1/2 C canned sliced mushrooms
1 Tbsp chopped pimento or green pepper
    (optional)
Baked patty shells, hot buttered toast or
    toasted English muffins

In a saucepan, melt butter. Stir in flour, salt, and mace. Cook, stirring, until foamy. Remove from heat and blend in milk. Cook and stir until thickened. Stir in crab, mushrooms, and pimento or green pepper. Heat until hot and serve in patty shells, or on toast, or on toasted English muffins. Serves 4.

CORNED BEEF CASSEROLE

Potatoes
Carrots
1 onion
2 Tbsp oil
Salt
Pepper
Cabbage
1 can corned beef
2 C water

Saute chunks of potatoes and carrots and onion in oil, enough for your family. Salt and pepper to taste. Lay wedges of cabbage on top and crumble corned beef on top of the cabbage. Add water and cover. Steam until done.

TUNA A LA KING

1/2 C flour
1/2 C butter
3 hard cooked eggs
1/2 can pimento
1/2 pkg frozen peas
1 small can mushrooms
1 large can tuna
1 tsp MSG
1 tsp salt
2 C milk

Heat butter; add flour, stir into a smooth paste. Heat milk and add to flour mixture. Stir constantly until smooth and thickened. Dice hard cooked eggs and pimento. Add to sauce. Cook frozen peas 2 minutes and drain. Add peas and mushrooms to white sauce. Drain oil from tuna and pour boiling water over tuna in sieve. Dice and add all ingredients to sauce. Do not cook after, or mixture will scorch. Serve in individual pie shell or over hot toast. Serves 6.

TUNA EGGS

1/3 C chopped dry-roasted peanuts
1/2 C thinly sliced green onions
3/4 C shredded Cheddar cheese
8 eggs
1 Tbsp water
1/4 tsp each salt and dill weed
1/8 tsp pepper
3 Tbsp butter or margarine
1 7-oz can tuna, drained

Combine the peanuts, onions, and cheese; set aside. Beat together the eggs, water, salt, dill, and pepper.

Melt butter in a large frying pan over medium-low heat; add eggs, then break the tuna into bite-sized pieces and distribute evenly over top. Cook slowly, gently lifting the cooked portion from the bottom to allow the uncooked egg to flow underneath. Cook just until set to your liking. Transfer to a serving platter and sprinkle with cheese mixture. Serves 4.

MEATLESS POTATO CASSEROLE

8 C reconstituted dehydrated cubed potatoes
   or fresh potatoes
1/4 C melted butter
2 Tbsp minced onions or 1/4 C chopped
   green onions
1 can cream of chicken soup
1 pt sour cream
2 C grated Cheddar cheese
Salt to taste

Mix all ingredients together and place in a greased 9x13 pan. Top with buttered bread crumbs. Bake at 350° for 45 minutes or until browned on top.

Note: Chicken may be added to this recipe.

BARBECUE SAUCE

1/3 C vinegar
2/3 C water
1 1/2 Tbsp prepared mustard
1/3 C brown sugar
1/4 tsp pepper
1 tsp salt
Pinch of cayenne pepper
2 lemon slices
1 large onion, sliced
2 Tbsp butter or margarine
2/3 C catsup
1 1/2 Tbsp Worcestershire sauce

Combine all ingredients. Cook 20 minutes. Pour over ribs, chicken, beef, or turkey. Bake.

IMPOSSIBLE TACO PIE

1 lb ground beef
1/2 C chopped onion
1 envelope taco seasoning mix
1 4-oz can chopped green chiles, drained
1 1/4 C milk
3/4 C Bisquick
3 eggs
2 tomatoes, sliced (optional)
1 C shredded Monterey Jack or Cheddar
   cheese

Heat oven to 400°. Grease a 9x13 pan. Cook and stir beef and onion until brown; drain, stir in seasoning mix. Spread in pan and top with chiles. Blend milk, baking mix and eggs until smooth, 15 seconds in a blender on high. Pour into pan. Bake for 25 minutes. Top with tomatoes and cheese. Bake 8 to 10 minutes longer or until knife inserted in center comes clean. Cool for 5 minutes. Serve with sour cream, chopped tomatoes, shredded lettuce and shredded cheese if desired. Serves 8.

IMPOSSIBLE CHEESEBURGER PIE
(makes its own crust)

1 lb ground beef
1 1/2 C chopped onion
1/2 tsp salt
1/4 tsp pepper
1 1/2 C milk
3/4 C Bisquick
3 eggs
2 tomatoes, sliced
1 C shredded cheese

Heat oven to 400°. Grease pie or cake pan. Brown beef and onion; drain. Stir in salt and pepper. Spread in plate. Blend milk, baking mix and eggs until smooth, 15 seconds in a blender on high. Pour into plate. Bake 25 minutes. Top with tomatoes, sprinkle with cheese. Bake until knife inserted in center comes out clean, 5 to 8 minutes. Cool 5 minutes. Serves 8.

MOCK TAMALE CASSEROLE

1 lb ground beef
1 large onion, chopped
Dash of salt
3/4 C uncooked cracked wheat
1 can tomato soup
1/2 tsp garlic powder
2 C boiling water
1 can corn or 2 C dehydrated sweet corn,
    reconstituted
1 tsp parsley
2 tsp chili powder
2 C grated cheese

Saute ground beef and onions, place in casserole. Add remaining ingredients, mix well. Bake at 325° for 1 hour. During the last 5 minutes, sprinkle with grated cheese. Leftovers are good served with corn chips or as taco or tostada filling.

CHEESE BALL
(Christmas or holidays)

3 4-oz pkgs cream cheese
1 lb Cheddar cheese, grated
1 C chopped green olives
2 Tbsp prepared mustard
2 cans deviled ham
2 Tbsp chopped chives

Mix all ingredients together well and roll into a ball. Roll ball in chopped walnuts, if desired. Chill.

MOCK ENCHILADA

EXCELLENT!

4 Tbsp oil
3 Tbsp chopped onions
2 cans tomato sauce or 1 qt canned tomatoes
1 4-oz can green chili peppers, chopped
2 tsp chili powder
1 tsp cumin
1/4 C sugar
1/4 tsp pepper
5 Tbsp dehydrated whole eggs, reconstituted
    in 1/2 C water or 4 eggs
1 can evaporated milk
12 tortillas
1 lb Jack or Cheddar cheese

Put oil and onions in a sauce-pan and saute but do not brown. Add tomato powder and water, chili peppers, spices, and sugar. Simmer for 5 minutes. Lightly beat eggs, water, and evaporated milk. Remove tomato mixture from heat. Quickly stir in egg mixture.

Cover the bottom of a 9x13 pan with sauce. Make layers of tortilla, sauce and cheese until all is used. Bake at 350° for 30 minutes. Serves 8 to 10.

SPINACH CHICKEN WITH RICE

1/4 C dehydrated peas, reconstituted
6 slices bacon, chopped
1/4 C onions, reconstituted
1 garlic clove, crushed
1 14-oz can whole tomatoes
1 3-oz can pimentos, drained
2 tsp paprika
1/4 tsp ground saffron
1 tsp salt
2 1/2 C water
1 1/3 C rice, washed
1 large can chicken or turkey

Cook peas in reconstituted liquid for 20 or 30 minutes or until tender. Set side.

Cook rice in water for 20 minutes, or until tender. Set aside.

In large frying pan, cook bacon until crisp. Reserve 2 to 3 Tbsp drippings. Transfer bacon to paper towels to drain. Add onion and garlic to drippings and saute for 5 minutes. Add tomatoes, pimentos, paprika, and saffron. Cook another 5 minutes. Stir in rice, peas, bacon, and chicken. Place in a covered casserole dish and place in oven for 35 minutes. Serves 4.

CHICKEN PILAF

1/4 C dehydrated butter, reconstituted
1 large can chicken or turkey
1/4 tsp salt
1/8 tsp black pepper
1/2 tsp dried tarragon
1/2 C dehydrated mushrooms, reconstituted
2 C rice
1 1/2 tsp dehydrated chicken bouillon diluted
    in 2 1/2 C boiling water
1/2 C evaporated milk

Cook mushrooms for 1/2 hour in liquid they have been reconstituted in. Drain. Carefully mix in the chicken bouillon and evaporated milk. Add all spices and gently add chicken and butter (do not over-stir). Bring to a boil and cover. Cook 20 minutes or until rice is tender and all liquid is evaporated. Serves 4.

MEATLESS BURRITOS

1 C lentils
2 C water
1/2 C rice
Powder garlic (to taste)
powder onions (to taste)
1 tsp salt

Boil lentils 10 minutes. Add rice. Cover and steam 20 minutes. Add more water if needed.

To cook -- Put lentil mixture on tortillas. Add hot sauce and cheese. Roll up and fry in oil pan.

CHICKEN WITH RICE AND RAISINS

1 C uncooked brown rice
2 1/2 C water
1/2 C golden raisins
1/2 C orange juice
4 C cubed chicken or canned turkey
1/4 C flour
1 tsp dried tarragon
1/2 tsp paprika
1/ tsp salt
1/8 tsp white pepper
2 Tbsp dehydrated reconstituted butter
1 Tbsp oil
3/4 C evaporated milk
3/4 C nonfat powdered milk,
     reconstituted
1 tsp dehydrated chicken bouillon
     dissolved in 1 C water

Lightly butter a 2-quart casserole dish. Place rice and water in medium saucepan. Cover and cook until tender and all water is absorbed.

In small saucepan combine raisins and orange juice. Bring to boil. Reduce heat and simmer for 5 minutes. Set aside.

Mix flour, tarragon, paprika, salt and white pepper together. In skillet, melt butter and add oil. Stir in flour mixture. Remove from heat. In a blender, whirl nonfat milk, evaporated milk and bouillon. Whisk into flour mixture and cook until thickened. Add raisins and orange mixture. Preheat oven 350°. Arrange rice in buttered casserole dish. Cover with 1/2 of sauce and top with chicken. Pour remaining sauce on top and bake uncovered for 30 minutes. Serves 6.

SALMON AND RICE

1 large can salmon
1 1/4 C evaporated milk
1/2 tsp nutmeg
1/4 C butter
1/8 C dried chopped onion, reconstituted
10 oz cooked rice
2 hard boiled eggs, chopped
1/2 tsp salt
1/4 tsp black pepper
2 tsp curry powder

In saucepan, combine salmon, evaporated milk and nutmeg, stirring just to mix. Cook mixture, stirring occasionally, for 3 to 5 minutes or until fish is heated through. Remove from heat. Set aside.

In large saucepan melt butter. Add drained onions and cook until translucent but not brown, about 5 minutes. Stir in cooked rice and half of the eggs. Next add the salmon mixture and seasonings. Remove from heat and sprinkle remaining eggs on top. Serve immediately. Serves 4 to 6.

RICE WITH CANNED SHRIMP

1/4 C butter
2 Tbsp olive oil
1/4 C dried chopped onion, reconstituted
1 garlic clove, finely chopped
1 red pepper, chopped or 1 small jar
    pimentos
1/3 C dehydrated mushrooms, reconstituted
1/2 tsp basil
1 tsp salt
1/8 tsp black pepper
2 C rice
2 cans shrimp, drained or 12 oz fresh shrimp
3 3/4 C boiling water
1/2 C Parmesan cheese

In large fry pan, melt half of the butter in olive oil over medium heat. Add onions, garlic, red pepper and drained mushrooms. Saute for about 5 minutes but do not brown. Add seasonings and rice. Reduce heat to low and cook for 5 more minutes stirring occasionally. Stir in shrimp carefully. Add boiling water and cover. Cook 15 to 20 minutes or until done. Remove the pan from heat and stir in remaining butter and Parmesan cheese. Serves 4 to 6.

LENTILS OVER RICE

1 large onion, chopped
1 carrot, chopped
1 Tbsp olive oil
1/2 tsp thyme leaves
1/2 tsp marjoram leaves
2 C chicken broth
1 C water
1 C uncooked lentils
2 8-oz cans tomato sauce
1/4 C chopped parsley
6 C cooked brown rice

In a large pot, saute onion and carrots in the olive oil for about 3 minutes. Add thyme and marjoram and saute for 1 minute. Add chicken broth, water, lentils, tomato sauce, and parsley. Simmer for 1 hour. Add more water if necessary. Serve over cooked brown rice.

Note: low fat recipe

BAKED BARLEY

1 C pearl barley
1/4 C dried chopped onion, reconstituted
1/3 C dehydrated sliced
    mushrooms, reconstituted
5 Tbsp butter
1 tsp dehydrated chicken bouillon
    or dehydrated beef bouillon dissolved in
    2 C boiling water
Salt
Pepper

In a skillet, saute onions and mushrooms in butter until tender, about 5 minutes. Stir in barley and continue cooking until it is browned lightly. Pour the mixture into a buttered casserole dish and add 1 cup bouillon. Cover and bake at 350° for about 30 minutes. Uncover and stir in remaining cup of bouillon. Add salt and pepper to taste. Cover and continue baking until all the liquid is absorbed and the barley is tender. Serves 4 to 6.

BARLEY AND ALMOND CASSEROLE

2 Tbsp butter
1/3 C slivered almonds
1/4 C butter
1 C barley
1 chopped onion
1/2 C fresh parsley, minced
1/4 C chives or green onion, minced
1/4 tsp pepper
1/4 tsp salt
1 14-oz cans beef or chicken broth

Heat 2 Tbsp butter; add almonds and stir fry until toasted, set aside. Melt 1/4 cup butter in a pan, add barley and onion. Saute until tender. Remove from heat. Stir in almonds, parsley, chives, salt and pepper. Spoon into a 1 1/2 quart casserole. Heat the concentrated broth to boiling. Blend into barley mixture. Bake at 375° for 1 hour, or until barley is tender and water is absorbed.

CURRIED BROWN RICE

1 1/2 C brown rice
3 C water
1 clove garlic, minced
1/2 C chopped onion
1/2 C chopped green pepper
1/2 C raisins
1/4 tsp curry powder
1 C water
2 Tbsp margarine or butter
1/2 tsp salt

Cook rice in 3 cups of water for 45 minutes. Saute garlic, onion, and green pepper in butter. Add raisins, curry powder, and water. Simmer for 10 minutes. Combine with cooked rice and cook together on low heat for another 15 minutes.

MUSHROOM BARLEY PILAF

1 lb fresh or canned mushrooms
1 C chopped onion
1 Tbsp margarine or butter
1 1/2 C uncooked pearl barley
1 4-oz can pimento, chopped
2 C chicken broth
1/4 tsp pepper

Pre-heat oven to 350°. Wash, dry and slice mushrooms. Saute onions and mushrooms in margarine in a large skillet for 4 to 5 minutes. Transfer to a large casserole dish. Add barley and pimento. Stir in broth and pepper. Cover and bake for 50 to 60 minutes or until barley is tender. Additional water may be needed during cooking if mixture seems dry. Can also be cooked on stove top in a large kettle on low heat for 45 minutes.

HAM AND FRIED RICE

2 C rice
3 C water
1/2 tsp salt
1 Tbsp butter
2 dehydrated whole eggs, reconstituted
4 Tbsp vegetable oil
1/2 C dehydrated string beans,
    reconstituted
1 C cooked ham cut in small pieces
1/2 tsp black pepper
1/8 C dehydrated chopped onions,
    reconstituted
1 tsp coriander

Put rice, water and salt in saucepan; cover and cook over medium heat for 15 to 20 minutes. Remove from heat and set aside.

In frying pan, melt the butter. Add eggs and cook 2 or 3 minutes. Stir with a fork until they are just set. Set aside in bowl.

Add oil to fry pan. Heat and saute onions for 2 minutes. Add cooked rice, beans, ham, and pepper. Cook, stirring constantly, for 2 minutes or until rice is well coated with oil. Add eggs and coriander. Continue stirring for 2 more minutes. Serves 4.

VEGETABLE RICE

2 C rice, washed and soaked in cold water
    for 30 minutes
3 1/8 C water
1 tsp salt
1/4 C butter
1/8 C dried chopped onions, reconstituted
1 qt jar whole tomatoes, drained and
    chopped
1 small jar pimentos, chopped
1 tsp celery salt
1/3 C dehydrated broccoli, reconstituted
1/3 C dehydrated mushrooms, reconstituted
1/4 tsp cayenne pepper

Drain rice and place in a large saucepan. Pour in water and add salt. Bring to boil. Cover and reduce heat to low, simmer for 15 to 20 minutes or until rice is tender. Remove from heat and set aside.

In large frying pan, melt butter. Saute drained onions and mushrooms for about 4 minutes. Add tomatoes, pimentos, celery salt, and broccoli. Cook for 10 minutes, or until tender. Season with salt and cayenne pepper.

Add rice to pan and stir. Cook until heated throughout. Serve.

Note: As other options, add a can of tuna or crab. Canned chicken or turkey is also delicious.

CURRIED RICE AND CARROTS   LOW FAT

1 C dehydrated sliced carrots,
    reconstituted
3/4 C uncooked white rice
1 tsp curry powder
1 green onion, sliced
1/4 C dehydrated raisins, reconstituted
2 tsp dehydrated chicken bouillon
    reconstituted in
1 1/2 C boiling water

Cook carrots for 1/2 hour and set aside.

Place rice in a shallow baking dish. Place in oven. Set oven to preheat 400°. Remove rice after 8 to 10 minutes or when lightly browned. Butter a 1 1/2 quart casserole dish. In casserole dish combine drained carrots, curry powder, green onions, raisins, and toasted rice. Stir in boiling bouillon. Bake uncovered for 25 minutes or until rice is done. Before serving fluff with a fork. Serves 4 to 6.

INDIAN CURRY DISH

6 C cooked rice
Juice of 1 to 2 lemons
1 to 2 tsp curry powder
6 C fresh mixed vegetables, peas, broccoli,
    cauliflower, peppers, carrots, or green
    onion
1 Tbsp oil
2 Tbsp mustard seed
1/4 tsp ground cumin
1/2 tsp salt
1/8 tsp cayenne pepper
1/4 C. chopped almonds
1/4 C chopped unroasted cashews
1/2 C raisins
2 C plain low-fat yogurt

Cook rice and drain well. Chop vegetables into medium sized chunks. Add oil and spices to chopped vegetables and stir until well coated. Cover and simmer until nearly tender Do not overcook. Mix with rest of ingredients and rice. Preheat oven 325°. Bake in a 9x13 dish for 40 minutes.

LOW FAT

SPINACH AND RICE CASSEROLE

1 10-oz pkg chopped, frozen spinach or
    canned spinach, drained well
1/2 C chopped onion
1/4 C sliced mushrooms
1 Tbsp olive oil
3 Tbsp whole wheat flour
2 C low-fat cottage cheese
3 eggs or 3 dehydrated eggs, reconstituted
3 C cooked brown rice
1/4 tsp pepper
1/2 tsp thyme
1/2 tsp garlic powder
1/2 tsp salt
1 Tbsp sesame seeds
1 Tbsp Parmesan cheese

Pre-heat oven to 350°. Thaw frozen spinach, drain. Saute onions and mushrooms in the oil. Combine with flour, cottage cheese, eggs, uncooked spinach, cooked brown rice, and seasonings. Pat into a shallow 9x12 baking dish. Top with sesame seeds and Parmesan cheese. Bake for 40 to 50 minutes.

BROWN RICE WITH BROCCOLI

2 onions, chopped
2 stalks celery, chopped
1 Tbsp margarine or olive oil
3 C chopped fresh broccoli or 3 C
    dehydrated broccoli, reconstituted
2 cans cream of celery soup
1/4 C Parmesan cheese
5 C cooked brown rice
4 drops tabasco sauce
1 8-oz can sliced water chestnuts, drained
4 Tbsp soft bread crumbs

Pre-heat oven to 350°. In a large skillet, saute the onions and celery in margarine until clear. Cook broccoli until barely tender and drain well. Mix broccoli with soup and cheese. Add celery and onions. Stir in rice, tabasco sauce, and water chestnuts. Mix well. Pour into a lightly oiled casserole dish and top with bread crumbs. Bake for about 20 to 30 minutes.

MEATLESS RICE AND BROCCOLI CASSEROLE

1 small chopped onion
3 Tbsp melted butter or margarine
1 pkg frozen or 1 lb fresh chopped broccoli
    or 2 C reconstituted dehydrated broccoli
1 can cream of mushroom soup 1 can cream
    of chicken soup
1 C cooked rice
1/2 C grated Cheddar cheese
1/2 C milk
1/2 tsp salt

Mix all ingredients together and pour into a large buttered casserole dish. Bake at 350° for 45 minutes.

Optional: Add 1 cup cooked chicken or ground beef.

SPANISH RICE

1 C uncooked long grain white rice
1 clove garlic
1 Tbsp olive oil
1 medium onion, chopped
1 green pepper, chopped
1 16-oz can tomatoes, reserve liquid
3/4 tsp chili powder
1/4 tsp marjoram leaves
1/2 tsp salt

Brown the rice and garlic in the oil in a 10-inch skillet. Add enough water to the tomato juice to make 2 cups. Pour into skillet and add remaining ingredients. Bring to a boil. Reduce heat to low, cover and cook for 20 minutes or until rice has absorbed all the liquid. Remove from heat. Let stand covered for 10 minutes before serving.

RICE AND WHEAT PILAF

3 Tbsp butter or olive oil
1/8 C chopped dried onion, reconstituted or
    1 onion, chopped
1 large green pepper, chopped
2 C celery, chopped
2 C rice, uncooked
2 C whole wheat, cooked
2 1/2 tsp chicken bouillon diluted in 3 3/4 C
    boiling water

In a medium saucepan, melt butter, saute onion, green pepper, and chopped celery until limp. Add the remaining ingredients, and bring to a boil. Cover and simmer for 20 minutes.

Delicious suggestion: serve with Chicken Filling for Crepes, pg. 99.

BROWN RICE AND SAUSAGE CASSEROLE

6 C cooked brown rice
1 lb Italian sausage
1 1/4 C chopped onion
1 C green pepper, chopped
1 C chopped celery
1 C sliced water chestnuts
1 4-oz can mushrooms
1 to 2 cans cream of mushroom
1 Tbsp chopped parsley

Brown sausage. Drain well. Add green pepper, onion, and chopped celery. Saute until limp. Add remaining ingredients. Bake 1 hour at 350°.

PILAF WITH CURRANT AND PINE NUTS

1 C long grain rice
1 Tbsp margarine or butter
1 10 1/2-oz can condensed beef broth
3/4 C water
1/4 C currant or raisins
2 Tbsp toasted pine nuts or slivered almonds

In a 10-inch skillet, stir rice in margarine over medium heat until lightly browned. Carefully add broth, water, and currants. Bring to boiling; reduce heat. Cover and simmer 15 to 20 minutes or until rice is tender and liquid is absorbed. Transfer to serving dish and sprinkle with nuts. Serves 6.

SPICED RICE WITH ALMONDS

3 Tbsp slivered almonds
2 Tbsp cooking oil
1 medium onion, thinly sliced
1 clove garlic, minced
1 C long grain rice
1/4 tsp ground cardamon
1/8 tsp ground ginger
Dash ground red pepper
Dash ground cinnamon
Dash ground cumin
Dash ground nutmeg
1 3/4 C chicken broth

In a medium saucepan, stir almonds in hot oil until lightly browned; remove and drain on paper towels. Add onion and garlic to saucepan. Cook and stir until onion is tender but not brown. Stir in uncooked rice, cardamon, ginger, red pepper, cinnamon, cumin, and nutmeg. Cook and stir about 3 minutes to brown the rice. Add chicken broth. Bring to boiling; reduce heat. Cover and simmer for 15 minutes; do not lift cover. Remove from heat. Let stand, covered, for 10 minutes. Stir in almonds before serving. Serves 4.

LOW FAT

BLACK BEANS AND RICE

3 C black bean sprouts*
2 C rice sprouts*
3/4 C water
1 large onion, finely chopped
2 cloves garlic, crushed
1 green pepper, finely chopped
1 bay leaf
1 tsp salt
1/2 tsp pepper
1/4 C olive oil
1/4 lb ham, finely chopped or 1 can Spam

May use rice and beans without sprouting

Heat 2 tablespoons olive oil in a large skillet and add half of the onion, garlic, green pepper, salt, and pepper. Saute until tender, then add beans, rice, bay leaf, and water. Cook, covered, over low heat until beans are tender, about 30 minutes. Remove bay leaf and let mixture stand 5 minutes. Meanwhile heat ham in remaining 2 tablespoons of olive oil. When lightly sauted, add remaining onions, garlic, green pepper, and seasonings. Serve ham mixture over beans and rice. Serves 4.

* See SPROUTING section in the front of the book for detailed information on sprouting seeds.

PLEASE see the front of the book for further information on SPROUTING DRY BEANS, SOAKING DRY BEANS, AND COOKING TIPS FOR BEANS.

CROCK POT CHALUPA

EXCELLENT!

1 lb pinto beans
2 or 3 lbs pork roast
7 C water
1/2 C dried chopped onions
2 cloves garlic, minced
1 Tbsp salt
2 Tbsp chili powder
1 Tbsp cumin
1 tsp oregano
1 4-oz can chopped green chiles
Corn chips

Put all ingredients, except corn chips, in crock pot. Cover and simmer about 5 hours or until beans are done and roast falls apart. Serve with corn chips and a choice of toppings. Makes 5 quarts.

Toppings:
Chopped tomatoes
Chopped avocado
Chopped onions
Grated Cheddar cheese
Shredded lettuce

CROCK POT BEANS

1 lb navy beans or great northern beans
6 C water
1/2 C molasses
2 tsp dry mustard
2 Tbsp dried chopped onions
1/4 tsp pepper
1/4 tsp thyme
1 tsp ginger
2 tsp salt
4 slices bacon, diced

Rinse beans well and combine with water in a crock pot. Cook at high setting for 3 hours. Add remaining ingredients. Cook at high setting 4 additional hours, stirring occasionally.

CROCK POT CHILI

1 lb pinto beans
1 C water
1 C diced onion
1 clove garlic, minced
3/4 C diced celery
1/2 lb lean ground beef
3/4 lb pork steak, cut in 1/2 inch cubes
1 29-oz can tomatoes
1 6-oz can tomato paste
1 chicken bouillon cube <u>or</u> 1/2 tsp chicken
   bouillon
1 1/2 tsp salt
1 tsp cumin
2 1/2 Tbsp chili powder

Wash and soak beans overnight. Drain. Lightly brown meat and onions. Add all ingredients to crock pot, along with 1 cup water, or more if needed. Cover, cook on low for 10 to 12 hours. Top with grated Cheddar cheese.

EXCELLENT!

MARLENE'S FAVORITE CHILI BEANS

1 lb dried kidney beans (or may use canned)
1/2 lb bacon slices, cut into 1" slices
   (optional)
4 cloves garlic, chopped
3 onions, finely chopped
1 green bell pepper, diced
3/4 lb lean ground beef
1 Tbsp chili powder
1/2 tsp cayenne pepper
1 Tbsp ground cumin
1 qt canned tomatoes
2 cans tomato sauce
1 Tbsp brown sugar
1 Tbsp dried leaf oregano
1 tsp salt
1 tsp freshly ground pepper

Optional:
If available add 1 fresh anaheim and 1 fresh jaloppa pepper seeded and chopped fine

Topping:
1 C shredded Cheddar cheese
1/2 C sour cream

If using dried kidney beans, wash, cover generously with water and cook until done.

Fry bacon pieces in a large saucepan. Drain, saving the grease. In the reserved bacon grease, fry the garlic, onions, and bell pepper for about 2 to 3 minutes. Add the ground beef and cook, stirring often, until the beef is browned. Add the chili powder, cayenne and cumin and saute another minute or so. Add the fried bacon pieces and remaining ingredients, except topping, and bring to a boil. Cook gently until thick, about 20 minutes.

Serve topped with the Cheddar cheese and a dollop of sour cream. Serves 4-6.

QUICK REFRIED BEANS

2 1/2 C water
1 tsp salt
1 tsp ham bouillon or base
3/4 C pinto bean flour
1/4 tsp cumin
1/2 tsp chili powder
Picante sauce, optional

Bring water, salt and bouillon to a boil in a small saucepan. Whisk in the bean flour and seasonings. Cook, while stirring, over medium heat for 1 minute, or until mixture thickens. Reduce heat to low, cover pan and cook 5 minutes. Add Picante sauce to taste, if desired, (mixture thickens as it cools).

REFRIED BEANS

1 1/2 C uncooked pinto beans
1/4 C chopped onion
2 cloves garlic, minced
2 Tbsp olive oil
1 tsp ground cumin

Soak beans overnight in water. The next day boil beans in 6 C fresh water until tender, about 2 to 3 hours.

Saute onions and garlic in oil until clear. Add a little water if onions stick. Mash half the beans and add to onion and garlic. Continue to saute for 10 minutes, stirring. Add cumin, and remaining beans. Continue cooking until they are warmed through. Water or liquid from beans may be added to keep beans soft and mushy.

MEXICAN SPICE MIX

5 tsp cumin
5 tsp chili powder
2 1/2 tsp black pepper
5 Tbsp dried chopped onion
5 Tbsp dried garlic
2 1/2 tsp salt

Whirl in blender and store in covered bottle.

MEXICAN REFRIED BEANS

3 Tbsp Mexican Spice Mix (pg. 125)
3 C cooked pinto beans

Add Mexican Spice Mix to drained cooked pinto beans along with 1 cup reserved bean liquid. Cook for 20 minutes. Mash with an electric mixer. Add more water, if necessary. Serve hot or reheated. Great for tacos, enchiladas, burritos or dip.

BEAN PIZZA

EXCELLENT!

2 C cooked pinto beans
1/2 lb ground beef
1 C dried chopped onions
1 8-oz can tomato sauce
2 tsp chili powder
1 tsp cumin
1/2 tsp salt
1/2 C chopped green pepper
1 small can sliced olives
1 lb frozen bread dough thawed, or 1 recipe
    pizza dough
1/2 lb grated Monterey Jack cheese
Red pepper flakes to taste
Guacamole recipe (below)

Mash 1 C beans and set aside remaining cup of beans. Brown the beef with onions in large skillet. Stir in mashed beans, tomato sauce, chili powder, cumin, and salt. Simmer 10 minutes. Pat or roll dough to cover bottom of greased 14 inch pizza pan or a cookie sheet. Spread with bean-beef mixture. Top with remaining green pepper, olives, whole beans, and cheese. Sprinkle with red pepper flakes. Bake in pre-heated 400° oven for 15 min or until crust is browned. Cut into wedges. Top each serving with Guacamole.

(To make this pizza meatless, omit the beef and increase the beans to 3 cups, mashing 2 of the cups).

GUACAMOLE

Mash 1 medium avocado with 1 clove garlic, minced, and 1 Tbsp lemon juice. Add liquid red pepper sauce and salt to taste. Stir in 1/4 cup chopped tomatoes. Cover with plastic and chill.

BEAN BURRITOS

2 C drained, cooked, pinto, pink, or kidney
    beans
1/2 C peeled and finely chopped tomatoes
1/4 C chopped green pepper
1/4 C chopped onion
2 Tbsp diced green chiles
1 small clove garlic, minced
2 Tbsp oil
1/2 C shredded Monterey Jack cheese
1/4 tsp salt
Bottled hot pepper sauce
6 flour tortillas (8 inch)
Taco sauce
Dairy sour cream (optional)
Tomato wedges (optional)

Mash the drained beans. Saute chopped tomatoes, green pepper, onions, chiles and garlic in oil. Add mashed beans, cheese, salt and hot pepper sauce to taste. Heat thoroughly. Wrap tortillas in foil and heat at 350° for 10 minutes. Place about 1/4 cup bean mixture along center of each tortilla and roll up. Serve with taco sauce or top each with sour cream and tomato wedges.

IRENE'S WONDERFUL BAKED BEANS

4 C kidney beans, cooked
4 C small white beans, cooked
4 C lima beans, cooked
2 cans pork & beans
10 slices bacon **or** ham **or** Spam
3 onions, diced
2 tsp dry mustard
2 cloves garlic, diced
1/3 C molasses, dark
1/4 C vinegar
2 cans crushed tomatoes (4 C)
1/2 C brown sugar
1/2 C smoked barbecue sauce
1 tsp Worcestershire sauce

Drain all of the beans, then mix all ingredients together and simmer slowly for about 2 hours, adding brown sugar during last hour of cooking.

Can also bake in oven at 350° for about 2 hours.

SOYBEANS AND CORN

2 C soybeans
2 C dehydrated sweet corn, reconstituted
Chopped parsley
Salt
1 cube butter or margarine

Soak soybeans overnight and sprout for 3 days (sprouting is optional).

Cover soybeans with water and cook for 3 or 4 hours. Liquid may evaporate so add more water if needed. However, the last hour, let water evaporate out. Watch carefully in order not to burn. Cook corn separately until desired tenderness. Combine corn, soybeans, parsley, butter, and salt. Serve warm.

Note: The corn and soybeans make a complete proteins.

SOYBEAN AND CARROT LOAF

2 C cooked soybeans
2 large carrots
1/4 medium onion
1/2 C nuts
2 eggs
1/8 tsp allspice
1 tsp salt
1 tsp dry mustard
1/2 C grated cheese

In a blender mix first 5 ingredient for about 3 minutes on high speed. Add spices and pour into a loaf pan. Cover top with grated cheese. Bake at 325° for 45 minutes.

SOYBEANS FOR SANDWICHES

Soak soybeans overnight and sprout for 3 days.

Cook 5 hours. Grind.

EXCELLENT!

EGG FILLING

2 boiled eggs, mashed
1/2 C soybeans prepared as above
1 dill pickle, chopped
1/3 C green olives, chopped (optional)
3 green onion, chopped
Mayonnaise
Salt to taste

Mix above ingredients together. Spread on bread.

EXCELLENT!

TUNA FILLING

1/2 C soybeans prepared as above
1 can tuna, drained
1/2 C celery, chopped
1 sweet or dill pickle, chopped
Mayonnaise

Mix above ingredients together and season to taste. Spread.

PEANUT BUTTER FILLING

1/4 C peanut butter or 1/4 C reconstituted
    peanut butter powder
1/2 C soybeans prepared as above
Honey

Mix above ingredients and refrigerate any unused portion.

NAVY BEANS WITH SAUSAGE

1 C navy beans, cooked and drained
1 lb pork sausage
2 Tbsp butter
1 medium onion, chopped
2 tsp flour
3/4 C stock
Squeeze of lemon juice
Salt
Pepper

In a skillet, fry the sausage until brown on all sides, pricking them to release the fat. Discard all but 2 or 3 tablespoons fat. Add cooked beans and cook over brisk heat until they are lightly browned and have absorbed all the fat. Transfer to a serving dish and keep hot.

Wipe out the skillet. Heat the butter and brown the onion; stir in flour. Pour in stock and bring to a boil, stirring. Simmer for 10 minutes. Add lemon juice. Pour mixture over beans and sausage. Season and serve hot.

EXCELLENT!

LIMA BEAN SAUSAGE CASSEROLE

2 C lima beans
1 lb bulk pork sausage
1 Tbsp dried chopped onion
1/8 tsp garlic powder
1/8 tsp MSG
1/4 tsp rosemary leaves
1/4 tsp thyme leaves
1 8-oz can tomato sauce
1/4 C butter
1 C dry bread crumbs
1 Tbsp parsley flakes

Wash and soak lima beans overnight. Cook until done but not mushy.

Crumble sausage in pan; add onion, garlic, MSG, and cook until sausage is browned, stirring and breaking up sausage. Crush rosemary leaves and add to sausage along with thyme and tomato sauce. Simmer for 15 minutes. Drain lima beans; add to sausage. Mix well. Transfer to a 1 1/2 quart casserole dish. Melt butter; stir into bread crumbs and parsley flakes. Toss lightly. Spoon over top of bean mixture. Bake at 350° for 1 hour or until golden brown.

SOUR CREAM LIMAS

EXCELLENT!

1 lb baby lima beans
6 C water
1/4 C melted butter
1/2 C brown sugar
1/4 C molasses
2 Tbsp prepared mustard
1 tsp salt
1 C sour cream

Soak beans overnight. Cook 2 to 3 hours. Drain thoroughly. Combine butter, brown sugar, molasses, mustard, and salt. Mix with drained beans. Stir in sour cream. Spoon into baking dish. Bake at 350° for 30 to 40 minutes or until bubbly.

BLACK BEANS AND RICE

LOW FAT

1 1/4 C uncooked black beans
4 C water
1 clove garlic, minced
1 small onion, peeled and stuck with 3 whole cloves
1/2 tsp salt
1 Tbsp oil
1 C chopped onion
1 green pepper, chopped
4 C cooked rice (1 1/2 C uncooked)

Soak bean overnight. The next day, bring beans to a boil. Reduce heat to moderate. Cook for 1 hour. Add garlic, onion with clove, and salt. Cook for 1 hour longer. Remove whole onion with clove from beans and discard.

Saute chopped onion and green pepper in oil briefly. Add to beans. Stir and cook a few minutes to blend flavors. Serve black beans over cooked rice and top with Salsa (below).

SALSA

1 16-oz can tomatoes, drained
3/4 C diced red or white onions
2 cloves garlic, chopped
1 Tbsp wine vinegar
1 tsp oil
3 dashes tabasco sauce

In a small bowl, break up tomatoes with a spoon. Mix in remaining ingredients. Cover and refrigerate to let flavors blend.

EASY SALSA

LOW FAT

2 clove garlic
3 dried hot red peppers
1 jar whole tomatoes
1/2 tsp cumin (or more)
1/2 tsp oregano

Mix together in blender or food chopper.

BAKED NAVY BEANS

1 lb uncooked navy beans
3 Tbsp brown sugar
3/4 tsp salt
1 tsp dry mustard
1/3 C dark molasses
1/2 C ketchup
2 onions, chopped
1/2 lbs bacon, fried crisp and drained

Soak beans overnight in enough water to cover. Drain and place in saucepan. Cover with water and simmer covered for 1 to 2 hours.

Mix beans with brown sugar, salt, mustard, molasses, ketchup, and onions. Pre-heat oven 325°. In a 2 quart casserole pan, pour in beans and bacon. Cover and bake for 5 to 6 hours, adding more water if needed.

BEAN STROGANOFF

LOW FAT

3 C chopped mushrooms
2 medium onions, sliced
1 tsp olive oil
1/4 C flour
3/4 C beef or chicken bouillon
4 tsp Worcestershire sauce
1/8 tsp marjoram leaves
1/8 tsp chili powder
1/8 tsp thyme leaves
Dash nutmeg
1/2 tsp garlic powder
6 C cooked pinto beans
1 1/2 C sour cream or plain low fat yogurt
1 tsp fresh lemon juice

In a large skillet, saute mushroom and onions in oil until tender. Mix flour and bouillon, Worcestershire sauce, and spices. Add to skillet and cook until thick. Stir in cooked drained beans and stir over low heat until heated through. Remove from heat and stir in sour cream or yogurt and lemon juice. Serve over cooked rice.

SOYBEAN SOUFFLE

3 C cooked soybeans, soaked and simmered
    for 5 or 7 hours
3 Tbsp minced green onion
1 Tbsp parsley
1/2 C milk or tomato juice
1 Tbsp wheat germ
Salt to taste
3 slightly beaten egg yolks
3 egg whites, beaten until stiff

Mash, grind, or blend soybeans until smooth. Add remaining ingredients except egg whites. Mix well. Carefully fold in egg whites. Place in a souffle dish and bake at 325° for 25 to 30 minutes.

SOYBEAN SAUSAGE PATTIES

2 C soybeans, cooked
1 C lima beans, cooked
1 C navy beans, cooked
2 Tbsp chopped green onions
2 tsp salt
1/8 tsp paprika
1 Tbsp oil
1/4 tsp sage
1/4 tsp thyme
1/4 tsp marjoram
1 beaten egg
2/3 C milk
1 C cornmeal

Grind soybeans, lima beans, and navy beans together until smooth. Add green onions, salt, paprika, oil, sage, thyme, and marjoram. Mix together. In a small bowl combined egg and milk. Shape bean mixture into sausage shapes and dip into egg mixture. Dip each sausage into cornmeal to cover both sides, and place in a well greased baking dish. Bake at 400°, turning once. Allow to brown.

LIMA BEANS AND RICE

2 lbs lima beans, barely cooked with liquid
2 lbs rice, uncooked
4 Tbsp olive oil
2 large onions, chopped
2 or 3 slices bacon, chopped
2 C water

Brown rice in 4 Tbsp olive oil. Put barely cooked lima beans and their liquid, in a large heavy saucepan. Place rice and water on top of beans, do not stir. Set aside. In fry pan, saute onion and bacon. Place on top of rice, cover and cook on very low heat for 30 minutes. Do not mix or stir until completely cooked.

WINTERTIME LIMAS

1 C dried large lima beans
Salt
1 lb pork-sausage meat, cut in patties and
    browned (reserve fat)
1 medium onion, chopped
1 3-oz can chopped mushrooms, drained and
    liquid reserved
2 Tbsp flour
2 tsp dry mustard
1 C milk
1 small bay leaf, crushed
2 Tbsp lemon juice
Pepper

In a saucepan, bring 4 cups water to boil. Add washed limas and boil 2 minutes. Cover, remove from heat and let stand 1 hour. Simmer 1 hour, or until tender. Add 1 tsp salt last half hour. Drain and reserve liquid. Put beans in shallow 2 quart baking dish and top with sausage patties. Saute onion and mushrooms in 2 Tbsp sausage fat a few minutes. Add mushroom liquid to bean liquid, then add enough water to measure 1 cup. Sprinkle flour and mustard over onion mushroom mixture and simmer, stirring, 1 minute. Add liquids and milk, bring to boil and cook, stirring, until thickened. Add bay leaf and lemon juice. Season with salt and pepper to taste and pour over beans and pork patties. Bake at 350° for 30 to 40 minutes. Serves 4.

BEEF AND BEAN ENCHILADAS

1 lb ground beef
1/2 C chopped onion
1 pkg taco seasoning mix
2 C cooked beans, mashed
1 4-oz can chopped green chiles
1/2 C beef bouillon or beef broth
1 4-oz can enchilada sauce
8 flour tortillas
Shredded cheese

Brown ground beef and onion in large skillet; drain. Stir in taco seasoning mix, beans, green chiles, beef bouillon and 1/2 cup of the enchilada sauce. Cook on medium heat until thickened, stirring occasionally, about 10 to 14 minutes. Remove from heat. Fill each tortilla with a scant 1/3 cup meat mixture. Roll up tightly. Place seam-side down in a 9x13 baking pan. Pour remaining sauce over enchiladas. Top with remaining meat mixture and sprinkle with cheese. Bake at 375° for 15 to 20 minutes. Cool slightly before serving. Serves 6 to 8.

TRIPLE EGG PASTA
(tender rich noodles)

EXCELLENT!

2 C flour
3 large egg yolks <u>or</u> 2 egg yolks and
   1 whole egg <u>or</u> 3 dehydrated eggs,
   reconstituted
3 to 6 Tbsp water

On a work surface, place a large bowl. Mound flour in bowl and make a deep well in center. Place eggs in well. With a fork, beat eggs lightly and stir in 2 Tbsp water. Using a circular motion, begin to draw flour from sides of well. Add 1 more Tbsp water and continue mixing until flour is moistened. If necessary, add more water a little at a time. When dough becomes stiff, use your hands to finish mixing. Pat into a ball and knead a few times to help flour absorb liquid.

Clean and lightly flour the work surface.

If you have a pasta machine, knead dough by hand for 3 or 4 minutes or until no longer sticky. Then use machine. Sprinkle with flour if needed.

If you plan to use a rolling pin, knead dough by hand for 10 minutes, or until smooth and elastic. This is important. Cover and let rest for 20 minutes.

With pasta machine or by hand, roll out one fourth of the dough at a time to desired thickness. Keep unrolled portion covered. When all the dough has been rolled, cut strips into desired shapes.

Cook according to recipe directions.

#1

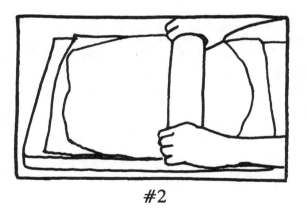

#2

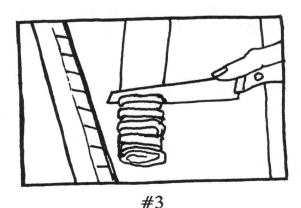

#3

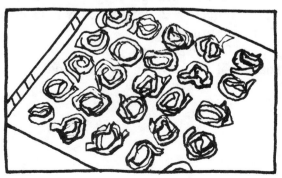

#4

ALL PURPOSE PASTA

2 C flour
2 large eggs or 2 dehydrated whole eggs, reconstituted
3 to 6 Tbsp water
Additional flour for kneading

LOW FAT

Use the directions of Triple Egg Pasta recipe (above) for mixing and kneading.

EXCELLENT!

SPINACH PASTA

1/2 pkg (10 oz) frozen chopped spinach
2 C flour
2 large eggs or 2 dehydrated whole eggs, reconstituted
Additional flour for kneading

Cook spinach. Let cool, then squeeze out as much of the liquid as possible. Mince finely. You should have 1/4 cup of spinach.

Use the directions of Triple Egg Pasta recipe (above) for mixing, except mix the spinach in with the eggs.

LOW FAT

RYE PASTA

2 C rye flour or 1 C white flour with 1 C rye flour
2 large eggs or 2 dehydrated whole eggs reconstituted
4 to 8 Tbsp water
Additional flour for kneading

Use the directions of Triple Egg Pasta recipe (above) for mixing, but use a pasta machine to roll out. Note: Rye flour makes a stiffer dough.

LOW FAT

WHOLE WHEAT PASTA

1 3/4 C whole wheat flour
1/4 C toasted wheat germ
2 large eggs or 2 dehydrated whole eggs reconstituted
3 to 6 Tbsp water
Additional wheat flour for kneading

Use the directions of Triple Egg Pasta recipe (above) for mixing. Note: Dough makes excellent noodles for lasagna, even when rolled thicker.

RYE NOODLE REUBEN

EXCELLENT!

1 recipe Rye Pasta or 1 8-oz pkg rye or
    wheat noodles
Boiling salted water
1 Tbsp butter or margarine
1/2 can corned beef
1 8-oz can sauerkraut, drained
1 Tbsp Dijon mustard
1 tsp caraway seeds
1 C shredded Swiss cheese

Cut fresh rye pasta into medium wide noodles about 10 inches long. Cook noodles in a large kettle of boiling salted water for 4 to 6 minutes, or until tender.

Meanwhile, in a frying pan over medium heat, melt butter, add corned beef and cook until heated through. Add sauerkraut, mustard and caraway seeds. Cook and stir until heated. Drain noodles and toss with sauerkraut mixture in fry pan. Remove from heat. Toss with cheese and serve immediately. Serves 6.

SAVORY BAKED NOODLES

1 recipe Spinach Pasta or 1 8-oz pkg spinach
    noodles
Boiling salted water
1 1/2 C large curd cottage cheese
1 C sour cream
1 clove garlic, minced or pressed
3 green onions, thinly sliced
1 tsp Worcestershire Sauce
1/4 tsp liquid hot pepper seasoning
2 Tbsp butter, melted or 2 Tbsp dehydrated
    reconstituted butter
1/2 C grated Parmesan cheese

Cut fresh pasta into medium wide noodles about 4 inches long. Cook noodles in large kettle of boiling salted water until done. Drain and rinse with cold water.

In a bowl, combine cottage cheese, sour cream, garlic, green onions, Worcestershire sauce, liquid hot pepper seasoning, and melted butter. Gently stir in noodles. Turn mixture into greased 1 1/2 quart casserole dish. Sprinkle with Parmesan cheese. Bake at 350° for 30 minutes. Serves 6.

LOW FAT

SOY PASTA

EXCELLENT!

1 C white flour
1 C soy flour
2 large eggs
3 to 6 Tbsp water

Use directions for triple egg pasta, pg. 135. Excellent with lemon cream sauce, pg. 235.

BEEF STROGANOFF WITH NOODLES

EXCELLENT!

1 recipe All Purpose Pasta (recipe above) <u>or</u>
   1 8-oz pkg noodles
Boiling salted water
2 lbs round steak <u>or</u> 2 lbs hamburger
3 Tbsp oil, divided
1 tsp salt
1/4 tsp pepper
2 Tbsp wine vinegar
1/4 C dehydrated chopped onions, reconstituted
1/3 C dehydrated mushrooms, reconstituted <u>or</u> 1 small can mushrooms
1 clove garlic, chopped
3 Tbsp flour
1 tsp beef bouillon, reconstituted in 2 C boiling water
2 Tbsp tomato powder, reconstituted
1 bay leaf
1/2 C sour cream
2 Tbsp chopped parsley

Cut meat across grain in 1/4 inch slices. In wide fry pan over medium heat, brown 1/2 of the meat in about 1 1/2 Tbsp of oil. Set aside and brown remaining meat, or brown the hamburger in oil. Add salt, pepper, and wine vinegar. Transfer to a 3-quart casserole dish. Add remaining 1 1/2 Tbsp oil to pan and cook drained onions over medium heat, stirring, until golden. Add drained mushrooms and garlic and cook until limp. With slotted spoon, transfer vegetables to casserole dish.

Blend flour into drippings in frying pan and cook, stirring until flour is golden. Remove from heat and gradually stir in beef bouillon, and tomato paste. Return to heat and bring to a boil, stirring continually. Add bay leaf. Pour over meat. Cover and bake at 350° for 1 1/2 hours or until meat is tender.

Cut fresh pasta into medium wide noodles. Just before serving, cook noodles in boiling water for 4 minutes. (Follow package directions for packaged noodles.) Drain. Place in a casserole dish. Mix sour cream into meat mixture and pour over noodles. Sprinkle with parsley. Serves 6.

CRAB SPAGHETTI CASSEROLE

6 oz spaghetti
Boiling salted water
2 Tbsp butter or olive oil
1/4 C dehydrated chopped onions,
    reconstituted
1/2 C dehydrated creamy soup base,
    reconstituted in 1 1/2 C water
1 C evaporated milk
1 Tbsp each, Worcestershire sauce, Dijon
    mustard
1 or 2 cans crab meat
2 hard boiled eggs, diced
1/2 C thinly sliced water chestnuts
1 2-oz jar sliced pimentos
Salt
Sprinkle of cayenne pepper
2/3 C shredded sharp cheese or 1/2 C
    dehydrated cheese powder, reconstituted

Cook spaghetti in boiling water until done, drain.

In 3-quart pan, melt butter or oil and saute reconstituted onions about 2 minutes. Stir in reconstituted creamy soup base and evaporated milk. Add Worcestershire and mustard. Add spaghetti and mix well. Gently stir in crab, eggs, water chestnuts an pimentos. Season to taste with salt and red pepper. Put spaghetti mixture in a shallow 2-quart baking dish. Sprinkle with cheese or spread reconstituted cheese on top. Bake at 375° for 25 to 35 minutes. Serves 6.

TUNA SPAGHETTI PIE

6 oz spaghetti
Boiling salted water
2 Tbsp dehydrated butter or margarine,
    reconstituted
1/3 C Parmesan cheese
2 dehydrated whole eggs, reconstituted
1 10-oz pkg frozen chopped spinach
 2 cans tuna, drained and flaked
1/4 C dried chopped onions, reconstituted
1 C small curd cottage cheese
1 Tbsp Dijon Mustard
1/2 tsp dill weed
1/2 tsp garlic salt
1 C (4 oz) shredded Swiss cheese

Cook spaghetti in boiling water. Drain. Combine spaghetti with butter, Parmesan cheese, and eggs. Spread over bottom and sides of a well greased 9" pie plate.

Press excess liquid out of spinach. Mix remaining ingredients together, reserving 1/2 cup of Swiss cheese for top. Blend well. Spread into spaghetti-lined pan. Bake at 350° for 30 to 45 minutes or until set. Sprinkle remaining 1/2 cup of Swiss cheese on top and bake for 5 minutes longer. Serves 6.

TURKEY TETRAZZINI

6 Tbsp butter or margarine
5 Tbsp flour
1 1/2 tsp dehydrated chicken bouillon
    reconstituted in 2 1/2 C boiling water
1 1/4 C evaporated milk
1 Tbsp lemon juice
3/4 C grated Parmesan cheese
1/3 C dehydrated mushrooms, reconstituted
12 oz spaghetti
Boiling salted water
1 to 2 cans cooked turkey (3 to 4 cups
    chopped)
Salt
White pepper

In 2-quart pan, melt 3 Tbsp butter over medium heat. Mix in flour and cook, stirring, until bubbly. Remove pan from heat. With a wire whip, mix in chicken bouillon and evaporated milk, beating until smooth. Return to heat. Cook, stirring, until thickened. Stir in Parmesan cheese and lemon juice. Measure out 1 cup of sauce and set aside.

Melt remaining 3 Tbsp butter in frying pan. Add drained mushrooms and saute for 2 minutes.

Cook spaghetti in boiling water until done. Drain. Combine spaghetti with larger portion of sauce. Add mushrooms and canned turkey. Mix lightly. Add salt and pepper to taste. Turn into greased 2 quart casserole dish. Spoon the 1 cup of sauce evenly over surface. Cover. Bake at 375° for about 45 minutes or until hot and bubbly. Serves 6.

MACARONI AND SAUSAGE BAKE

1 1/2 lbs mild sausage or spicy Italian
    sausage
6 oz macaroni
Boiling salted water
1/2 C dehydrated cheese reconstituted to 1 C
1 tsp Italian spice
1/2 tsp salt
1/2 tsp pepper
Dash of cayenne pepper
1/2 C dehydrated sweet peas, reconstituted
1/2 C canned milk

Cook reconstituted peas for 1/2 hour in their liquid.

Remove and discard sausage casings. Crumble sausage into wide frying pan and cook over medium heat until browned, about 6 minutes. Drain and set aside.

Cook macaroni in boiling salted water until done. Drain. Turn into large bowl. Add sausage, cheese, Italian spice, salt, pepper, cayenne pepper, drained peas, and milk. Toss lightly to blend ingredients. Turn into 2 1/2 quart baking dish. Bake covered at 350° for 20 minutes or until bubbly. Serves 6.

SPAM AND MUSHROOM SPAGHETTI

3 Tbsp butter
1/3 C dried chopped onions, reconstituted
1/2 lb dehydrated sliced mushrooms,
    reconstituted or 1 can mushrooms
3/4 C tomato juice or 1/3 C dehydrated
    tomato powder reconstituted to 3/4 C
1/2 tsp rubbed sage
1/2 tsp nutmeg
1/3 C canned milk
1/4 C chopped parsley
1/2 C Parmesan cheese
2 C ham, chopped or 1 can Spam, chopped
6 oz spaghetti
Boiling salted water

In a large frying pan over medium heat, melt butter; add drained mushrooms. Saute 2 minutes. Add tomato juice, sage, nutmeg, and canned milk. Boil uncovered over high heat, stirring occasionally. Boil about 5 to 8 minutes. Stir in parsley and cheese. Add ham or Spam.

Boil spaghetti in salted water. Drain. Return spaghetti to kettle. Pour sauce over spaghetti and toss gently. Sprinkle servings with Parmesan cheese. Serves 4.

GREEN CHILI PASTA

6 strips bacon, diced
1/4 C dried chopped onion, reconstituted
8 oz spaghetti
1 can (about 1 lb) Italian Style tomatoes
1 tsp dehydrated beef bouillon reconstituted
    in 2 C boiling water
1 4-oz can green chiles
2 Tbsp red wine vinegar
Salt
Pepper
Grated Parmesan cheese

In dutch oven over medium heat cook bacon until crisp. Remove bacon and drain on paper towels. Set aside. Discard all but 1/4 cup drippings. Add drained onions to drippings and saute until limp. Break spaghetti into 2-inch pieces (should be 2 cups). Add to onions and continue cooking for 2 minutes. Add tomatoes and their liquid. Break up tomatoes with a spoon. Add beef bouillon, chiles, and vinegar. Stir well. Cover and simmer until spaghetti is tender and most of the liquid is gone. About 15 minutes. Season to taste with salt and pepper. Turn into serving dish and top with bacon. Pass cheese at the table. Serves 4-6.

EZEKIEL BREAD

1-1/2 C Ezekiel flour (pg. 227)
3/4 tsp baking powder
1 tsp salt
1-1/3 C milk
2 eggs
1/4 C oil, margarine or melted shortening

Beat together; pour into greased 9x9 pan and bake at 450° for 25-30 minutes or until done.

EZEKIEL POUND CAKE

1 C butter
6 eggs
2-3/4 C sugar
3 C Ezekiel flour (pg. 227)
1/2 tsp salt
1/4 tsp baking powder
1 C dairy sour cream
1 tsp vanilla

Beat together, pour into 10-inch greased tube pan and bake at 350° for about 1-1/2 hours, or until done.

EZEKIEL APPLESAUCE CAKE

2-1/2 C Ezekiel flour (pg 229)
1-3/4 C sugar **or** 1 C honey
1-1/2 tsp baking powder
1-1/2 tsp salt
1 tsp cinnamon
1/2 tsp cloves
1/2 tsp ginger
1/2 tsp allspice
1/2 tsp nutmeg
1/2 C shortening **or** margarine
2 C applesauce
1/2 C raisins
1/2 C walnuts

Beat together and pour into greased 13x9x2 pan and bake at 350° for 45 minutes or until done.

NOTE: See page 229 for Ezekiel flour.

BREADS

HINTS FOR BETTER BREAD

For lighter bread, grind wheat fine.

Do not over-rise bread, only until it doubles in size.

Do not tear bread dough, always cut it.

Do not put pans too close together in the oven.

Let the yeast double in water before adding to dough.

Do not add too much flour. Use only the full amount of flour, if necessary. Keep dough soft but not sticky.

Always knead dough for 10 minutes.

Use good flour! Poor grade flour makes poor bread. Old wheat sometimes makes heavier bread.

1,000 milligrams of Vitamin C added to 100% whole wheat bread recipe will make a much lighter bread. It is a natural dough conditioner.

MARLENE'S NEVER-FAIL BREAD

EXCELLENT!

6 Tbsp yeast
1 C warm water
1 Tbsp sugar
1/2 C dehydrated potato flakes
4 C boiling water
1/2 C non-fat powdered milk
1 1/2 C cold water
1 C oil
1 C honey or sugar
2 Tbsp salt
5 Tbsp dehydrated whole eggs, reconstituted
8 C wheat flour and 8 C white flour, or 15
    C wheat flour*, or 16 C white flour

Dissolve yeast and sugar in warm water and set aside.

Add potato flakes to boiling water and set aside.

Dissolve powdered milk in cold water. Add oil, honey or sugar, salt, eggs, and mix. Add potato mixture. Mix well and add yeast. Add wheat flour and continue mixing well. Gradually add white flour. Mix well. Knead 10 minutes (important). If dough is too sticky, add a little more flour, however, be careful not to make too dry.

Cover; let rise in warm place until double. Punch down dough; form into 7 loaves. Place loaves in greased loaf pans, 9x5x3 inches. Let rise to the size of loaf you desire. . .almost double. Bake at 350° for 20 minutes.

*If using 100% wheat flour, do not use stone ground flour for it will be too heavy. Use commercial flour or very finely ground flour.

NOTE: With this recipe you can make cinnamon rolls, donuts, hot dog or hamburger buns, dinner rolls, and/or coffee cakes.

EXCELLENT!

CRACKED WHEAT ROLLS OR BUNS

Using **Marlene's Never-Fail Bread** recipe, substitute the 16 cups flour with the following:

1 C cracked wheat (soak in the boiling water
    mixture)
2 C oats
2 C wheat bran
2 C white flour
8 C whole wheat flour

Proceed as directed in bread recipe. If desired, can eliminate oats and wheat bran and increase cracked wheat to 2 cups and whole wheat flour to 11 cups.

This recipe makes excellent buns for school lunches. Delicious with cheese and mayonnaise.

MARLENE'S ALMOND PASTE SWEET BREAD

6 Tbsp yeast
1 C warm water
1 Tbsp sugar
1/2 C dehydrated potato flakes
3 1/2 C boiling water
1/2 C non-fat powdered milk
1 1/2 C cold water
1 C oil
1 C honey or sugar
2 Tbsp salt
5 Tbsp dehydrated whole eggs, reconstituted
8 C wheat flour
8 C white flour
or 16 cups white flour

Dissolve yeast and sugar in warm water and set aside.

Add potato flakes to boiling water and set aside.

Dissolve powdered milk in cold water. Add oil, honey or sugar, salt, eggs, and mix well. Add potato mixture. Mix well and add yeast. Add wheat flour and continue mixing well. Gradually add white flour. Mix well. Knead 10 minutes (important). If dough is too sticky, add a little more flour being careful not to make dough too dry.

Cover; let rise in warm place until double.

Divide dough into 2 parts. Roll first part into a rectangle and cut in three more rectangles (see diagram #1). Separate and put Almond Paste Filling (below) down the middle of each rectangle (see diagram #2). Sprinkle with raisins. Stretch ends around the filling (see diagram #3), and proceed to braid bread (see diagram #4). Brush the top with beaten egg whites and sprinkle with sliced almonds and 1 tsp. sugar. Set aside in a warm area to rise until doubled in size. Bake at 350° for 25 minutes or until light brown. Cool slightly and glaze with Sugar Glaze (below).

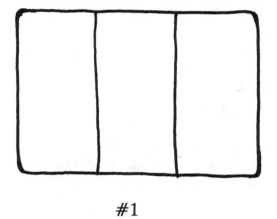

#1

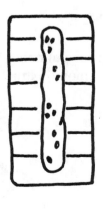

#2

#3

#4

ALMOND PASTE FILLING

1 C butter, softened
2 C sugar
1 C almond paste
1 Tbsp almond flavor
Raisins

Crumble almond paste into a large bowl. Whip in butter and sugar until smooth. Add almond flavoring.

SUGAR GLAZE
(for all coffee cakes or cinnamon rolls)

2 C powdere sugar
1 Tbsp frozen orange juice concentrate
1 tsp vanilla
1/2 tsp almond flavoring
1/2 tsp rum flavoring (optional)
1 Tbsp lemon juice

Whip all ingredients together until smooth. If mixture is too dry add a little hot water. Drizzle over coffee cake or rolls.

HOW TO MAKE ALMOND PASTE

1/2 C almonds ground very fine
3/4 C powder sugar
1 egg, beaten
1/2 tsp almond extract

Mix sugar and ground almonds well. Mix in beaten egg and almond extract, knead until well mixed.

PARMESAN HERB TOPPING

EXCELLENT!

(for rolls or bread sticks)

1/4 C olive oil
1 C butter
1 C Parmesan cheese
2 tsp dried parsley flakes
1 Tbsp dried basil
1/2 tsp salt
1/2 tsp garlic powder (optional)

Melt butter and add all other ingredients. Mix. Dip bread sticks or dinner rolls before baking.

To make Parmesan Rolls, use the Never-Fail Bread recipe (pg. 144) with 1/2 wheat flour or all white flour. Grease muffin tins or cupcake pans. Dip small balls of dough into topping and place them in the cups. Let rise until double. Bake at 350° for 10 to 15 minutes or until golden brown.

To make Parmesan Bread Sticks, use the same dough. Roll dough into a long 6 inch rectangle. Cut into 1 inch strips or smaller. Dip each strip into topping and place on a baking sheet. Bake at 350° for 10 to 12 minutes or until golden brown.

GLAZED POTATO DOUGHNUTS

To make Glazed Potato Doughnuts, use the Never-Fail Bread recipe (pg. 144) with all white flour. Let the dough rise until doubled in size. Punch down, and roll dough 1/3 inch thick on a lightly floured board. Cut with a doughnut cutter and place on floured cookie sheet. Let rise until doubled in size. Carefully place each doughnut in hot peanut oil. Fry until done. String doughnuts on a dowel and place over a large bowl. Pour Glaze (recipe below) over them. Glaze will drip back into the bowl.

DOUGHNUT GLAZE

2 C powdered sugar
1 Tbsp orange juice concentrate
1/2 tsp almond flavoring
1 tsp vanilla
Lemon juice

Mix all the ingredients together to form a smooth liquid glaze. Pour over warm doughnuts.

DILLY CASSEROLE BREAD

1 pkg. dry yeast or 1 Tbsp yeast
1/4 C warm water
1 C cottage cheese, heated to lukewarm
2 Tbsp sugar
2 tsp instant dried onion
1 Tbsp oil
2 tsp dill seeds
1 tsp salt
1 beaten egg <u>or</u> egg powder, reconstituted
2 - 2 1/2 C sifted wheat flour, ground fine

Soften yeast in warm water. Combine in a mixing bowl, the cottage cheese, sugar, onion, oil, dill seeds, salt, egg, and softened yeast. Add flour gradually, beating well. Cover and let rise in a warm place until double in size, 50 to 60 minutes. Stir dough down, turn into a well-greased 1-quart casserole and let rise in a warm place until light. Bake at 350° for 40 to 50 minutes or until golden brown. Brush with softened butter and sprinkle with salt.

SWEET RYE BREAD

2 Tbsp dry yeast
1/3 C warm water
2 1/4 C hot water
3/4 C brown sugar
1/2 C molasses
2 Tbsp shortening
1 1/2 Tbsp salt
1 tsp anise flavoring
1 1/2 C white flour
4 1/2 C white flour
3 C rye flour

Dissolve yeast in warm water. Pour 2 1/4 cups of hot water over brown sugar, molasses, shortening, salt, and anise flavoring and mix well. When luke warm, add 1 1/2 cups of white flour and the yeast mixture. Stir well then add 4 1/2 more cups of white flour and 3 cups of rye flour. Knead dough for 10 minutes. Shape into long loaves like French bread. Let rise until doubled in size. Bake at 375° for 30 minutes.

SKY HIGH BISCUITS

2 C flour
1 C wheat flour
4 1/2 tsp baking powder
2 Tbsp sugar
1/2 tsp salt
3/4 tsp cream of tarter
3/4 C butter or margarine
1 egg, beaten
1 C nonfat powdered milk, reconstituted

In a bowl, combine dry ingredients. Cut in butter until mixture resembles course cornmeal. Add egg and milk, stirring gradually and briefly. Knead lightly on a floured board. Roll or pat gently to a 1-inch thickness. Cut into 1- to 2-inch biscuits. Place on a greased 9-inch square pan. Bake at 450° for 12 to 15 minutes.

ENGLISH MUFFINS

4 C flour
1 tsp salt
1 Tbsp dry yeast
1/2 C warm milk or 1/2 C nonfat powdered
    milk, reconstituted
1 C warm water
3 Tbsp sugar
1/4 C butter, softened
Corn meal

Sift flour and salt together. Combine yeast with warm milk and set aside for 5 minutes. Mix in water and sugar. Work in 2 cups flour mixture and let stand 1 1/2 hours.

Beat in softened butter and remaining flour. Place dough on a board which has been covered lightly with cornmeal. Cover and let rise.

Roll out dough 1/2 inch thick on the cornmeal covered board. Cut in 4 1/2-inch circles (use a tuna fish can). Let stand 20 min.

Heat a lightly-oiled electric fry pan or hot griddle. Place muffins in fry pan and cover with lid. Fry for 5 to 7 minutes.

Turn and fry second side for another 5 to 7 minutes.

BRAN ENGLISH MUFFINS

1 Tbsp yeast
1/2 C warm water
1 C scalded milk
2 tsp honey
1 tsp salt
1 C unprocessed bran flakes
1 1/2 C whole wheat flour
1 1/2 C oatmeal
1/4 C rye flour
3 Tbsp soft butter

Dissolve yeast in warm water. Blend in scalded milk, honey, and salt. Add bran flakes. Sift remaining dry ingredients together. Beat one half of flour mixture into liquid and bran mixture. Cover and allow to double in volume, about 1 hour.

Beat in soft butter and remaining flour, saving about 3/4 cup for the board. Cut into rounds 3 inches in diameter with dough 3/4 inch thick. Cover and let rise on floured board until double, about 20 to 30 minutes.

Carefully lift on a lightly oiled electric griddle. Bake at 300° uncovered for 10 to 12 minutes on each side.

FOUR-GRAIN ENGLISH MUFFINS

4 to 4 1/2 cups all purpose flour
1 pkg quick-rise dry yeast
1/2 C whole wheat flour
1/2 C toasted wheat germ
1/2 C quick oats, uncooked
1 C nonfat powdered milk
3 Tbsp sugar
2 tsp salt
2 C water
1/4 C oil
1/4 C cornmeal

In a large mixer bowl, combine 2 cups flour, yeast, whole wheat flour, wheat germ, oats, dry milk, sugar, and salt. Mix well. In saucepan, heat water and oil until very warm (120° to 130°). Add to flour mixture. Blend at low speed until moistened; beat 3 minutes at medium speed. By hand, gradually stir in enough remaining flour to make a firm dough. Knead on floured surface, 5 to 8 minutes. Place in a greased bowl, turning to grease top. Cover; let rise in warm place until double, about 30 minutes.

Punch dough down. On surface sprinkled with cornmeal, roll dough to 1/2 inch thickness. Cut into 3-inch circles. Place muffins on ungreased cookie sheets. Cover, let rise in warm place until double, about 15 minutes. Bake on lightly oiled electric griddle or skillet at 325° for about 8 minutes on each side until deep golden brown. Cool.

SPICY BEAN MUFFIN

1 C cooked pinto beans
3/4 C nonfat powdered milk, reconstituted
2 egg whites
1/4 C vegetable oil
1/2 C brown sugar
1 1/2 C flour or 3/4 C each whole wheat
    flour and white flour
2 tsp baking powder
1/2 tsp baking soda
1/2 tsp salt
1/2 tsp cinnamon
1/4 tsp each nutmeg and cloves
1/2 C raisins

Puree beans with milk in blender until smooth. Transfer to bowl. Beat egg whites, oil, and brown sugar. Combine remaining ingredients. Fold into bean mixture, mixing just until dry ingredients are moistened. Spoon into greased or paper-lined muffin cups. Bake at 400° for 15 to 18 minutes. Makes 12 muffins.

FLOUR TORTILLAS
(makes 11 large)

2 C unsifted flour
1 tsp salt
1/4 C lard or shortening
1/2 C luke warm water

Put flour in a mixing bowl and sprinkle with salt. Stir to mix. With pastry blender or two knives, cut in lard until particles are fine. Add water gradually. Toss with a fork to make a stiff dough. Form into a ball and, on a lightly floured board, and knead thoroughly until smooth and flecked with air bubbles.

At this point you can grease the surface of the dough, cover tightly and refrigerate for as long as 24 hours before using it. This will make the dough easier to handle.

Let dough return to room temperature before rolling out. Divide dough into 11 balls. Roll as thin as possible on a lightly floured board, or stretch and pat with floured hands until thin or roll between 2 pieces of waxed paper.

Drop onto a very hot ungreased griddle. Bake until freckled on one side, about 20 seconds. Lift edge with spatula and turn. Bake second side. Cool tortillas. Wrap air tight and refrigerate or freeze until ready to use.

POCKET BREAD

1 Tbsp yeast
2 C water
4 C flour, divided
1 tsp salt

Dissolve yeast in water. Add 2 cups of flour and beat until smooth. Add salt and remaining 2 cups of flour. Knead until smooth, about 10 minutes. Let rest 15 minutes. Cut into 8 equal pieces. Lightly roll into patties about 1/4 inch thick. Transfer to floured wax paper. Let rest 45 minutes, uncovered. Preheat oven to 500°. Do not grease cookie sheet. Peel off wax paper and put on cookie sheet. Place in oven. Do not open oven for 4 minutes. Reach in and turn bread over. Bake 1 to 4 minutes longer. Do not let brown. Put bread on a towel on top of the stove, stacked on top of each other and cover with a towel. When ready to use, cut in half and separate sides. Fill.

Note: To form pockets well, roll dough evenly, roll only to a thickness of 1/4 inch, no thinner, and keep dough sticky.

Fillings:

2 lbs lean hamburger
Salt
Pepper
Garlic salt
1 lb mild cheese
1 chopped onion
2 chopped tomatoes
1 chopped green pepper
1 small can mushrooms
1 small can green chiles

Brown hamburger and sprinkle with salt, pepper, and garlic salt. Just before serving stir in remaining ingredients. Stuff into pockets and serve warm.

Avocado
Cucumber, chopped
Onion, chopped
Tomato, sliced
Alfalfa sprouts
Bacon bits
Mayonnaise

Mash avocado and mix with remaining ingredients. Place in pockets and serve.

SESAME SANDWICH FILLING

1 ripe avocado
2 Tbsp cream cheese
1 tsp lemon juice
1 tsp mayonnaise
2 Tbsp sesame seeds
1 tsp soy sauce
Salt to taste

This sandwich filling is made by mashing the ingredients together.

QUICK TUNA ANCHOVY SPREAD

1 can tuna, drained
1 can anchovies, drained
1/8 tsp each, dry mustard and oregano leaves
1 Tbsp pickle relish
1 tsp lemon juice
1/4 C French dressing
Dash of cayenne pepper

In a bowl, carefully break tuna into bite-sized pieces. Coarsely chop anchovies and add to tuna. Add mustard, oregano, cayenne pepper, pickle relish, lemon juice and French dressing. Toss lightly. Marinate in refrigerator for 1 hour. Serve with crackers or as a sandwich filling.

EXCELLENT!

100% WHOLE WHEAT BREAD

1/2 C warm water (110°)
2 Tbsp yeast
1 Tbsp sugar
5 C hot water
7 C whole wheat flour
3/4 C oil
3/4 C honey or sugar
2 Tbsp salt
5 to 6 C whole wheat flour

Mix yeast, warm water, and sugar and set in a warm place. Combine 5 cups hot water with whole wheat flour, oil, honey, and salt. Mix well. Add yeast mixture and remaining flour. Knead 10 minutes. Let rise until double. Push down then divide dough into equal portions and shape into loaves. Place into greased loaf pans. Let rise only 1/2 (approximately even with the top of pan) Bake at 350° for 40 minutes.

NOTE: To make lighter wheat bread add 1,000 mg Vitamin C crushed or powdered to wheat flour.

POLISH RYE

2 pkg active dry yeast
3/4 C warm water, about 110°
1 Tbsp sugar
1 C flour
3 C buttermilk
2 tsp salt
4 tsp caraway seed
6 C rye flour
Toasted Rye Crumbs (directions below)
1 C unprocessed bran
3 C whole wheat flour

Combine yeast and water; let stand 5 minutes to soften. Stir in sugar and flour and let stand uncovered, until thick and bubbly, about 30 minutes.

Meanwhile, in a 2 quart saucepan, heat buttermilk to 110°, then blend into yeast mixture along with the salt, caraway, rye flour, rye crumbs, and bran. Mix well. Set aside.

Add 1 to 1 1/2 cups whole wheat flour to yeast mixture and beat on low speed with a dough hook until thoroughly moistened. Mix in 3/4 to 1 cup whole wheat flour; beat 10 minutes, scraping bowl sides often. Dough will be very stiff and just slightly sticky. Scrape dough down from bowl sides. Cover with plastic wrap and let rise in a warm place until doubled in volume, about 1 1/2 hours.

Punch down dough and knead briefly on floured board. Divide into 3 equal portions. Shape each into a smooth round or oval. Grease two 12x15 baking sheets. Set two loaves well apart on one sheet, and one loaf on the other, Cover lightly with plastic wrap and let rise in a warm place until doubled, about 1 1/2 hour.

Bake uncovered at 350° for 40 minutes or until browned. Makes 3 loaves.

Toasted Rye Crumbs:
Toast 6 to 8 slices dark rye bread. Break into pieces and whirl in a blender or food processor.

SOURDOUGH RYE BREAD

1 C corn flour or fine cornmeal
3 C rye flour
3 1/2 C warm water
1 C sourdough starter
3 tsp caraway seed
2 pkgs active dry yeast
3 Tbsp salad oil
2 Tbsp molasses
2 tsp salt
7 to 8 C flour
4 Tbsp cornmeal

In a large bowl, stir together the corn flour, 1 cup of rye flour, 1 1/2 cups of the water, the sourdough starter, and caraway seed. Cover and let stand at room temperature until very bubbly, at least 4 hours or overnight.

In another large bowl, combine yeast and the remaining 1/4 cup water and let stand about 5 minutes to soften. Stir in the oil, molasses, salt, 1/2 cup of the flour, and the sourdough mixture.

Add remaining 1/2 cup rye flour and 3 cups of the flour. Beat, using a dough hook, 10 minutes; dough will be soft. Scrape dough from bowl sides. Cover with plastic wrap and let rise for about 1 1/2 hour or until doubled in volume.

Punch down dough and knead briefly on a floured board. Divide dough and shape into smooth rounds. Grease a baking sheet; sprinkle with cornmeal. Place loaves in opposite corners of baking sheet. Cover lightly with plastic wrap and let rise in a warm place until doubled, about 1 1/2 hours.

Bake uncovered at 350° for 40 minutes or until browned.

CORN BREAD

1/4 lb butter
1 C sugar
2 eggs
1 C yellow cornmeal
1 1/2 C flour
1/2 tsp salt
2 tsp baking powder
1 1/2 C milk

Cream margarine and sugar, add eggs, and cornmeal. Sift flour, baking powder and salt. Add 1/3 flour mixture at a time. Bake at 375° for 35 minutes.

Variety: Add blueberries or raspberries.

PUMPERNICKEL BREAD

3 pkg active dry yeast
1 1/2 C warm water (110°)
4 tsp salt
2 Tbsp shortening
1 Tbsp caraway seed
2 3/4 C rye flour
2 3/4 to 3 1/4 C white flour
Cornmeal
1/2 C molasses

Dissolve yeast in warm water. Stir in molasses, salt, shortening, caraway seed and rye flour. Beat until smooth. Mix in enough white flour to make dough easy to handle.

Turn dough onto lightly floured board. Cover; let rest 10 to 15 minutes. Knead until smooth, about 5 minutes. Place in greased bowl; turn greased side up. Cover; let rise in warm place until doubled, about 1 hour. Punch down dough. Cover; let rise again until doubled, about 40 minutes.

Grease baking sheet and sprinkle with cornmeal. Punch down dough. Divide in half. Shape each half into round, slightly flat loaf. Place loaves in opposite corners of baking sheet. Cover and let rise 1 hour. Heat oven to 375°. Bake 30 to 35 minutes. Makes 2 loaves.

QUICK LEMON NUT BREAD

2 1/2 C flour
1 C sugar
3 1/2 tsp baking powder
1/2 tsp salt
1/2 C water
1/3 C shortening, melted
2 eggs, beaten
1 1/2 Tbsp fresh, grated lemon peel
1/2 C fresh, squeezed lemon juice
1/2 C chopped nuts
1/2 C raisins

In a large bowl, sift together dry ingredients. Combine water, shortening, eggs, lemon peel, and juice; add to flour mixture. Stir just until blended (don't over mix). Stir in nuts and raisins. Pour into greased 9x5x3 inch loaf pan. Bake at 350° for 1 hour and 15 minutes or until toothpick inserted in center comes out clean. Cool 10 minutes; remove from pan. Cool on wire rack.

ORANGE ROLLS

4 Tbsp sugar
5 Tbsp shortening
1 tsp salt
1 C scalded milk
1 Tbsp dry yeast dissolved in 1/4 C warm
    water
2 eggs
3 1/2 to 4 C white flour
Butter, softened
1 C sugar
Grated orange peel

Mix sugar, shortening, and salt in scalded milk. Cool to lukewarm. Add dry yeast which has been mixed with warm water. Add eggs; then stir in white flour and knead for 5 minutes in a mixer or 10 minutes by hand.

On a lightly oiled counter top pat or roll dough to about 4x24 inches. Spread onto dough soft butter, then sugar and grated orange peel. Roll length wise and pinch edges securely. With thread cut roll into 24 slices and put in oiled muffin tins. Let rise about 1 hour. Bake at 350° for 12 to 15 minutes or until lightly browned.

SPICY CORN CRISPS

1 C cornmeal
1 clove garlic, pressed
1 1/2 tsp cayenne pepper
1 1/2 tsp ground cumin
1 1/2 tsp chili powder
1/4 tsp salt
2 Tbsp butter or margarine
1 C boiling water
About 1 1/3 C all purpose flour
Salt for the tops
Paprika for the tops

Preheat the oven to 375°. In a large bowl or in the food processor, mix the cornmeal, garlic, cayenne, cumin, chili powder, and salt. Add the butter and boiling water and blend well. Allow the mixture to cool and rest for 10 minutes. It will thicken slightly. Slowly blend in the flour, using just enough to form a dough that will hold together in a cohesive ball. Divide the dough into 3 equal portions for rolling.

On a floured surface or pastry cloth, roll as thin as possible, to about 1/16 inch thick. Sprinkle lightly and evenly with salt and paprika roll over the top of the dough lightly with the rolling pin. Cut the dough into 2 inch triangles or squares. Arrange them on an ungreased baking sheet. Bake for 10 to 12 minutes. Cool on a rack.
These crackers will crispen as they cool. If they are not crisp enough after cooling, put them back into the oven for a few minutes longer and allow them to cool again. Makes about 150.

OATMEAL BUTTER CRACKERS

1 1/2 C all purpose flour
1 1/2 C rolled oats (oatmeal)
1/2 tsp salt
1 Tbsp sugar
6 Tbsp butter or margarine, melted and
    cooled
About 1/2 C milk

Preheat the oven to 325°. Stir together the flour, oats, salt, and sugar in a large bowl or in the food processor. Cut in the butter until the mixture resembles coarse meal. Blend in enough of the milk to form a dough that will hold together in a cohesive ball. Divide the dough into 2 equal portions for rolling.

On a floured surface, or pastry cloth, roll as thin as possible, to about 1/16 inch tick. Using a spatula, rolling pin, or your hands, transfer the rolled dough gently onto a large baking sheet. With a sharp knife, score the dough into 2 inch squares without cutting all the way through the dough. Prick each square 2 or 3 times with the tines of a fork. Bake for 20 to 25 minutes, turning over after 15 minutes, until crisp. Cool on a rack. Break into individual crackers when cool. Makes 50 to 60.

EXCELLENT!

PIZZA CRUST

2 C flour
1 C warm water
1 Tbsp yeast
1 Tbsp sugar
1 tsp salt
1 Tbsp oil

Work all ingredients together, mixing well. Set aside for 5 minutes. Bake at 350° for 5 minutes the remove and add toppings. Return to oven and continue baking for another 5 to 10 minutes, or until toppings are warm and cheese is melted.

OAT BRAN SQUARES

1 1/2 C oat bran
1/2 C all purpose flour
1/4 tsp salt
Pinch of baking soda
4 Tbsp butter or margarine, softened
1 tsp honey
1/4 C hot water

Preheat the oven to 325°. Combine the oat bran, flour, salt, and baking soda in a large bowl or in the food processor. Cut in the butter until the mixture resembles coarse meal. Dissolve the honey in the hot water and blend it into the flour mixture. If the dough is too wet for rolling, quickly add a little more flour. Divide the dough into 2 equal portions for rolling.

On a floured surface or pastry cloth, roll to about 1/8 inch. With a sharp knife, cut the dough into 2 inch squares. Place them on a lightly greased or parchment-lined baking sheet. Prick each square in 2 or 3 places with the tines of a fork. Bake for 18 to 22 minutes, or until medium brown. Cool on a rack. Makes 50 to 55.

Variations: Substitute wheat bran for oat bran. For a more delicate cracker, roll the dough thinner and reduce the baking time to compensate.

JAN'S DINNER ROLLS

2 C milk
2 tsp salt
1/2 C sugar (scant)
2 Tbsp yeast (2 packages)
1/2 C warm water

6 C flour white or wheat or 1/2 and 1/2
2 eggs

In a pan, heat the milk to scalding point. Cool to warm. In a separate bowl mix the yeast in the warm water along with the sugar and salt. Let stand until dissolved and yeast starts to rise. Add to warm milk. Then add 3 cups of the flour, stir well. Let rise until doubled. Add the eggs, one at a time, and about 3 more cups of the flour, stir well. Cover and let rise again. Roll out and shape into desired rolls. Dip in melted butter and place in pan. Let rise to double. Bake at 350° for 15 minutes or until done.

GRAHAM CRACKERS

EXCELLENT!

1. Mix together:
    1/2 C evaporated milk <u>or</u> 1/4 C non-fat powdered milk
    1/2 C water
    2 Tbsp lemon juice <u>or</u> vinegar

2. Beat well in large bowl:
    1 C dark brown sugar
    1/2 C honey
    1 C oil
    2 tsp vanilla
    2 eggs beaten <u>or</u> 2 dehydrated eggs, beaten lightly

3. Combine above mixtures and add:
    1 tsp salt
    1 tsp baking soda
    6 C whole wheat flour (approx.)

4. Divide into 4 equal parts. Place each on a greased and floured cookie sheet and roll to 1/8" thick. Prick with a fork.

5. Bake at 375° for about 15 minutes, or until light brown. Cut in squares immediately.

WHEAT THINS

1 1/2 C all purpose flour
1/2 C whole wheat flour
1/2 C sugar
1/4 tsp salt
2 Tbsp butter or margarine, softened
1/2 to 2/3 C milk
Salt for the tops (optional)

Preheat the oven to 325°. In a large bowl or in the food processor, combine the flours, sugar, and salt. Cut the butter into the flour until the mixture resembles coarse meal. Blend in the milk slowly, using only enough to form a dough that will hold together in a cohesive ball. Divide the dough into 2 equal portions for rolling.

On a floured surface or pastry cloth, roll the crackers thin, 1/16 to 1/8 inch. If desired, lightly sprinkle the tops with salt and gently roll over the dough with your rolling pin. With a sharp knife, cut the crackers into 2 inch squares. Transfer them to an ungreased baking sheet. Prick each cracker in 2 or 3 places with the tines of a fork. Bake for 20 to 25 minutes, or until the crackers are lightly browned. Cool on a rack. Makes 95 to 100.

JULIE'S DANISH PASTRIES

DOUGH;
1 C milk, scalded
1/4 C granulated sugar
1 tsp salt
1 1/4 C butter
1/2 C warm water
2 Tbsp yeast
3 eggs, beaten
1 large orange rind, grated
1 large lemon rind, grated
1/2 tsp each, vanilla extract, lemon extract,
    almond extract
1 tsp cinnamon
3 C whole wheat pastry flour
3 to 4 C all purpose flour
Orange juice
Evaporated milk

Combine the milk, sugar, salt, and 1/4 cup of the butter and cool to lukewarm. Dissolve the yeast in the warm water. Combine the milk mixture with the yeast, add eggs, orange rind, lemon rind, extracts, and enough flour to make a soft dough. Turn onto a board and knead for about 10 minutes, until smooth and elastic. Place in buttered bowl and butter top of dough. Cover and let rise in a warm place for about 1 hour, or until doubled in bulk.

Punch the dough down, Roll out to a rectangle and mark into thirds. Thinly slice 1/3 cup of butter onto the middle section and fold on end of the dough over it. Fold the second end of dough over that. Turn the dough so that one short end is nearest you. Roll the dough into a rectangle, divide into thirds, add the next 1/3 cup of butter, repeat procedure. Continue rolling and folding until all the butter is worked into the dough.

Shape as desired (see recipes below). Preheat oven to 375°. Let rise. Just before placing pastries in oven, brush with evaporated milk. Bake 10 to 15 minutes of until golden brown. Immediately upon removal from oven, brush with orange juice. Let cool, then drizzle with glaze. Makes about 40 pastries.

CHEESE FILLING

1 lb cream cheese, softened
6 Tbsp granulated sugar
2 Tbsp orange juice
1 Tbsp grated orange rind

Mix ingredients well. Roll pastry dough into rectangle. Cut into squares 2x2 inches. Spread filling diagonally down square. Pinch opposite ends and fold over. Let rise.

FIGURE EIGHTS

Apricot jam
Raspberry jam

Roll out dough into rectangle about 8 inches long. Cut lengthwise into strips 1 inch wide. Twist; fashion and twist ropes into figure eights. Just before baking, fill with jam.

BUTTER HORNS

1/2 C almond paste
1/4 tsp almond extract
1/4 C powdered sugar
1/2 to 1 C flour
Evaporated milk

Combine ingredients. Add enough flour to make mixture crumbly and dry appearing. Roll dough into rectangle 6 inches wide. Overlap into thirds lengthwise, so it sort of resembles a jelly roll. Cut into 1 inch widths. Just before baking, brush with evaporated milk. Place crumbly mixture on top; drizzle with more evaporated milk.

BEAR CLAWS

1 C mincemeat
Vanilla wafers, crumbled

Add enough wafers to mincemeat so that it is not too runny. Roll dough into rectangle 6 inches wide. Spread mincemeat on one side, lengthwise, leaving edges free. Fold over and pinch seams. Cut 2 1/2 inches wide, then cut 3 toes, twist the toes out. Let rise.

DANISH PASTRY DIAGRAMS

WENDY'S SOURDOUGH WHITE BREAD

EXCELLENT!

1 or 2 Tbsp salt
2 Tbsp yeast
2 C mashed potatoes (can use reconstituted
    dried potatoes)
1/2 C sugar
1/2 C oil
2 C sourdough starter
6 C hot water
18 to 20 C white flour

Mix all ingredients in bread mixer for 6 minutes or knead by hand for 10 minutes, adding last 2 cups of flour slowly. Do not let dough get stiff. Let rise to double. Push down and shape into 6 loaves. Let rise to double again. Bake at 350° for 30 minutes.

DESSERTS

WHEAT PUDDING

6 C water
1 1/2 C wheat flour, coarse grind
1/2 C sugar
3 eggs, separated
1/2 C milk or reconstituted nonfat powdered
    milk

Bring 4 of the 6 cups of water to a rolling boil. Whirl wheat flour and remaining 2 cups of cold water in a blender. Pour wheat mixture into boiling water, beating continually. Cook 10 minutes on low heat, stirring continually so as not to burn.

In blender, whirl milk, egg yolks, and sugar. Add to cooked wheat, stirring continually. Beat egg whites until very stiff. Beat 1 cup of the hot wheat mixture into egg whites, then add remaining wheat mixture. Serve in dishes topped with strawberry jam and whipped cream. Can also be topped with ice cream.

RICE PUDDING FOR BABIES

1/2 C white rice
1 C water
1/2 C or less sugar
1 Tbsp cornstarch
2 eggs, separated
1 C milk

Mix rice and water in a saucepan. Heat to boiling, stirring once or twice. Reduce heat, cover and simmer for 15 minutes without removing the cover. Stir cornstarch into sugar and add to slightly beaten egg yolks and milk. Stir into cooked rice. Continue cooking until thick. Beat egg whites until stiff. Whip into rice mixture. Serve.

HOT FUDGE SAUCE

EXCELLENT!

2 C sugar
1/2 C dehydrated margarine, reconstituted or
    1 cube margarine
1/4 C syrup
1/4 C cocoa
1/2 C evaporated milk
1/4 tsp salt
1 tsp vanilla

Combine all ingredients except vanilla. Bring to a boil over medium heat, stirring constantly. Boil 1 minute. Stir in vanilla.

WHOLE WHEAT CREAM PUFFS

1/2 C butter or shortening
1 C water
1 C unsifted whole wheat flour
4 eggs

Bring shortening and water to boil; turn off heat and add flour all at once. Stir vigorously until mixture leaves sides of pan and forms a ball. Remove from heat. Add eggs one at a time, beating after each. Place balls of dough on ungreased cookie sheet, making 12 large or 16 medium puffs. Bake for 15 minutes at 400° then bake 30 to 45 minutes at 350° or until bubbles of moisture disappear from shells. Cool and fill. Makes 12 to 16.

EXCELLENT!

CREAM PUFF FILLING

2 C nonfat powdered milk, reconstituted
3/4 C sugar
5 1/2 Tbsp flour
1/8 tsp salt
2 eggs, beaten
1 tsp vanilla
1 C whipped cream

Scald milk. Mix sugar, flour, and salt together. Add to hot milk. Stir constantly over low heat until thickened. Cool over hot water in a double boiler for 15 min. Gradually add cooked mixture to beaten eggs. Return to double boiler and cook 3 to 4 minutes, stirring constantly. Chill. Add whipped cream and vanilla. Fill cream puffs.

HONEY RICE PUDDING

3/4 C honey
Pinch of salt
3 C nonfat powdered milk, reconstituted
3 slightly beaten eggs or 3 dehydrated whole
  eggs, reconstituted
1 1/2 tsp vanilla
3 C cooked brown rice
1 tsp grated lemon peel
1 C raisins or 1 C dehydrated reconstituted
  raisins

Stir all ingredients together and pour into greased baking dish. Set baking dish in a flat pan containing an inch of hot water. Bake at 325° for 1 hour or until set.

BREAD PUDDING

4 slices bread
2 Tbsp butter or margarine
1/3 C brown sugar
1/2 tsp cinnamon
1/3 C raisins
3 eggs, lightly beaten
1/3 C sugar
1 tsp vanilla
Dash of salt
2 1/2 C nonfat powdered milk, reconstituted,
  scalded

Heat oven to 350°. Butter a 1 1/2 qt casserole pan. Spread lightly toasted bread with butter. Sprinkle with brown sugar and then cinnamon. Cut bread into rectangles. In casserole arrange rectangles in single layer. Sprinkle with raisins.

Blend eggs, sugar, vanilla, and salt. Gradually stir in milk. Pour mixture over bread. Place casserole in pan of very hot water, 1 inch deep. Bake for 65 to 70 minutes or until knife inserted comes out clean. Serve warm or cold.

EASY CHRISTMAS PUDDING

EXCELLENT!

2 C brown sugar
4 Tbsp butter
5 C hot water

2 Tbsp butter
1 C sugar
1 C milk
2 C flour
1/2 tsp each nutmeg and cinnamon
2 tsp soda
1/4 tsp salt
1 C raisins
1/2 C nuts

In a pan, boil the first three ingredients; set aside.

Mix the remaining ingredients together and place in a 9x12 pan. Pour the above hot sauce over the top and bake at 350° for about 40 minutes.

NEVER FAIL PIE CRUST

EXCELLENT!

4 C flour
1 3/4 C shortening, cold
2 Tbsp sugar
1 tsp salt
1 C cold water
1 Tbsp vinegar
1 egg or 1 dehydrated whole egg, reconstituted

Mix flour, sugar, and salt in a mixing bowl. Using a pastry blender, cut shortening in until particles are size of small peas. Mix water, vinegar, and egg together, then sprinkle over mixture and toss with a fork until moistened. (More water can be added if necessary.) Divide into four equal parts and roll out. Do not handle more then necessary. Shape into crust, and place in freezer for 15 minutes before adding filling. Bake at 350°.

Yield: 50 tarts or 2 9-inch two-crust pies.

WHOLE WHEAT PIE CRUST

2 C whole wheat flour (fine)
1 tsp salt
5 Tbsp cold water
2/3 C lard, cold

Sift flour and salt. Remove 1/3 of this flour and make a paste by adding water. Cut lard into remaining flour until it is size of peas. Add paste and stir into ball. Roll out and chill in pans. When ready to use, fill with filling and bake.

SOYBEAN PIE
(Tastes like Pumpkin Pie)

EXCELLENT!

1 1/2 C ground cooked soybeans
1 2/3 C reconstituted nonfat powdered milk
3/4 C evaporated milk
1 C brown sugar
1 1/2 tsp cinnamon
1 1/4 tsp ginger
3/4 tsp cloves
1 1/2 tsp nutmeg
3 tsp grated lemon peel
2 eggs, slightly beaten or 2 dehydrated reconstituted eggs

In a blender, whirl together cooked soybeans, milk, and evaporated milk. Add sugar and spices and lemon peel. Add to eggs and mix well. Pour into an unbaked pie shell. Bake at 400° for 15 minutes. Turn oven down to 350° and continue baking for 45 minutes or until done. Serve with whipped cream or ice cream.

PINTO BEAN PECAN PIE

1/2 C sugar
3/4 C brown sugar
1/2 C butter or 1/2 C dehydrated butter,
    reconstituted
1 heaping C mashed cooked pinto beans
2 dehydrated whole eggs, reconstituted or 2
    fresh eggs
1/4 C Karo syrup
1 tsp vanilla
1/2 C chopped nuts, pecans or walnuts
1 9-inch unbaked pie shell

Blend sugars, eggs, and butter until creamy. Add pinto beans, Karo syrup, and vanilla. Blend well. Pour into unbaked pie shell. Top with chopped nuts. Bake at 375° for 20 minutes then at 350° for an additional 25 minutes. Can be served with whipped cream or ice cream. Can use as a tart filling.

PUMPKIN PIE

1 large can pumpkin
1 C honey
2 Tbsp flour
1 1/2 C reconstituted nonfat powdered milk
1 large can evaporated milk (1 3/4 C)
4 dehydrated whole eggs, reconstituted
1 tsp each salt, cinnamon, and nutmeg
1/4 tsp ginger

Prepare pie crust and bake in a 350° oven for 4 minutes.

Mix pumpkin, honey, seasoning, and flour together with milk and evaporated milk. Heat to boiling point and remove from stove.

Add the eggs which have been beaten. Mix well. Pour mixture into slightly baked pie crusts. Return to oven and bake for 45 minutes or until knife inserted comes out clean.

Note: For variety, spread a thin layer of mincemeat on the bottom crust and carefully pour pumpkin filling on top.

PUMPKIN PECAN PIE

3 dehydrated whole eggs, reconstituted
1 C pumpkin
1 C brown sugar or 1 C honey
1/2 C Karo Syrup
1/2 tsp cinnamon
1/4 tsp salt
1 C pecans, chopped

Combine all ingredients together except for nuts. Pour into unbaked pastry shell. Top with nuts. Bake at 350° for 40 minutes.

EXCELLENT!

CRANBERRY MINCEMEAT PIE

4 C fresh or frozen cranberries
1 C water
4 large apples, cored and coarsely chopped
1/4 lb beef suet, finely diced
1 C light or dark molasses
1/4 C cider vinegar
1 tsp each ground allspice and cinnamon
1/4 tsp ground nutmeg
2 1/2 C firmly packed brown sugar
3/4 C finely chopped mixed candied (glace) fruits
2 C raisins
1 C nuts, coarsely chopped
Whipped cream or ice cream (optional)

In a 5- to 6-quart kettle, combine cranberries and water. Cover and cook over high heat until cranberries pop open, about 5 minutes.

Add apples, suet, molasses, vinegar, spices, brown sugar, candied fruits, and raisins; stir to mix well. Bring to a boil, then reduce heat and let simmer, uncovered, over medium heat, stirring occasionally, for about 1 hour. Cool. Will keep in refrigerator up to 1 month.

Prepare pastry for a 9-inch double crust pie. Mix 4 to 5 cups of mincemeat with 1 C coarsely chopped walnuts or pecans. Spoon into bottom pastry shell. Place remaining shell on top of pie; seal edges and prick top with a fork.

Bake at 375° for about 1 hour. Top with ice cream or whipped cream, if desired.

DRIED APPLE PIE

2 C dehydrated apples, reconstituted
1/2 C brown sugar
1/2 C white sugar
1/4 tsp salt
1 tsp cinnamon
1/2 tsp ginger
1/4 tsp cloves
1 can evaporated milk
1 9-inch double crust pie

Cook and mash apples. Cool. Mix all ingredients in order given. Pour into bottom pastry shell. Place remaining shell on top of pie; seal edges and slit top with a knife. Bake at 425° for 15 minutes, then reduce heat to 350° and bake an additional 45 minutes.

EXCELLENT!

ALMOND PEACH PIE CUSTARD

1 9-inch single pie crust
1 C drained canned peaches
2 Tbsp dehydrated butter, reconstituted
3 fresh eggs or 3 Tbsp reconstituted egg powder
1/2 C sugar
1/2 tsp salt
1/4 tsp nutmeg
1/2 tsp each vanilla and almond flavoring
1/2 C light corn syrup
2/3 C evaporated milk
1 12-oz pkg sliced almonds

Preheat oven to 375°. Drain peaches. Place butter, eggs, sugar, salt, nutmeg, and vanilla in medium bowl. Add almond extract. Beat with wire whip or beater until smooth. Gradually stir in corn syrup and evaporated milk until well blended. Stir in drained peaches and almonds. Pour into unbaked pie shell. Bake 35 to 40 minutes or until filling is set. Cool slightly. Serve warm or cool.

EXCELLENT!

IMPERIAL MOUSSE

1 Tbsp unflavored gelatine
1/2 C cold water
1/2 C boiling water
1/2 C sugar
2 C sour cream
1 tsp vanilla
1/2 tsp almond flavoring
Raspberries and whipped cream

Dissolve gelatine in cold water and let set 5 min. Add boiling water and stir until completely dissolved. Add sugar and stir well. With wire whip, blend in sour cream and flavorings. Refrigerate until set, at least 6 hours or overnight. Serve topped with raspberries and whipped cream. Makes 4-6 servings.

CRUSTY LEMON PIE

EXCELLENT!

1 9-inch single pie crust
2 lemon
2 C sugar, divided
4 eggs
3 Tbsp flour
Whipped cream

Prepare crust and refrigerate while making filling.

Peel lemons, being careful to remove all the white membrane. Slice lemons paper thin (less than 1/8 inch thick). Remove seeds. Measure 1 tbsp lemon peel and set aside. Add 1 cup sugar to lemon slices; set aside. In a medium bowl, lightly beat eggs, flour, and remaining sugar until smooth. Gently stir in lemons and shredded peel. Pour into unbaked pie shell. Bake at 350° for 45 min. Serve with whipped cream.

PECAN TARTS

EXCELLENT!

2 C chopped pecans
1/2 C butter
2 C brown sugar
6 eggs, beaten
1 tsp vanilla
3/4 T lemon juice

In a small saucepan, melt butter and stir in brown sugar, mixing well. Add remaining ingredients.

Use 1 recipe of Never Fail Pie Crust (pg. 168). Roll pie crust out on a lightly floured board. Using tart tins, cut around each tin and gently press dough into bottoms. Spoon filling into each tin, being careful not to spill. Bake at 350° for 20 minutes. Makes 50 tarts

BUTTER TARTS

3/4 C each of raisins, and currents
2 eggs, beaten
3/4 Tbsp lemon juice
1/2 C melted butter
1 1/2 C brown sugar
1 tsp vanilla

Bring raisins and currents to boil in 1 C water. Remove from heat and drain. Mix with all remaining ingredients.

Use 1 recipe of Never Fail Pie Crust (pg. 168). Roll pie crust out on a lightly floured board. Using tart tins, cut around each tin and gently press dough into bottoms. Spoon filling into each tin, being careful not to spill. Bake at 350° for 20 minutes. Makes 50 tarts.

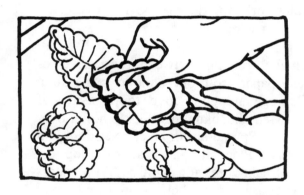

JULIE'S ALMOND CHOCOLATE CAKE

6 oz semisweet chocolate
1/2 C plus 3 Tbsp butter
3/4 C sugar
4 eggs, separated
3/4 C ground almonds
3/4 C whole wheat flour

Frosting:
6 oz almond paste
1 C semisweet chocolate chips
Apricot jam
Almond slices

Grease an 8-inch springform cake pan. Preheat oven to 350°.

To make cake, melt chocolate in a double boiler over low heat. Cream butter and half the sugar in a medium bowl until light and fluffy. Stir in chocolate, egg yolks, and ground almonds. In a separate bowl, beat egg whites until stiff; fold in remaining sugar. Fold egg white mixture into chocolate mixture. Fold in flour. Turn batter into prepared pan. Bake 40 to 45 minutes, or until done. Do not overbake. Cool on a wire rack.

To make frosting, between two sheets of waxed paper, roll out almond paste to a circle large enough to cover top and sides of cake. Melt chocolate in a double boiler over low heat. Spread a thin layer of apricot jam over cake. Place almond paste over top and sides of cake, pressing lightly. Trim excess almond paste. Spread chocolate evenly over cooled cake. Arrange sliced almonds on cake while chocolate is soft. (see picture)

LINZERTORTE

EXCELLENT!

3/4 C plus 2 Tbsp butter or margarine, softened
3/4 C plus 2 Tbsp sugar
3 eggs or 3 dehydrated whole eggs, reconstituted
1/8 tsp each salt and cloves
1/2 tsp cinnamon
Grated peel of 1/2 lemon
1 scant cup plain cookie crumbs
1 1/4 C ground almonds
2 C white flour, sifted or 1 C white flour and 1 C pastry wheat flour
1 C raspberry jam
1 egg yolk, beaten

Grease a 10-inch springform cake pan. Cream butter and sugar in a large bowl until fluffy. Add 3 eggs, one at a time, with salt, cloves, cinnamon, and lemon peel. Mix cookie crumbs and almonds. Stir into egg mixture. Fold in flour to make a soft dough. Refrigerate for 2 hours.

Preheat oven to 375°. Roll or pat 2/3 of the dough to a 10 inch round. Return remaining ground of dough in greased pan. Shape it so it is about 3/4 inch high around the edges. Spread jam over dough. Roll out remaining dough about 1/8 inch thick. Cut 1/2 inch wide strips with a pastry cutter. Arrange strips in a lattice pattern over jam. Brush with egg yolk. Bake for 40 minutes or until pastry is lightly browned. Cool in pan about 30 minutes. Remove to a rack to cool.

EGGLESS CHOCOLATE CAKE

3 C flour
2 C sugar
1/2 C cocoa
2 tsp baking soda
2 tsp vanilla
1 tsp salt
2 C water
3/4 C vegetable oil
2 Tbsp vinegar

Mix together dry ingredients. Add remaining ingredients and beat for 3 min. Pour into a greased 9x13 pan. Bake at 350° for 35 to 40 minutes.

EXCELLENT!

MARLENE'S FAVORITE CHOCOLATE FROSTING

2 1-oz squares unsweetened chocolate (melted)
1/2 C butter, melted
1 egg
1 tsp vanilla
2 3/4 C powdered sugar
milk, if needed

Put all ingredients in a mixing bowl except milk. Beat until the right thickness. Add milk if needed. Will frost a whole cake.

WHOLE WHEAT CHIFFON CAKE

1/2 tsp cream of tartar
10 egg whites or dehydrated egg whites,
   reconstituted
2 C sifted pastry (fine grind) wheat flour
1 1/2 C sugar
1 tsp salt
3 tsp baking powder
1/2 C oil
4 egg yolks or dehydrated whole eggs,
   reconstituted
3/4 C cold water
1 tsp lemon rind, grated
1 tsp vanilla
1 tsp lemon flavoring
2 Tbsp cornstarch

Sift dry ingredients together. Make a well and add oil, egg yolks, water and flavorings. Beat until very smooth. Beat egg whites and cream of tartar until very stiff; pour egg yolk mixture slowly over beaten egg whites, folding gently until barely blended. Don't stir. Pour into angel cake pan. Bake at 350° for 45 to 55 min.

PINEAPPLE FILLING

1/2 C sugar
3 T cornstarch
1/2 tsp salt
3/4 C pineapple juice
1 C crushed pineapple, well drained
1 Tbsp butter
1 tsp lemon juice

Mix all ingredients and bring to a rolling boil for 2 minutes, stirring constantly. Chill before using.

EXCELLENT!

CRANBERRY DESSERT

12 oz. fresh cranberries
1 1/2 C sugar

3/4 C broken walnuts, toasted
3/4 C orange marmalade
Juice of 1 lemon
Whipped cream or ice cream

Wash and drain cranberries. Mix with the sugar and place in shallow baking pan. Cover with a lid or alum. foil. Bake at 350° for 1 hour. Mix remaining ingredients together and stir into the baked cranberries. Serve with whipped cream or ice cream.

POPPY SEED CAKE

EXCELLENT!

4 large eggs or 4 dehydrated whole eggs, reconstituted
1 1/2 oil
2 C sugar
3 C unsifted flour or 1 1/2 C white flour and 1 1/2 C pastry wheat flour
1/2 tsp salt
1 1/2 tsp baking soda
1 12-oz can evaporated milk
1/2 C chopped walnuts (optional)
2 oz. poppy seeds
1 tsp almond flavor

Beat eggs well. Add oil and beat, then add sugar and beat well. Alternately, add flour (sifted with soda and salt) and the milk. Mix well, fold in nuts and poppy seeds. Bake in an ungreased 10" angel cake tube pan, 350° for 1 hr 15 min. Frost with Lemon Glaze (below).

LEMON GLAZE

EXCELLENT!

2 Tbsp lemon juice
1 C powdered sugar

Mix and beat together well or until smooth. Pour over warm cake.

ZUCCHINI CAKE (OR BREAD OR MUFFINS)

2 C chopped raw zucchini
1 C oil
3 eggs
1 C brown sugar
3 C flour (half wheat and white)
1 tsp salt
1/4 tsp baking powder
1 tsp soda
2 tsp cinnamon
1 C sugar
1 Tbsp vanilla
1/2 C chopped nuts or raisins

Put zucchini, oil and eggs in blender and blend until mixed; pour into bowl. Stir in sugars and remaining dry ingredients. Add vanilla and nuts. Mix well. Pour into 2 greased loaf pans or muffin cups or bundt pan. Bake at 325° for 1 hour.

WARM GOLDEN PINEAPPLE CHEESE CAKE

2 C unsifted flour or 1 C white flour and
    1 C pastry wheat flour
1/4 tsp salt
1/2 tsp baking powder
2/3 C butter or margarine
1/3 C sugar
2 egg yolks
2 Tbsp evaporated milk
1/2 tsp grated lemon peel

Cheese Filling:
1 8-oz can crushed pineapple
4 Tbsp butter or margarine
2/3 C sugar
2 8-oz pkgs cream cheese
1 egg yolk
1/4 C evaporated milk
1/2 C golden raisins
1 tsp grated lemon rind

Set cream cheese in a warm place to soften. In a large bowl, sift flour with salt and baking powder. With a pastry blender, cut in butter until mixture resembles course crumbs (see diagram #1). Add sugar, egg yolks, evaporated milk, and grated lemon peel. Toss lightly with a fork. Mix with hands just until pastry holds together. Turn out on a lightly floured surface; roll over to coat with flour. Knead until smooth, about 2 minutes (see diagram #2). Shape pastry into a ball and wrap in waxed paper. Refrigerate for 30 minutes.

For filling, drain crushed pineapple, reserving liquid. Pre-heat oven to 350°. Lightly grease a 10-inch springform pan; remove side. Beat butter, sugar, and cream cheese on high speed until mixture is well blended. Add egg yolk. Beat until smooth. Add crushed pineapple, raisins and grated lemon peel, set aside.

Place 3/4 of the dough into the bottom of springform pan. Cover with a 10 inch square sheet of waxed paper. Refrigerate remaining pastry. Roll out pastry on bottom of pan (see diagram #3). Remove waxed paper. Bake 12 minutes, or until golden brown. Cool. Assemble pan with baked pastry on bottom. Pour filling into pan spreading evenly.

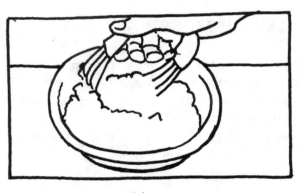

#1

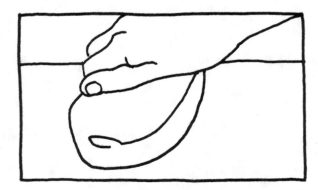

#2

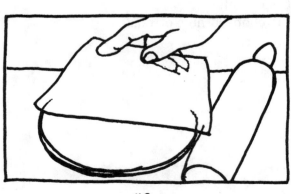

#3

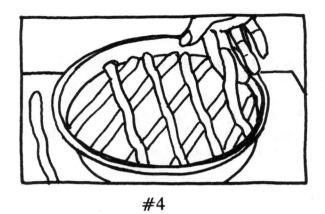

#4

Cut half of the reserved pasty into 5 equal pieces. On a lightly floured surface, roll out 10-inch strips. Place pastry strips 1-1/2 inches apart over filling. Trim. Make 5 more 10-inch strips. Lay in a criss-cross fashion over other strips (see diagram #4). Bake 40 minutes or until golden brown. Cool 10 minutes, sprinkle strips with powdered sugar. Remove side of pan and serve warm. Top with whipped cream if desired.

MARGARET'S CHOCOLATE CHIFFON CAKE

2 C flour
1 3/4 C sugar
1/3 C cocoa
3 tsp baking powder
1 tsp salt
1/2 C oil
7 egg yokes
3/4 C cold water
1 tsp vanilla
7 egg whites
1/2 tsp cream of tartar

Mix first five ingredients together. Make well in flour. Add next four ingredients beating well. Set aside.

Beat egg whites and cream of tartar until stiff. Fold into egg batter and place in ungreased tube pan. Bake at 350° for 1 hour. Invert pan until cooled.

HONEY CAKE

6 Tbsp butter
3 dehydrated whole eggs, reconstituted
1/2 C plus 1 Tbsp sugar
1/8 tsp vanilla
1 1/4 C white flour or finely ground wheat
    flour
1 tsp baking powder
3 Tbsp evaporated milk

Grease a 10-inch springform cake pan. Pre-heat oven to 400°.

Melt butter and cool slightly. Put eggs, sugar, and vanilla into medium bowl. Beat until pale and creamy, about 5 to 10 minutes.

Sift flour and baking powder together, then fold into mixture. Stir in melted butter and evaporated milk. Turn batter into pan and smooth the surface. Bake for 15 minutes or until top is just firm.

Meanwhile, make topping. Do not turn oven off. Spread topping carefully over partially cooked cake. Return cake to oven and bake 15 minutes longer or until almonds are browned. Leave cake in pan until topping begins to set, then transfer to rack and cool.

Topping:
8 Tbsp butter
1/4 C plus 2 Tbsp sugar
1/4 C honey
3 Tbsp evaporated milk
1 1/4 C sliced almonds
1/2 tsp cinnamon
Grated peel of 1/2 orange

Melt butter in small saucepan. Add sugar, honey, evaporated milk, almonds, cinnamon and orange peel. Stir well. Bring to a boil and remove from heat.

WHEAT CARROT CAKE

1 C sugar
1/2 C olive oil
2 eggs, beaten or 2 dehydrated whole eggs, reconstituted
1 1/2 C grated carrots or sliced carrots, reconstituted
1/2 C flour
1/2 C wheat flour
1/2 tsp salt
1 tsp baking soda
1 tsp cinnamon
1/4 C each ground coconut, nuts, and raisins

Combine sugar and oil. Add eggs. Mix well. Add grated carrots. Slowly stir in sifted dry ingredients. Add ground coconut, nuts and raisins. Pour batter into lightly greased and floured 9x9 cake pan. Bake at 400° for 20 to 30 minutes or until it tests done. When cool, frost.

NOTE: recipe can be doubled and poured into a lightly greased and floured bundt pan. Bake 50 to 60 min.

Frosting:

1 8-oz pkg cream cheese, softened
1/4 C margarine
2 1/2 C powdered sugar
Hot water, if needed

Cream together the cream cheese, margarine, and sugar. Add a little hot water, 1 teaspoon at a time, until you reach spreading consistency. Mix well.

SOUR CREAM CHOCOLATE BUNDT CAKE

6 Tbsp soft butter or margarine
2 eggs
1 1/2 tsp baking powder
1 tsp cinnamon
1 6-oz pkg semisweet chocolate chips
1 C plus 1 Tbsp sugar
1 1/3 C unsifted flour
1 tsp soda
1 C sour cream

Mix butter with the 1 cup sugar until blended, then beat in eggs, one at a time. Mix together dry ingredients, add to creamed mixture. Mix in sour cream. Pour batter into a greased and floured 9x13 baking pan. Scatter chocolate bits evenly over the batter, then sprinkle with the remaining 1 Tbsp sugar. Bake at 350° for 35 minutes or until cake first begins to pull away from sides of pan. Serve warm or cooled, cut in rectangles.

CHEESE CAKE
(medium/large pan)

EXCELLENT!

3 8-oz pkgs cream cheese
1 C sugar
6 eggs
2 tsp vanilla

Beat the cream cheese until creamy, add other ingredients and mix well. Pour into prepared graham cracker crust. Bake at 350° for approximately 50 minutes to 1 hour.

CHEESE CAKE ALMOND TOPPING

EXCELLENT!

1/4 C butter
1/2 C sliced almonds or pecans
1/2 C brown sugar
3 Tbsp whipping cream

Melt butter. Add almonds or pecans and stir over medium heat until lightly toasted. Stir in brown sugar and whipping cream. Bring quickly to a boil and boil 1 minute. Immediately drizzle evenly over hot cake.

GERMAN PLUM CAKE

1/2 C soft butter
3 eggs
1 C unsifted flour
1/2 C sugar
1/2 tsp vanilla
purple plums cut in half, seeded

Cream butter and sugar. Beat eggs in, one at a time. Stir in vanilla and flour. Spread in a shallow 9x13 baking pan and top with plums, peaches, and/or apricots. Sprinkle with cinnamon sugar. Bake at 375° for 40 minutes.

EXCELLENT!

CREAM CHEESE FROSTING FOR CARROT CAKE

1/2 C butter or margarine
1 8-oz cream cheese
1 16-oz powder sugar
2 tsp grated orange rind
1 tsp vanilla

Combine butter and cream cheese in large bowl, beat until light and fluffy. Add sugar, orange rind, and vanilla, mixing well. Spread on cake.

FRUIT COCKTAIL CAKE

2 C flour
1 tsp salt
1 1/2 C sugar
2 tsp baking soda
2 eggs
1 can fruit cocktail (do not drain)

Topping:
1/2 C chopped nuts
1/2 C brown sugar

Frosting:
1/2 C butter or margarine
1 1/2 C sugar
2 tsp vanilla
1 C evaporated milk
1 tsp brandy flavoring

Combine all ingredients in order given. Pour into a prepared 9x13 pan. Sprinkle top with topping. Press down lightly. Bake at 350° for 45 minutes. Remove from oven and pour frosting over cake while hot.

Bring to a boil and boil for 10 minutes.

EXCELLENT!

MARGARET'S CARROT CAKE

1-1/2 C whole wheat flour
2/3 C white flour
2 tsp **ea** baking soda and cinnamon
1/2 tsp **ea** salt and nutmeg
1/4 tsp ginger
1 C **ea** brown and white sugar
1 C buttermilk
3/4 C oil
4 eggs
1-1/2 tsp vanilla
4 large carrots, grated
1 8-oz can crushed pineapple, drained
1 C chopped walnuts
1 C coconut
1/2 C raisins

Combine first 7 ingredients; set aside. In separate bowl, combine sugars, buttermilk, oil, eggs and vanilla. Stir until well blended. Add flour mixture, carrots, and remaining ingredients; stir until barely blended. Grease and line with waxed paper an 11x17 pan or three 8" round pans. Pour into pans; bake at 350° for 30 min. or until toothpick inserted in center comes out clean. Cool on racks 10 min. Remove from pans and remove waxed paper.

After completely cooled, frost with cream cheese frosting. Refrigerate overnight before cutting. Excellent for wedding sheet cake.

MARLENE'S FRUIT CAKE

EXCELLENT!

1 C raisins
1 C dates
2 C light raisins
1 C candied cherries
1 C candied pineapple
6 C mixed candied fruit
3 tsp cinnamon
2 tsp allspice
1 tsp cloves
1 C apricot nectar
2 C almonds, coarsely chopped
3 C walnuts, coarsely chopped

1 C butter
1 C margarine
1 C brown sugar
2 C sugar
10 eggs, beaten
4 1/2 C sifted flour
1 tsp baking soda
1 tsp salt
1 tsp baking powder
2 tsp vanilla

Mix first 12 ingredients together and set aside for 1 hour.

Whip butters and sugars until light and fluffy. Add eggs, blend well. Add remaining ingredients. Add the above fruit/nut mixture. Pour into prepared pans (instructions below). Place pans on a cookie sheet (this prevents burning of the fruits). Bake at 250° for 2 1/2 to 3 1/2 hours.

Place on cooling racks. Remove the papers while cakes are still warm.

To age, dip a clean cloth in apricot nectar, wring out well and wrap around the cakes. Let cakes age for about a week.

Note: This recipe makes a heavy fruit cake. If a lighter cake is preferred, simply double the quantities for the dough part but prepare only a single recipe of the fruits/nuts portion. Either way, it is excellent.

To prepare pans for baking, cut patterns of the baking pans from brown paper bags and again from waxed or parchment paper. (If using parchment paper, you won't have to grease it.) To assemble, grease a loaf pan, place in it a layer if the brown paper, grease it, place on it a layer of the waxed paper, grease it. Then pour the batter into the prepared pan.

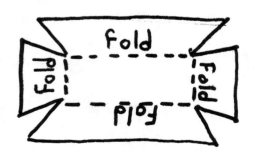

MARGARET'S APPLESAUCE CAKE

2 C chopped raw apples **or** 1 C applesauce
1 egg, lightly beaten
1 C sugar
1/4 C oil
1 C flour
1 tsp salt
1 tsp baking soda
1 tsp cinnamon
3/4 C raisins
3/4 C chopped nuts

Mix apples or applesauc
and oil. Mix together, then auu,
and dry ingredients. Do not beat too
mix only until everything is moistened.
Pour into greased 8" square pan and bake at
350° for 30 min. Top with Caramel
Frosting, pg. 193.

Note: For larger cake, double everything
except sugar -- use 1 1/2 cups.

MADGE'S OATMEAL CAKE

1 1/2 C oatmeal
2 C boiling water
1 1/2 C sugar
1 1/2 C brown sugar
3/4 C oil
3 eggs
1 1/2 tsp vanilla
2 C plus 4 Tbsp flour
1 1/2 tsp baking soda
1 tsp salt
1 tsp cinnamon

Pour boiling water over oatmeal and set
aside to soak. Cream together sugars, oil,
eggs, and vanilla. Sift dry ingredients
together. Add to creamed mixture,
alternating with oatmeal. Pour into a 9x11
pan and bake at 375° for 50 minutes.

BROWN SUGAR FROSTING

1 cube margarine
1 C brown sugar
1/2 C milk
1 C coconut
1 C chopped nuts

Mix ingredients together and bring to a boil
in small pot. Boil for 1 minute. Spread
over hot cake.

CARAMEL FROSTING

1/2 C butter or margarine
1 C brown sugar
1/4 C canned milk
2 C powder sugar

Melt butter in pan, add brown sugar and
milk. Bring to boil and boil 1 minute.
Whip in powder sugar and spread on cake.

LEMON-YOGURT CAKE

2 3/4 C flour
1/4 tsp salt
2 tsp baking powder
1 C butter or margarine
2 C sugar
1 1/2 tsp grated lemon peel
1 tsp lemon extract
5 eggs, separated
1 C unflavored yogurt
Powdered sugar

Mix together the flour, salt, and baking powder. In a large bowl, beat the butter and sugar until creamy, scraping bowl several times. Beat in lemon peel, lemon extract, egg yolks, and half the yogurt. Reduce speed to low and gradually mix in half the flour mixture, scraping sides of bowl as needed. Mix in remaining yogurt and remaining flour. Beat egg whites until stiff peaks form. Carefully fold into batter until well blended.

Spoon batter into a well greased Bundt pan or a 10-inch tube pan. Bake at 350° for about 1 hour or until a pick inserted in center comes out clean. Cool on a rack (do not invert) for 15 minutes, then turn out of pan and cool completely. Before serving, sift powdered sugar over top.

SUNFLOWER SEED COOKIES

1 C butter, softened
2/3 C sugar
1 C brown sugar, packed
2 eggs
1 tsp baking powder
1 tsp vanilla
Pinch of salt
1 C whole wheat flour
1 C white flour
2 C rolled oats
1 12-oz pkg chocolate chips
1 C sunflower seeds

Cream butter with sugars and eggs until light and fluffy. Beat in baking soda, vanilla and salt. Blend in flours and oats to make stiff dough. Stir in chocolate chips. Roll into balls then roll in sunflower seeds. Place 2" apart on cookie sheets which have been greased, or lined with parchment paper. Bake at 375° for 8 to 10 minutes. Don't overbake. Cool few minutes then remove to wire racks. Makes 6 dozen.

BASIC YULE LOG

5 eggs (separated)
1/2 C sugar
1 tsp vanilla
1/2 C flour
1/2 tsp baking powder
1/2 tsp salt

Separate eggs. Beat yolks until thick and lemon-colored. Gradually add sugar. Beat until thick. Add remaining ingredients. Set aside. Whip egg white until stiff. Gently mix into yoke mixture. Spread evenly in jelly roll pan that has been greased and lined with waxed paper and greased again. Bake at 350° for 10 to 12 minutes. Turn out onto a towel sprinkled with powdered sugar. Roll gently and cool on wire rack. Fill and frost (recipes below).

RASPBERRY FILLING

Raspberry jam
1 C cream, whipped

Fold jam into whipped cream. Unroll cake and spread cream evenly over it. Roll up cake and place seam side down on serving dish. Frost with your favorite chocolate frosting.

CLEAR LEMON FILLING

1 C sugar
3 Tbsp cornstarch
1/2 tsp salt
1 C water
2 Tbsp lemon rind
1/2 C lemon juice
2 Tbsp butter
4 egg yolks

Mix ingredients together in a saucepan, except for egg yolks. Bring to a rolling boil and then boil 1 minutes. Beat in 4 egg yolks, return to heat and continue cooking for 1 minute more. Chill.

PINEAPPLE FILLING

1/2 C sugar
3 Tbsp cornstarch
1/2 tsp salt
3/4 C pineapple juice
1 C crushed pineapple, well drained
1 Tbsp butter
1 tsp lemon juice

Mix all ingredients together in a saucepan. Bring to a rolling boil and boil for 2 minutes, stirring constantly. Chill before using.

CHRISTMAS YULE LOG - CHOCOLATE

5 egg yolks
5 egg whites
1/4 C wheat flour
3 Tbsp cocoa
1/4 tsp baking powder
1/4 tsp salt
1 C powdered sugar
1/4 tsp cinnamon
1/2 tsp almond flavoring

Beat egg yolks until thick and lemon colored. In a separate mixing bowl, sift together flour, cocoa, baking powder, salt, powdered sugar, and cinnamon. Add beaten egg yolks; beat well. Add almond flavoring. In separate bowl whip egg whites until stiff peaks form. Gently fold into the egg yolk batter.

Spread in a jelly roll pan which has been greased and lined with waxed paper and greased again. Bake at 350° for 10 to 12 minutes. Turn out onto a towel which has been dusted with powdered sugar, then gently roll up and cool on a wire rack.

Filling:
1 C whipping cream
2 Tbsp powdered sugar
1 tsp vanilla (option)

For filling: Whip cream and powdered sugar until stiff. If desired, flavor with vanilla. Unroll cake and spread cream evenly over it. Roll up cake and place seam side down on serving dish. Frost with your favorite chocolate frosting or Mocha Butter Cream (below).

MOCHA BUTTER CREAM

1/2 C butter
1 C powdered sugar
1 Tbsp cocoa
1 tsp instant Postum or Pero
2 egg yolks

Cream butter, add powdered sugar, cocoa and Pero. Beat until fluffy. Add egg yolks and blend thoroughly.

CARAMEL FROSTED FILBERT ROLL

EXCELLENT!

5 eggs, separated
3/4 C sugar
1/3 C graham cracker crumbs
1 tsp baking powder
1 tsp vanilla
1/8 tsp each salt and cream of tartar
1 C ground filberts
Filling (below)
Caramel Frosting (below)
2 Tbsp chopped filberts

Filling:
1 C whipping cream
2 Tbsp powdered sugar
1 tsp vanilla (optional)

Caramel Frosting:
1/4 C butter
1/2 C firmly packed brown sugar
2 Tbsp milk
3/4 C powdered sugar

Beat egg yolks until light and lemon colored. Gradually add all but 2 tablespoons of sugar and beat until thick. Mix in crumbs, baking powder, and vanilla. Beat egg whites until foamy, add salt and cream of tartar, and beat until stiff. Beat in the remaining sugar. Fold egg whites into the yolk mixture alternately with the ground filberts.

Grease a 10x15 jelly roll pan, line bottom with waxed paper and grease again. Pour in batter and smooth. Bake at 350° for 20 minutes. Let stand 5 minutes, then turn out onto a large cloth lightly dusted with powdered sugar. Lightly roll up and cool on a wire rack.

For filling: Whip cream and powdered sugar until stiff. If desired, flavor with vanilla. Unroll cake and spread cream evenly over it. Roll up cake and place seam side down on serving dish. Frost with Caramel Frosting and decorate with nuts.

Melt butter in a small saucepan and stir in brown sugar. Bring to a boil and cook over low heat, stirring constantly, for 2 minutes. Pour in milk and cook, stirring until it comes to a full boil. Remove from heat and let cool until lukewarm. Gradually add powdered sugar and beat until smooth.

APPLESAUCE CUSTARD PIE
(Open Face)

4 C unsweetened applesauce*
1/2 C margarine or butter, melted
2 C sugar
Dash salt
6 Tbsp flour
1 Tbsp vanilla
4 egg yolks
4 egg whites

*If applesauce is already sweetened, add only 1 cup sugar.

Mix all ingredients together, except egg whites. Whip egg whites. Fold into above mixture. Bake in an unbaked pie shell until brown at 375° for about 45 minutes.

BLUEBERRY CRISP

2 1/2 C rolled oats
2 1/2 C sifted whole wheat pastry flour
4 tsp baking powder
1 1/2 C honey
1 1/2 C butter
1 tsp salt
3 1/2 C blueberries
1/2 C honey
1/2 tsp cinnamon

In a mixing bowl, combine oats, flour, baking powder, honey, butter, and salt, and mix with a pastry blender. Divide into two portions and spread one portion in shallow pan. Combine blueberries, honey, and cinnamon and cover mixture in pan. Cover with the rest of the first mixture. Bake at 350° for 15 minutes, then raise temperature to 375° for 15 minutes.

DIET LEMON SNOW

1 envelope Knox gelatin
1 1/2 C water, divided
1/3 C sugar or sweetener
1/4 C lemon juice
2 tsp grated lemon rind
1 unbeaten egg white

Sprinkle gelatin on 1/2 C of the water to soften. Add sugar or sweetener. Place over low heat and stir until gelatin is dissolved. Remove from heat and add remaining water, lemon juice, and lemon rind. Chill to slightly thicken, then add unbeaten egg white and beat with a beater until fluffy. Spoon into dessert dishes and chill.

CHOCOLATE CHIFFON PIE

1 envelope unflavored gelatin
3 egg yolks
1/3 C sugar
1/4 tsp salt
1 tsp vanilla
2 1-oz squares unsweetened chocolate
1/2 C water
3 egg whites
1/2 C sugar
1 9-inch baked pastry shell

Soften gelatin in 1/4 cup cold water. Beat egg yolks until thick and lemon colored. Gradually beat in the 1/3 cup sugar; add salt and vanilla. Combine chocolate and 1/2 cup water. Stir over low heat until blended. Add softened gelatin; stir to dissolve. Immediately beat chocolate mixture into egg yolk. Chill, stirring occasionally, until mixture is partially set.

Beat egg whites to soft peaks. Gradually add 1/2 C sugar, beating to stiff peaks. Fold small amount of egg whites into chilled chocolate mixture. Then spoon about half the chocolate mixture over remaining egg whites; fold in just until blended. Repeat with remaining chocolate. If necessary, chill until mixture mounds when spooned. Pile into cooled shell. Chill until firm Garnish with whipped cream.

CRACKER PIE

12 soda cracker squares
1 Tbsp baking powder
1 C walnuts, chopped
3 egg whites
1 C sugar
1 tsp vanilla
1 small carton fresh whipping cream (1 C)

Beat egg whites until stiff, adding sugar very slowly while beating. Add vanilla. Crush crackers and mix separately with baking powder and nuts. Fold into first mixture. Pour into greased pie plate. Bake at 325° for 20 minutes. Beat whipping cream, adding sugar slowly to taste, about 1/4 to 1/2 cup. Serve with pie.

RUM RAISIN RICE PUDDING

1 C raisins
1/4 to 1/3 C gold rum or 2 Tbsp
    rum flavoring
1 quart milk
1/2 C sugar
1 tsp salt
3/4 C uncooked long grain rice, rinsed and
    drained
1/2 tsp vanilla extract
1 tsp ground ginger
1 C heavy cream, whipped

In a small bowl, combine raisins and rum; set aside. In a 3-quart saucepan, combine milk, sugar, salt, and rice. Bring to boil over medium heat, stirring constantly. Cover, reduce heat and simmer 25 to 30 minutes, stirring constantly until rice is tender. Stir in vanilla, rum-raisin mixture and ginger. Cool to room temperature. Fold cream into rice; chill. Serves 8.

WHOLE WHEAT CANDY

3 Tbsp cocoa
1/2 C milk
2 C sugar
1 C cooked wheat, drained
1/4 tsp salt
1 tsp vanilla
2 C quick oats
1/2 C shredded coconut

Bring to a boil slowly, cocoa, milk, sugar, salt, and vanilla. Remove from heat and add oats, wheat, and coconut. Drop on waxed paper by teaspoonfuls. Put in refrigerator to set. Makes 30.

JAR OF FRUIT CAKE

1 qt bottled fruit (any kind)
4 tsp baking soda
2 C sugar
1 C oil
4 C flour or 3 3/4 C fine whole wheat flour
1 tsp salt
4 tsp cinnamon
1 tsp nutmeg
1 tsp cloves
1 C raisins dredged in flour
1 C chopped nuts (optional)

Blend bottled fruit in blender. Pour into a large bowl and add ingredients in order given (no need to sift together first). Mix until well blended. Pour into 2 well-greased and floured bread pans or 1 Bundt pan.
Bake at 350° for 1 hour.
Frost with Caramel Frosting (below).

CARAMEL FROSTING

EXCELLENT!

1 cube butter or 1/2 C dehydrated butter
   reconstituted with 2 Tbsp oil
1 C brown sugar
1/3 C evaporated milk
2 C powdered sugar
Pecans (optional)

Boil first 3 ingredients together for 1 minute. Add 2 C powdered sugar and beat well. Spread on cake. Optional: top with 1/2 cup chopped pecans.

CARAMEL POPCORN BALLS

8 C popped corn
3/4 C sugar
3/4 C brown sugar
1/2 C light corn syrup
1/2 C water
1 tsp salt
3/4 C butter or margarine

Measure popped corn into a large bowl. Combine sugars, corn syrup, water, and salt in a 2-quart saucepan. Heat to boiling over medium heat, stirring frequently. Cook, stirring constantly, to 260° on a candy thermometer or until a small amount of mixture dropped into very cold water forms a hard ball. Reduce heat to low; stir in butter until melted. Pour syrup in thin streams over popped corn. Stir until well coated. Cool slightly.

To form ball: Butter hands; shape mixture into 3 inch balls and place on waxed paper.

HONEY CANDY

2 C honey
1 C sugar
1 C cream

Combine ingredients and cook slowly until it reaches the hardball stage when tested in cold water. Pour onto buttered platter, and when cool enough to handle, grease or butter hands and pull until a golden color. Cut into pieces.

SPROUTED WHEAT CANDY

EXCELLENT!

1 C almonds
1 C raisins
1 C sprouted wheat
Coconut

Mix ingredients together. Grind twice in a food chopper or processor. Shape into balls; roll in coconut.

CHRISTMAS FUDGE

3 pkgs chocolate chips
1 8-oz jar marshmallow cream
1 cube margarine
1 tsp vanilla
2 C chopped nuts
4 1/2 C sugar
1 large can evaporated milk

Mix sugar and milk in saucepan. Bring to boil and boil exactly 10 minutes. Pour over remaining ingredients and mix thoroughly. Place in greased dish and let set in refrigerator 24 hours.

HONEY TAFFY

1 C honey

Cook honey to hard crack stage at 285°. Stir occasionally. Remove from heat and pour onto buttered platter. As outside edges cool, fold to center and start stretching while still hot. Pull until light and porous and until small strings develop. Cut into short pieces. Place in paper-lined metal can for 2 days to soften.

PEANUT BUTTER KISSES

1 C peanut butter
1 C honey
1 1/2 C nonfat milk powder

Mix peanut butter and honey together. Add the dry milk a little at a time. Work finished mixture into balls, and top with an almond or roll in sesame seeds.

SESAME BARS

5 California figs, soaked a little
1 C sesame seeds
2 C almonds
1 C sunflower or pumpkin seeds
1/3 C sesame seeds
2/3 C honey
Coconut

Grind figs, 1 cup sesame seeds, almonds, and sunflower seeds. Add 1/3 cup sesame seeds and honey. Press flat or make into a bar, then cut into pieces and roll in coconut.

PISTACHIO FINGERS

1-1/2 C butter, softened
2/3 C sugar
6 oz almond paste (2/3 C)
2 egg yolks
3-1/3 C flour

Frosting
2 C semisweet chocolate chips
1 C finely chopped pistachio nuts

Cream butter and sugar until blended. Add almond paste and egg yolks; beat until light. Blend in flour to make a smooth dough. Turn out onto lightly-floured board. Divide into 8 equal pieces, divide each piece in half. Roll each half into a 12" rope; cut each rope into 2" lengths. Place 2" apart on cookie sheets which have been greased and floured or lined with parchment paper. Bake at 350° for 10-12 minutes or until edges just begin to brown. Remove to wire rack and cool.

Frosting
Melt chocolate chips in small bowl over hot water. Stir until smooth. Dip both ends of cookies about 1/2" into melted chocolate, then dip into pistachios. Place on waxed paper; let set. Makes 6 dozen.

HONEY COOKIES

5 C whole wheat flour
1 tsp salt
1 tsp baking powder
1/2 tsp baking soda
1 tsp cinnamon
1 tsp ginger
1/2 tsp cloves
1/2 tsp nutmeg
1 C shortening
2 dehydrated whole eggs, reconstituted
2 C honey
1 tsp vanilla
1 C nonfat powdered milk, reconstituted

Sift dry ingredients together. Combine eggs, honey, shortening, and vanilla. Beat well. Add milk alternately with dry ingredients. Chill dough. Roll out and cut with cookie cutters or form into balls and flatten slightly. Bake at 375° for 8 to 10 minutes.

RANGER COOKIES

1/2 tsp baking powder
1/2 tsp salt
3/4 C oil
1 C brown sugar
1 C white sugar
2 eggs
2 C flour
2 C corn flakes
2 C rolled oats
1 tsp soda
1 C coconut
1 tsp vanilla

Cream first six ingredients then add remaining ingredients. Mix well. Bake at 350° for about 15 to 20 minutes.

WHOLE WHEAT PEANUT BUTTER COOKIES

1 C shortening
1 C peanut butter
1 C brown sugar
1 C white sugar
2 eggs or 2 dehydrated eggs, reconstituted
2 1/2 C sifted whole wheat flour*
1 tsp baking powder
1 1/2 tsp soda
1/2 tsp salt

Cream together shortening, peanut butter, and brown and white sugars. Add eggs 1 at a time and beat until light and fluffy. Add dry ingredients. Chill dough at least 1 hour. Roll into walnut-size balls and place 3 inches apart on a cookie sheet. Flatten cookie with a fork. Bake at 350° for 10 minutes or until set but not hard or brown. Do not overbake.

* If grinding your own wheat, grind it fine or double grind it.

HONEY WHEAT PEANUT BUTTER COOKIES

1/2 C shortening
1 C peanut butter
1 C brown sugar
1 C honey
2 eggs or 2 dehydrated eggs, reconstituted
2 1/2 C sifted whole wheat flour
1 tsp baking powder
1 1/2 tsp soda
1/2 tsp salt

Cream together shortening, peanut butter, and brown sugar. Add honey, mix. Add eggs 1 at a time and beat until light and fluffy. Add dry ingredients. Mix. Chill dough at least 1 hour. Roll into walnut size balls and place 3 inches apart on a cookie sheet. Flatten cookie with a fork. Bake at 350° for 10 minutes or until set, but not hard or brown. Do not overbake.

PEANUT BUTTER CRISSCROSS COOKIES

1 1/2 C flour
1/2 tsp baking soda
1/2 C butter or margarine
1 C chunky peanut butter
1/2 C packed brown sugar
1/2 C white sugar
1 egg
1 tsp vanilla

Heat oven to 375°. Mix flour and baking soda together; set aside. Beat butter and peanut butter in a large bowl with electric mixer until creamy. Add sugars and beat until fluffy. Beat in egg and vanilla until well blended. With mixer on low speed, gradually add flour mixture. Beat just until blended. Roll dough into 1" balls. Place 1-1/2 inches apart on ungreased cookie sheet. Flatten with fork, making crisscross design. Bake for 10 to 12 minutes until browned. Cool on cookie sheet 1 minute before removing.

PAN HONEY CAKE

1 1/4 C honey
1/2 C oil
1 C sugar
5 1/2 C whole wheat flour, finely ground
1 Tbsp baking powder
2 C ground almonds
2 tsp ground cinnamon
1/2 tsp allspice
pinch ground cloves
pinch salt
3 eggs, beaten
1 C chopped, mixed candied peel
3 Tbsp evaporated milk
Candied cherries
Blanched almonds

Bring honey, oil and sugar a to boil in medium saucepan, stirring constantly. Cool. Sift flour and baking powder into a large bowl. Mix in ground almonds, cinnamon, allspice, cloves, salt, eggs, and candied peel. Add cooled honey mixture. Knead to a dough. If dough is too soft, add a little more flour. Press into a ball and refrigerate for 1 hour.

Grease two 9x13 pans. Press dough into greased pans. Smooth surface and brush with evaporated milk. Cut into cookie-size squares and decorate with almonds and cherries. Bake at 375° for 25 to 30 minutes.

IRIS'S GINGER SNAPS

3/4 C shortening
1 egg
4 Tbsp molasses
1 tsp ginger
1 tsp cinnamon
1 C sugar
1/8 tsp salt
2 tsp soda
1 tsp cloves
2 C flour

Mix and chill. Roll into 1" balls, then dip balls in sugar. Bake at 375° for 15 minutes.

WHOLE WHEAT BROWNIE MIX

6 C whole wheat flour
4 tsp baking powder
4 tsp salt
8 C sugar
2 C unsweetened cocoa
2 C shortening (any kind)

Mix all dry ingredients together then cut in the shortening. Mix thoroughly. Pack loosely in quart jars. Refrigerate.

To use brownie mix, combine 2-1/2 cups of the Mix with 2 eggs, 1 tsp vanilla and 1/2 cup chopped nuts. Mix well. Spread in greased 9" square pan and bake at 350° for about 20 to 25 min. **Don't overbake.**

OATMEAL COOKIES

EXCELLENT!

1 1/3 C brown sugar
1 C shortening
2 eggs
1 tsp vanilla
1 C flour
1 tsp baking soda
1 tsp salt
1 tsp cinnamon
1/4 tsp nutmeg
2 C oatmeal
2 C raisins or 2 C chocolate chips (optional)

Mix all ingredients together in order given. Spoon onto greased cookie sheet. Bake at 350° for 12 minutes. Let cool 2 or 3 minutes on cookie sheet before removing.

OAT AND WHEAT JAM SQUARES

2 C rolled oats
1 3/4 whole wheat flour
1 C shortening or margarine
1/2 C chopped nuts
1 tsp cinnamon
3/4 tsp salt
1/2 tsp soda
1 1/2 C jam, (apricot, raspberry, plum) or
    Raisin Filling (below)

Combine all ingredients except jam in large bowl, beat until crumbly. Reserve 2 cups mixture and press the rest into a 9x13 greased pan. Spread jam evenly over the top and sprinkle with remaining mixture. Press gently until set. Bake at 400° for 25 to 30 minutes. Do not overbake. Cool and cut into squares.

RAISIN FILLING

2 C chopped raisins
1 C sugar
1 C water
1 tsp lemon juice
1 tsp corn starch

Combine and simmer 10 to 15 minutes. Stir often. Cool then use for filling in above cookies.

ORANGE OATMEAL COOKIES

2 C sifted whole wheat flour
1/2 tsp salt
1 tsp soda
1 tsp cinnamon
1/2 tsp nutmeg
1 C oatmeal
3/4 C shortening
1 C packed brown sugar
2 eggs or 2 dehydrated eggs reconstituted
2 Tbsp orange juice
1 Tbsp grated orange rind

Sift together dry ingredients. Add oatmeal to dry ingredients and set aside. Cream shortening and sugar. Add eggs and beat well. Add orange juice and rind. Combine with dry ingredients. Drop dough by teaspoonfuls 2 inches apart onto a greased cookie sheet. Flatten with fork dipped in flour. Bake at 375° for 10 minutes.

SNICKERDOODLES

1 C shortening
1 1/2 C white sugar
1 tsp vanilla
2 eggs or 2 dehydrated eggs, reconstituted
2 3/4 C sifted whole wheat flour
2 tsp cream of tarter
1 tsp soda
1/2 tsp salt

2 Tbsp white sugar
1 to 2 tsp cinnamon

Cream together shortening, sugar, and vanilla. Beat eggs in one at a time. Sift dry ingredients together then mix into shortening and egg mixture. Shape into walnut-size balls and roll into a cinnamon/sugar mixture. Place on an ungreased sheet and bake at 375° for 8 to 10 minutes. Do not overbake, they should be light brown.

BROWN SUGAR COOKIES
(cut out cookies)

EXCELLENT!

2 C brown sugar
2/3 C shortening
2 eggs, beaten
1/2 tsp vanilla
3 C flour
1 tsp baking powder

Cream sugar and shortening together until fluffy. Add beaten eggs slowly. Add vanilla. Sift dry ingredients together and add to egg mixture. Chill. Roll out on a lightly floured board. Cut into desired shapes. (A lid from a mayonnaise jar may be used for a cutter.) Carefully place on a greased cookie sheet. Bake at 375° for 8 minutes. Cool on rack and decorate with frosting below. (Pattern on pg. 248.)

Frosting:
2 C powdered sugar
2 egg whites
1/2 tsp vanilla

Mix ingredients together until smooth. Frosting should be fairly thick. Place in a pastry tube and draw faces on cookies. Let dry for several hours before serving or packaging.

RASPBERRY JAM CIRCLES

1 C margarine
1 C brown sugar
2 eggs or 2 dehydrated eggs, reconstituted
2 tsp vanilla
3 C whole wheat flour
2 tsp baking powder
1/2 tsp salt
1/4 tsp nutmeg
1/2 C raspberry or apricot jam, chilled

Cream margarine and sugar together until fluffy. Add eggs and vanilla slowly, beating well. Sift dry ingredients together and add to egg mixture, mixing well. Chill for 2 hours. Using a 2 inch cutter, cut dough into circles. Put 1/2 teaspoon jam in the center of each circle. Then cut a smaller hole in the center of another circle. Place on top of first circle and seal edges by pressing gently. Place on an ungreased cookie sheet. Bake at 375° for 10 to 12 minutes. Do not overbake. Cool and brush with a powdered sugar glaze. Tastes better if allowed to set overnight.

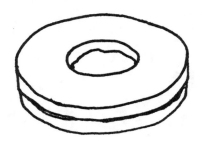

EXCELLENT!

TOFFEE SQUARES

1 C flour
1/2 tsp ground cinnamon
1/2 C butter or margarine
1/2 C packed brown sugar
1 egg, yolk and white separated
1/2 tsp vanilla extract
1 C (6 oz) semisweet chocolate chips, melted
1/2 C coarsely chopped nuts

Heat oven to 275°. Grease a 9 inch square baking pan. Mix flour and cinnamon. In a medium-size bowl, beat butter and sugar until creamy. Beat in egg yolk and vanilla. Stir in flour mixture just until blended. Spread dough in prepared baking pan. Brush top of dough with slightly beaten egg white. Bake 35 minutes or until lightly browned. Cool in pan on wire rack. Spread chocolate on top. Sprinkle with walnuts. Chill until chocolate is firm before cutting into squares.

SOUR CREAM COOKIES
(refrigerator cookies)

1 1/2 C sugar
2 C thick sour cream
2 eggs or 2 dehydrated eggs reconstituted
1 1/2 C whole wheat flour
2 tsp soda
1/2 tsp salt
1 tsp cinnamon
1/2 tsp nutmeg
1 C dehydrated ground raisins

Cream sugar, sour cream, and eggs together. Sift all dry ingredients together. Mix into egg mixture. Add more flour if needed to make a soft dough. Add ground raisins.

Mold into long roll about 2 1/2" in diameter. Wrap in waxed paper and chill.

Slice 1/8" to 1/4" thick. Place about 1 inch apart on a cookie sheet. Bake at 350° until set, about 12 minutes. Dough can be frozen.

FRAGILE HAZELNUT COOKIE SANDWICHES

(fill with apricot jam, top with icing)

EXCELLENT!

1 C butter
1/2 C sugar
1/2 lb hazelnuts or filberts, finely ground
2 1/2 C sifted cake flour

Cream butter with sugar until fluffy. Work in nuts and flour to make a smooth dough. Chill. Roll to 1/3 inch thickness between 2 sheets of waxed paper. Cut into small rounds or diamonds. Bake on cookie sheet at 350° for 10 to 15 minutes, or until golden brown. Cool and put 2 cookies together with apricot jam between. Spread with Thin Lemon Frosting (below). Makes 40 to 50 cookies sandwiches.

Thin Lemon Frosting:
1 C powdered sugar
Lemon juice
Green food coloring.

Mix all ingredients together, adding enough lemon juice to make a thin frosting. Beat until all lumps are gone. Spread over cookies and let set until dry.

LEBKUCHEN

(German pan cookie)

3 3/4 C sugar
1 1/4 C honey
6 Tbsp water
3 C chopped, unblanched almonds
1 1/2 C finely chopped mixed candied fruit
6 eggs, well beaten
3/4 C orange juice
8 1/4 C sifted flour
6 tsp cinnamon
3 tsp ground cloves
6 tsp ground cardamon
3 tsp soda
3 tsp baking powder

Combine sugar, honey and water in large saucepan. Bring to a boil. Remove from heat. Cool. Stir in almonds, fruit, eggs, and orange juice. Sift in flour, spices, soda, and baking powder and blend thoroughly. Store in tightly closed container at room temperature for 3 days to ripen. Spread in greased and floured pans. Bake at 325° for 35 to 40 minutes. Frost with Thin Orange Frosting (below). Makes a large amount.

Thin Orange Frosting:
1/2 C powdered sugar
2 Tbsp orange juice
1 to 3 Tbsp hot water
1/2 tsp vanilla or brandy flavoring.

Mix all ingredients together until smooth. Spread over baked cookies.

ALMOND PASTE FRUIT ROUNDS

EXCELLENT!

Cookie Base:
1/2 C butter
3 Tbsp powdered sugar
1 egg yolk
1 1/4 C flour

Beat butter, powdered sugar and egg yolk until creamy. Add flour and mix until dough holds together. Turn out half the dough at a time onto a lightly floured board and fold into a sheet about 3/16 inch thick. Cut into three inch rounds and place 1 inch apart on buttered baking sheets. Bake at 350° for about 10 minutes, or until faintly brown. Remove from oven but do not remove cookies from the baking sheet. Simply place the baking sheet on wire racks for 10 minutes, then decorate as instructed below.

Dough for Cookie Rings:
1/2 C each, granulated sugar and brown
    sugar
2 Tbsp flour
1/4 C egg whites (about 2 egg whites)
1/4 tsp almond extract
1 8-oz can almond paste
Raspberry and apricot jam

In a small bowl, stir together the sugars and flour. Add egg whites, extract and almond paste. Beat at medium speed until smoothly blended. Spoon into pastry bag with large star tip.

Using the filled pastry bag, press almond paste dough onto the cookie rounds, making a 3/8 inch thick circle around the edge with a line down the center. Return to a 350° oven and bake until topping is golden brown, about 15 minutes. Transfer to wire racks and cool. Fill cookie depressions with 1/2 tsp each raspberry and apricot jam.

PARTRIDGE AND PEARS

1 C butter
1 8-oz can almond paste
3/4 C sugar
1 egg
3 C flour

With an electric mixer or heavy wooden spoon, beat together butter, almond paste, and sugar until creamy. Beat in egg. Gradually mix in flour (unsifted) until thoroughly blended. You can shape cookies from dough either at refrigerator or room temperature. Keep dough tightly covered while you shape a few cookies at a time. (You will need Partridge and Pear cookie cutters.) Bake on an ungreased cookie sheet at 325° for 20 minutes or until lightly browned on the bottom. Cool.

KIFLINGS

1/2 C sugar
Scant 4 C flour
1/2 tsp almond extract
3 1/2 cubes butter
1 C ground almonds (1/2 lb)

Mix all ingredients well. Take a teaspoonful of dough and roll between palms of hands. Roll into crescent shape. Bake for 10 minutes at 300°. Roll in powdered sugar while warm.

CHRISTMAS BUTTER COOKIES

1 C butter
1/4 tsp salt
3/4 C sugar
1 egg
1 tsp vanilla
1/2 tsp almond extract
2 1/2 C sifted flour

Cream butter with salt until soft. Blend in sugar 1/4 cup at a time, until mixture is fluffy. Beat in egg, vanilla and almond. Stir in flour. Pack dough in cookie press; press shapes onto ungreased baking sheet. Bake at 400° for 8 to 10 minutes. Cookies should be set but not brown. Makes 6 dozen.

Chocolate variation: Blend into butter mixture one square 1-oz melted chocolate.

RAISIN FILLED NUTMEG COOKIES

4 C sifted flour
1 tsp soda
1/4 tsp salt
1 tsp nutmeg
1 C butter
1 1/2 C brown sugar
2 eggs

Combine dry ingredients. Cream butter; add sugar and beat until fluffy. Add eggs, blend well. Stir in dry ingredients. Place on floured board and roll about 1/8 inch thick. Cut with 2 1/2 inch cutter. Place on greased baking sheet. Fill with 1 tablespoon of filling(recipe below); moisten edge with water and put another on top. Press edges together with fork and prick cookie for vents. Bake at 375° for about 12 minutes. Makes 3 1/2 dozen.

Filling (date or raisin):
1 1/2 C raisins or dates
3/4 C sugar
3/4 C water
1 Tbsp lemon juice
1 1/2 tsp flour
1/4 tsp salt
3/4 C chopped nuts

Combine all ingredients, except nuts in saucepan. Cook over low heat, stirring until thick. Cool. Add nuts.

ALMOND PASTE BARS
(double recipe for large cookie sheet)

1 C butter
3/4 C sugar
1 egg, separated
1/2 C almond paste
1 tsp almond flavoring
2 C sifted flour
1 C sliced almonds

Beat butter and sugar until fluffy; add egg yolk. Mix in almond paste and extract; add flour until well combined. DO NOT OVER BEAT! Press on ungreased cookie sheet. Beat egg white until foamy (not stiff) spread over top and sprinkle with sliced almonds. Bake at 350° for 30 minutes.

EXCELLENT!

TOFFEE SQUARES

1 C butter, softened to room temperature
1 C brown sugar
1 egg yolk
2 tsp vanilla
1 7/8 C all purpose flour
6 1.65-oz milk chocolate bars
1 C chopped toasted almonds or pecans

In mixing bowl, cream together butter and brown sugar until light-colored and fluffy. Add egg yolk and vanilla. Gradually beat in flour until smooth and blended. (Dough will be thick.) Spread evenly on ungreased 16x14x1 inch baking pan. Bake at 350° for 15 minutes or until crust is golden brown and puffy. Remove from oven. Arrange unwrapped chocolate bars evenly over surface of crust. Let stand for 5 minutes to soften. Spread chocolate evenly over crust. Sprinkle with chopped nuts. Cool. Cut into squares.

EXCELLENT!

3 - LAYERED CHOCOLATE BARS

1/4 C butter or margarine
1/4 tsp salt
1 C sifted flour

Cream butter, salt and flour together. Pat into greased and floured pan. Bake at 350° for 15 minutes.

2 eggs, well beaten
1 C walnuts or pecans, chopped
1 tsp vanilla
2 Tbsp flour
3/4 C packed brown sugar
1/2 C coconut
1/4 tsp salt

Mix all ingredients together. Pour onto first layer and bake at 350° for 15 minutes. Cool before frosting.

1 Tbsp water
1/4 C white corn syrup
1 C semisweet chocolate chips

Melt over hot water, not boiling water. Blend thoroughly and put on as third layer.

DELICIOUS BEST BROWNIES

EXCELLENT!

1-1/4 C margarine
8 Tbsp cocoa
2 C sugar
4 eggs
2 C flour
1 C nuts, chopped

Frosting
1/2 C margarine
1/2 C unsweetened cocoa
3 C powdered sugar
1/4 C milk
1 tsp vanilla
1/2 C pecans (optional)

Melt margarine; add cocoa and sugar. Mix in eggs and flour, stirring well. Add nuts. Pour into greased 9x13" pan and bake at 350° for about 30 min. **Do not overbake**.

Frosting
Melt margarine; blend in cocoa and heat just until it comes to a boil, stirring constantly. Remove from heat. Mix in the milk, vanilla and powdered sugar. Beat until smooth and use to frost brownies.

MINIATURE CHOCOLATE PECAN TARTS

EXCELLENT!

Pastry
2 C flour
2 pkg (3 oz ea) cream cheese, cold, and cut into chunks
1 C butter, cold, and cut into chunks

Filling
2 Tbsp butter
2 1-oz squares unsweetened chocolate
1-1/2 C brown sugar, packed
2 tsp vanilla
2 eggs, beaten
Dash of salt
1-1/2 C chopped pecans

To prepare pastry:
Put flour into large bowl; cut in the cream cheese and butter. Mix until dough can be shaped into ball. Wrap in plastic and refrigerate 1 hour. Shape dough into 1" balls. Press each ball into ungreased miniature (1-3/4") muffin cups, spreading to cover bottom and sides with dough.

To prepare filling:
Melt butter and chocolate in heavy pan over low heat. Remove. Blend in sugar, vanilla, eggs and salt; beat until thick. Stir in pecans. Spoon about 1 tsp filling into each unbaked pastry shell. Bake at 350° for 20 to 25 min. or until lightly browned. Cool in pans on wire racks. Store in airtight containers. Makes 5 dozen.

SPRINGERLE
(white German cookie)

4 eggs, extra large
1 lb powdered sugar
1 Tbsp grated lemon rind
1 tsp anise extract
4 1/2 C sifted cake flour
1 tsp baking powder

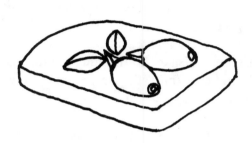

Beat eggs until lemon colored. Stir in sugar and beat until thoroughly blended. Add lemon rind and anise extract. Sift flour and baking powder together and add to the egg mixture. Dough will be stiff; work flour in well. Knead dough for 10 minutes. Dough should be smooth not sticky. Cover and let stand for 1 hour.

Roll dough to a thickness of 3/8 inch. Next roll with a decorated pin so that design is clearly impressed. Lightly grease a cookie sheet. Cut cookies and gently place on cookie sheet. Let sit, uncovered, at room temperature overnight.
Bake at 250° for 20 minutes. The top of the cookie should be light in color and the bottom barely browned. Remove from oven and let cool. Place cooled cookies in an air tight container for 1 week to soften.

MARSHMALLOW AND NUT BROWNIES

1 C butter or margarine
1 C unsweetened cocoa
2 C sugar
2 eggs
1 C flour
1/2 C buttermilk
2 tsp vanilla
2 C miniature marshmallows
2 C coarsely chopped walnuts
2 C semisweet chocolate chips

Combine butter and cocoa in heavy saucepan over low heat, stirring until smooth. Remove from heat and stir in next 5 ingredients; mix well. Spread on greased 12x16 cookie sheet. Bake at 350° for 25 min. or until center feels dry. Sprinkle with last 3 ingredients and return to oven for 3-5 min. or until topping melts together.

RASPBERRY HAZELNUT SCHNITTEN

EXCELLENT!

1/2 C. butter (room temp.)
1/3 C sugar
1 large egg white, slightly beaten
2 C flour
1 large egg
1/2 C raspberry jam
1/2 C coarsely chopped hazelnuts
1 C (6 oz) semi-sweet chocolate chips
2 Tbsp shortening

Beat butter and sugar until fluffy. Beat in eggs. Gradually stir in flour until blended. Divide dough in half. Wrap in plastic wrap and chill one hour or until firm enough to roll. Heat oven to 350°. Roll out each half of dough to a 12"x 5" rectangle between 2 sheets of wax paper. Peel top wax paper off both rectangles. Invert dough on cookie sheet two inches apart. Peel off other paper. Brush a one-inch wide border of egg white on each long side of rectangle. Fold long sides inward 1/2 inch, keeping borders even; seal any cracks. Carefully spread half of jam on each rectangle. Sprinkle nuts on top of preserves. Bake 10 minutes until just golden brown. While still warm, cut cookies into 16 and cool.

Melt chocolate chips and shortening and dip each end of cookie. Set aside.

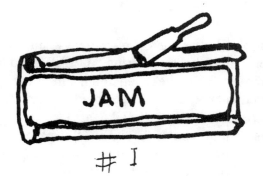

#1

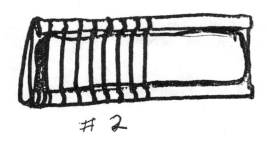

#2

#3

ESSENTIALS

WHITE SAUCE MIX

6 C flour
6 C dehydrated butter or margarine
1 1/2 Tbsp salt
1/2 C dehydrated chicken broth

Mix all ingredients together well. Store in an air tight container.

WHITE SAUCE

1 C White Sauce Mix (above)
2 C cold water

Whirl ingredients in a blender or use a wire whip. Mix until smooth. Bring to a boil, stirring constantly over medium heat until thickened.

Note: White Sauce is for use in casseroles, creamed vegetables, scalloped potatoes, soups, etc.

CREAM SOUP MIX

2 C nonfat powdered milk
3/4 C cornstarch
1/4 C instant chicken bouillon
2 Tbsp dried onion flakes
1 tsp basil leaves
1 tsp thyme leaves
1/2 tsp pepper

Combine all ingredients, mixing well. Store in an air tight container until ready to use.

CREAM SOUP

1/3 C Cream Soup Mix (above)
1 1/4 C cold water

Whirl ingredients in a blender or use a wire whip. Mix until smooth. Bring to a boil, stirring constantly over medium heat until thickened.

Note: Cream Soup can be a substitute in any recipe that calls for a can of condensed soup.

MAYONNAISE

2 egg yolks
1/4 tsp salt
Pinch of pepper
Pinch of dry mustard
3/4 C oil
2 Tbsp wine vinegar

In a bowl, beat egg yolks and seasonings with a small wire whisk. Add oil drop by drop; when 2 tablespoons have been added, mixture will be thick. Stir in 1 tablespoon wine vinegar. Remaining oil can now be added more quickly, 1 tablespoon at a time. Beat thoroughly between each addition. If using an electric blender, add remaining oil in a thin steady stream. When all oil has been added, add remaining wine vinegar.

Note: Mayonnaise curdles easily, so be sure to add oil drop by drop.

CREAM SAUCE
(for tuna-on-toast, stuffed baked potatoes, or noodles)

1/4 C dehydrated sweet peas
1 C warm water
3 C water
3/4 C dehydrated creamy soup base
1 tsp dill weed
2 tsp lemon juice
1/2 tsp dry mustard
1 can tuna
2 boiled eggs

Soak sweet peas in 1 cup warm water for 1 hour. Add peas and liquid to the 3 cups of water in a saucepan. Bring to a boil and boil for 20 minutes. Whip in creamy soup base. Add lemon juice, dill weed and dry mustard. Simmer until thick, about 1 minute. Add drained tuna and sliced boiled eggs. Salt to taste. If sauce is too thin, add 1 Tbsp corn starch mixed with 2 Tbsp cold water.

BISCUIT MIX

8 C flour
1 1/8 C dehydrated margarine
3/4 C powdered milk
1/2 C dehydrated eggs
1/4 C baking powder
1 Tbsp salt
2 tsp cream of tartar
1 tsp baking soda

Mix all ingredients together well. Store in an air tight container. Use as needed for recipes.

EGG SUBSTITUTE

1 tsp unflavored gelatin
3 Tbsp cold water
2 Tbsp plus 1 tsp boiling water

Place water in a bowl and sprinkle unflavored gelatin over water to soften. Beat; add boiling water and beat until dissolved. Place in the freezer to thicken. Remove from freezer and beat thickened gelatin at high speed until frothy. Equivalent of 1 egg.

WHIPPED TOPPING

1/4 C ice water
1/4 C nonfat powdered milk
1/4 C sugar
1 Tbsp lemon juice

Combine ice water and powdered milk in a bowl and beat until stiff, about 10 minutes. Add sugar, and lemon juice. Chill before serving. If separated, whip again.

SOURDOUGH STARTER

1 pkg active dry yeast
2 C unsifted flour
2 C warm water
1 Tbsp sugar
1/3 C nonfat powdered milk

Mix ingredients together beating vigorously. Cover with plastic wrap and let sit 2 to 5 days until good and sour. Stir down at least once a day. After dough is sour, keep refrigerated.

Caution: Sourdough should not touch metal until ready to bake so always mix with a wooden or plastic spoon and in a glass or plastic container.

To replenish starter, replace exactly what you take out. If you take out 1 cup sourdough, replenish with:
1/2 C flour
1/2 C warm water
1/4 tsp sugar
If you want to increase the amount of starter, add up to 2 1/2 times what you take out.

COTTAGE CHEESE
(made from nonfat milk)

1/4 rennet tablet dissolved in 2 Tbsp water
1 gal reconstituted nonfat powdered milk
1/4 C buttermilk
1 tsp salt
Cream

Heat milk to 90° over low heat. Cook for 30 minutes. It is important to keep temperature at 90°. Add dissolved rennet tablet and buttermilk. Let stand in warm room for 10 to 12 hours.

Cut curd into 1/2 inch squares. Place into a colander lined with a cheese cloth. Drain. Rinse curd in cold water and drain again. Let set a half day to drain.

Stir in salt, and add cream to your taste.

NOTE: This can be used in cream cheese recipes.
       The whey is high in protein and can be used in bread making.
       Thermometer can be bought at health food store.

TARTAR SAUCE

1/2 C mayonnaise
1 Tbsp lemon juice
2 Tbsp chopped pickle (dill)
1 Tbsp chopped onion
1 Tbsp chopped parsley
Dash Worcestershire sauce

Mix all ingredients well and serve with your favorite fish or meat dish.

EXCELLENT!

DILL SALMON SAUCE

1 C mayonnaise
1 tsp chervil
1 tsp tarragon
1 small onion, quartered
1/4 C lemon juice
Tabasco drops
1 tsp mustard
2 dill pickles
1 Tbsp capers
1/2 tsp Worcestershire sauce

Combine all ingredients and mix well.
Whirl in blender.

SHRIMP COCKTAIL SAUCE

EXCELLENT!

1/2 bottle catsup
1 Tbsp brown sugar
1/2 C tomato sauce
1 Tbsp prepared mustard
White vinegar
Garlic salt
Salt and pepper
Minced onion
Tabasco sauce
Minced celery

Mix all ingredients together and keep in refrigerator.

HOMEMADE PECTIN

1 lb apples, trimmed and thinly sliced
2 pints water

Combine apples and 1 pint of water in a kettle, cover. Bring to a boil and boil for 15 minutes. Strain free running juice through cheesecloth. Return pulp to kettle and add the remaining pint of water. Cook at lower temperature 15 minutes and let stand for 10 minutes, and strain again. Do not attempt to squeeze pulp. Allow to cool and gently squeeze remaining juice. Use stock immediately or freeze.

To can the stock, heat to boiling and pour into hot sterilized jars. Seal and invert jars to cool. Fruits such as pears, peaches, cherries, and berries such as strawberries, blueberries, elderberries, mulberries, and raspberries are to be used with the pectin.

CARMEL SAUCE
(for ice cream, puddings and cakes)

EXCELLENT!

2 C brown sugar
2 cubes butter or margarine
1/2 C corn syrup
1/2 C water

Bring all ingredients to a boil pour over cakes and puddings, etc.

FRUIT LEATHER

Make a puree of fresh fruit in a blender, or boil slightly, peels and cores and put through a ricer. Heat fresh puree to about 180° to stop enzyme action. Add a little honey if you like it a little sweet. If too thin, you may add ground chia seeds, about 1/8 cup to 1 cup puree. Chia seeds enhance the flavor and the nutrition. Pulp left over from jelly making may be used.

Line cookie sheets with plastic wrap, fastened down with tape. Spread puree on cookie sheet, 1/4 to 1/8 inch thick. Dry from 36 to 48 hours in the sun. COVER WITH SCREEN.

You may bring it in at sundown and place in an oven not over 85°, which will hasten the drying time. When dry, peel off original plastic wrap. Place in fresh wrap and roll into loose roll.

Keeps one month at room temperature, four months in refrigerator, or six months frozen. Excellent for snacks, camping, or back packing.

CANNED TOMATO COCKTAIL

20 lbs tomatoes (60 medium) unpeeled, cut
   in halves, stems removed
2 Tbsp salt
1 tsp celery salt
3 Tbsp Worcestershire sauce
2 tsp onion powder
1/4 tsp Tabasco sauce

Place all ingredients in a large canning kettle, boil for 5 minutes stirring frequently. Using a food mill, colander or sieve, strain juice gently. Reserve pulp for tomato sauce. Heat juice to boiling, pour into hot sterilized jars and process in boiling water for 10 minutes. Makes 4 quarts.

SPAGHETTI SAUCE

Reserved tomato pulp from above recipe
1 Tbsp dried oregano leaves
2 cloves garlic
2 Tbsp Worcestershire sauce

Blend ingredients together thoroughly. If necessary, puree can be run through a food mill or colander to remove seeds. Heat mixture to boiling and pour into sterilized jars. Process for 10 minutes in boiling water bath.

SPICY TOMATO CATSUP

12 lb tomatoes
2 large onions
1 red bell pepper
1 Tbsp mustard seed
1 Tbsp celery seed
1 Tbsp whole black pepper
1 Tbsp dried basil
2 tsp allspice
2 small dry hot chiles
1 large bay leaf
3 inch cinnamon stick
1 C honey or 1 1/2 C brown sugar
1 Tbsp salt
1 Tbsp paprika
1 C cider vinegar

In a blender, whip tomatoes, onions, and bell pepper after straining out skins and seeds. Boil gently 1 hour in an 8-quart kettle or until reduced to about half. Add mustard seed, celery seed, whole black pepper, basil, allspice, chiles, bay leaf, and cinnamon stick after tying loosely in a spice bag. Add honey or brown sugar, salt, and paprika to puree. Cook over medium heat about 2 hours until thick, stirring often. Add cider vinegar. Cook an additional 10 to 15 minutes. Remove spice bag. Catsup can be frozen of canned.

EXCELLENT!

WONDERFUL SALSA

6 C tomatoes
1 small can tomato paste
1 C chopped celery
1 C chopped onion
1 C chopped green pepper
1 4-oz can diced green chiles
1 tsp garlic salt
1 tsp chili powder
1 tsp cumin
1 tsp salt
1 tsp tabasco sauce
Small amount of sugar

Stir and simmer all ingredients for 1 hour and 15 minutes. Place in jars and boil 10 minutes for seal.

EXCELLENT!

HOW TO PRESERVE RAISINS

Put new crop raisins into a quart mason jar, leaving one inch air space. Use new sealing lid and ring. Bake in the oven at 150° for 3 hours. Let cool. They will seal and last 3 years.

CHILI SAUCE

24 C peeled chopped tomatoes
12 C chopped celery
8 C chopped onions
4 C chopped peppers, green or red
1 C salt
2 1/2 tsp pickling spice, tied in cloth bag
1 C brown sugar
8 to 10 C white sugar
4 or 5 C white vinegar
2 1/2 Tbsp black pepper
1 small hot pepper

Mix vegetable together and add salt. Set overnight. Drain liquid.

Bring remaining ingredients to a boil. Add drained vegetable and boil for 20 minutes. Remove spice bag. Fill jars with mixture. Seal. Process pints for 5 minutes and quarts for 10 minutes in boiling water.

EASY SWEET PICKLES

8 cucumbers, unpeeled, sliced thin
3 medium onions, white or yellow, sliced
    thin
2 green peppers or 1 red pepper and 1 green
    pepper, sliced thin
3 1/3 C sugar
2 C white vinegar
1/4 C salt

Mix first three ingredients together and place in a gallon jar. Combine remaining ingredients in a saucepan and bring to a boil. Pour over contents of gallon jar. Store pickles in refrigerator for up to 1 year. No processing necessary.

DILL PICKLES

20 C water
1 C salt
3 1/4 C vinegar

1 slice onion
1 tsp dill seed
1 garlic clove
1/8 tsp alum
1 sprig dill
1/8 tsp cayenne pepper
1 grape leaf (optional)

Bring water, salt, and vinegar to a boil. Place remaining ingredients in each quart jar and fill with canning pickles. Insert a wooden spoon to release air. Pour boiling water mixture into each jar; seal. Process in boiling water for 5 minutes. Makes about 6 quarts of pickles.

APPLE FILLING

2 1/2 C granulated sugar
2 C packed light brown sugar
1 C cornstarch
1 1/2 tsp salt
1 tsp ground nutmeg
Cinnamon
2 1/2 quarts water
2 Tbsp lemon juice
6 quarts thinly sliced, pared tart apples

Prepare quart jars and follow procedure as directed. Mix sugars, cornstarch, salt, cinnamon and nutmeg in a 4- quart Dutch oven; stir in water. Heat to boiling, stirring frequently. Reduce heat and continue cooking, stirring constantly, until thickened and bubbly, about 5 minutes. Stir in juice.

Pack hot jars 1/3 full with apple slices. Pour on enough hot syrup to cover slices; remove air bubbles with a spoon. Continue packing jars 1/3 at a time with apple slices and syrup. When filled to within 1 inch of tops, seal. Process in boiling water bath for 20 minutes.

PICKLED BEETS

4 quarts beets
3 C vinegar
1 C sugar
2 tsp salt

Cover beets with water and boil until almost done. Reserve 1 quart of the liquid. Drain beets and peel and slice. Add liquid to remaining ingredients and bring to a boil.

Fill jars with sliced beets and pour boiling liquid over them. Seal. Process in for 30 minutes in a boiling water.

FRESH FROZEN STRAWBERRY JAM

5 C strawberries
2 C sugar
1/3 C Karo syrup
4 Tbsp clear starch

Wash and slice strawberries; mash and set aside. Mix sugar and clear starch will then add to strawberries and Karo syrup. Let set for 10 minutes before filling containers and freezing.

POWDERED MILK can be a substitute in any recipe that calls for whole milk, evaporated milk, sweetened condensed milk, sour milk, buttermilk, yogurt, or scalded milk. Not only is it less expensive than fresh or canned milk products, but in most cases it contains the same nutrients (except for fat), with less cholesterol and fewer calories.

WHOLE MILK

1 C water
2/3 C nonfat powdered milk

If your recipe uses dry ingredients, you can mix the powdered milk with them and add the same amount of water as the recipe calls for milk. But if the recipe contains only liquid ingredients, mix nonfat powdered milk and water together thoroughly before adding to the recipe.

SWEETENED CONDENSED MILK

1/2 C hot water (not boiling)
1 C plus 2 Tbsp powdered milk (non-instant)
3/4 C granulated sugar
2 Tbsp butter

Put hot water and powdered milk in a deep narrow bowl. Mix until all milk is dissolved. Add sugar and butter and mix until dissolved. Can be stored in refrigerator for up to 2 weeks.

Note: This recipe can be used in place of one 16-oz can of Eagle Brand sweetened condensed milk in any recipe and you'll never know the difference.

BUTTERMILK

4 C water
1 C nonfat powdered milk
1/2 C buttermilk
Pinch of salt

Combine water and nonfat powdered milk. Stir to dissolve. Stir in buttermilk and a pinch of salt. Blend well. Allow to stand at room temperature overnight (10 to 12 hours). Stir until smooth, chill before serving. Keep in a covered container in the refrigerator. Save 1/2 cup of buttermilk to use for making another quart.

YOGURT

2 C warm water (100°)
1/2 C nonfat powdered milk
3 Tbsp plain yogurt that does not contain
    gelatin

Using clean utensils, pour warm water into a blender and turn it on low speed, slowly adding powdered milk. Blend well. Add plain yogurt. Blend again. Pour into jars or glasses. Place the jars neck deep in 100° water. Cover the pan with a lid, and set in a warm place by a heater. Sets in 4 hours. Chill immediately. It will refrigerate for up to 4 weeks.

Note: Yogurt can be used in place of sour cream in most recipes, i. e.: stroganoff, dips, salad dressing, etc. It can be used in place of buttermilk if about 1/3 cup of water is added per 2/3 cup yogurt. Yogurt can also be mixed with fresh fruits, jams, etc. and can be used to make milk shakes.

ALMOND SPROUT MILK

1/2 C sunflower seed sprouts (optional)
3/4 C almonds or almond sprouts
2 C cold water
2 Tbsp honey
Salt

Put all ingredients in a blender and whirl at high speed for 10 seconds.

SOUR MILK

1 C reconstituted powdered milk
1 Tbsp vinegar or lemon juice

Add vinegar to reconstituted powdered milk and allow to stand for 5 minutes.

Note: You can also use this mixture in place of buttermilk in a recipe.

SOUR CREAM

2 tbsp lemon juice
2 C creamed cottage cheese

Put ingredients into container, cover and blend until smooth and creamy. Use in place of sour cream in any recipe. This thickens as it is refrigerated.

CREAM CHEESE (OR RICOTTA)

2 C yogurt

Empty yogurt into cloth-lined sieve, cheese cloth, or old piece of nylon; set over bowl and let stand for 1/2 hour. Tie the corners of the cloth together to form a bag. Hang on kitchen faucet or lay a wooden spoon across a pan and let the yogurt drain for 12 hours or overnight. Save the cloth for the next batch. For a tangier taste age the yogurt for several days before making cheese. This will refrigerate for 2 weeks.

Note: This cheese has a sour taste, however, it can be used in place of and in most recipes that call for cream cheese. It can also be used in place of Ricotta cheese in most recipes.

RICOTTA (ITALIAN COTTAGE CHEESE)

1 qt milk or reconstituted powdered milk
1/4 C dry whey powder
2 Tbsp buttermilk

Combine the milk and dry whey powder then stir in buttermilk. Cover bowl and allow to incubate in cold oven for 24 hours. Transfer to saucepan and slowly bring to scalding (200°). It will separate into curds and whey. Drain though cheesecloth and allow to drain several hours. Salt as desired.

AU GRATIN POTATO

2 C dehydrated sliced potatoes
1/2 C powdered milk or canned milk
1/2 C cheese powder
1/2 tsp salt
3 C boiling water

Directions for use of oven
Preheat oven to 400°. Place potatoes in a 1-1/2 quart casserole dish. Mix powdered milk, powdered cheese, and salt together. Sprinkle over potatoes. Stir in 2 tablespoons butter or margarine and the boiling water. Bake at 400°, uncovered, for about 35 minutes or until potatoes are tender. Let stand a few minutes before serving.

Directions for stove top
In a 2 quart sauce pan, heat to boiling 4 cups water, 1/2 tsp salt. Add potatoes and cook until tender, about 20 minutes. Drain. Stir in 2 tablespoons butter or margarine, 1-1/2 cups milk, and cheese powder. Heat to boiling, stirring until sauce thickens. Let stand before serving.

DANISH CREAM SAUCE
(use over chicken breast or canned turkey)

1/2 lb butter or margarine
1 C flour
1 qt water
1 Tbsp custom chicken broth paste
1/8 tsp nutmeg
1/8 tsp salt
1/8 white pepper
1/8 tsp basil
1/8 tsp Rosemary
1/8 tsp thyme
1/8 tsp sage
1/4 C chopped fresh chives or dried chives
1 C sour cream

Make a rue from butter and flour. Cook 1 minute. Take from heat. Whip in water and chicken broth. Cook until thick. Add spices and cook 1 more minute. Add chopped chives and sour cream. Do not boil after adding sour cream.

CHEESE

(For additional information, see Rita Bingham's book on Powdered milk cheeses.)

Quick Soft-Pressed Cheese
2 C boiling water
1/3 C vegetable oil
4,000 mg. ascorbic acid powder (Vitamin C)
1 1/2 C dry milk powder (non-instant)

Blend water, milk, and oil, allowing foam to settle slightly. Pour into hot Pam-sprayed saucepan and heat to at least 160°. Add ascorbic acid and continue to stir until mixture curdles.

Rinse with warm water, then salt and put between two plates or into a cheese press. Apply weight or pressure and let set for 1/2 hour or longer, depending on how firm you want the cheese. Remove from press, rinse, wrap in plastic and refrigerate. This cheese can be sliced, grated, or crumbled. For smoky flavor, add up to 1/2 tsp Liquid Smoke flavoring and 1/2 tsp salt after rinsing curds.

Yellow Cheddar Cheese
4 C warm water
2/3 C vegetable oil
3 C dry milk powder (non-instant)
1-3/4 C white vinegar
6 Tbsp Cheddar cheese powder **or** add 1 cheese coloring tablet to water (these items are optional-- they give the cheese its yellow coloring and, if desired, they can be purchased at most health food stores).

Blend all ingredients (except cheese powder, if used). Pour into hot Pam-sprayed saucepan and heat to 115° to form curds.

Rinse and drain curds in warm water, and salt to taste. Add cheese powder, if used, and mix well. Put into cheese press or hang in cheesecloth bag and press out excess whey.

After 15 minutes, remove from press or cloth, wrap in plastic and refrigerate. Grate or slice as you would regular Cheddar cheese.

CHEESE MAKING DIAGRAMS

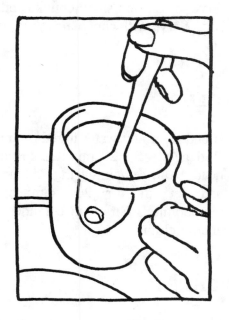

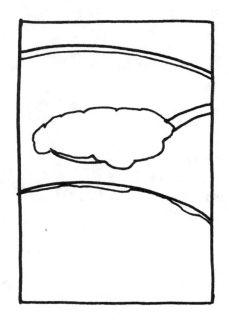

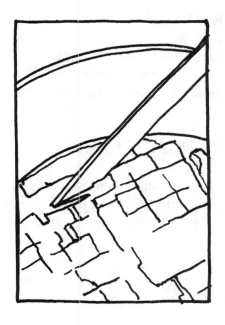

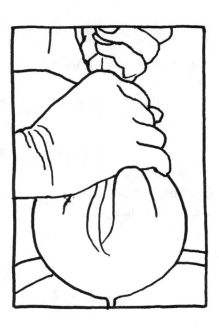

SOFT ICE CREAM

1 C nonfat powdered milk
1 C water
3 Tbsp honey

In a blender, mix all ingredients. Place in a shallow tray and freeze until solid. To serve, break into small chunks and beat until soft. Serve with chocolate syrup, fruit syrup, etc.

SOFT TOFU   LOW FAT

1 C soy flour
1 quart water
3/4 Tbsp lemon juice
3/4 tsp salt

Blend flour and water together until smooth. Boil gently for 20 minutes. Remove from heat. Add remaining ingredients, stir once and let sit for 20 minutes at room temperature. Strain in colander lined with cheese cloth.

FARMER'S CHEESE

1 1/3 C nonfat powdered milk
3 C hot water
1 Tbsp lemon juice

Mix ingredients together and put in a covered jar. Let stand in a warm place for 24 hours. Drain in a cheese cloth.

BABY FORMULA

1 12-oz can evaporated milk
1 1/2 (18 oz) water
1 1/3 Tbsp sugar (do not use Karo syrup)

Boil water for 5 minutes, add milk and sugar. Pour into prepared bottles and cover. Ready to use. Refrigerate unused portion.

WHOLE WHEAT CEREAL FOR BABIES

2/3 C whole wheat flour
2 1/2 C cold water
1/2 tsp salt

Beat all ingredients together in a blender until smooth. Cook in a heavy pot or double boiler for 30 minutes, stirring often.

GLUTEN

GLUTEN is a good source of protein. 1 cup of gluten equals 72 grams of protein. For additional information about Gluten see <u>Le Arta Moulton Book On Gluten</u>.

HAND METHOD
(makes 1 to 2 cups gluten)

Mix 3 cups cool water with 7 cups whole wheat flour. Knead well for 15 to 20 minutes.

Extract gluten from the kneaded dough by covering dough with water in a bowl. Work dough with your hands. Hold dough under cool tap water, working with your hands, wash until tap water runs clear. (Should feel like bubble gum). Be careful not to wash all the bran out.

Bake in a greased loaf pan with beef or chicken broth covering about 1/2 inch above gluten. Bake at 300° for 2 to 4 hours or until the gluten has a firm texture, springs back to the touch, and broth is nearly gone. Remove from oven and slice into steaks about 1/4 inch thick. Use in the recipes below.

QUICK METHOD
(makes 1 to 2 cups gluten)

Follow the above directions but instead of baking, form raw gluten into a long roll using wet hands. Slice and flatten pieces. Drop into seasoned broth and simmer for 30 minutes. Press out as much of the liquid as possible, or blot with paper towel. Place pieces on an oiled cookie sheet. Bake at 300°, turning once for 20 to 30 minutes. Use in the recipes below.

QUICK STEAK

Make Broth for Beef (below). After washing gluten, pinch off some gluten the size of a large walnut and flatten out to size of a thin steak. Or, slice baked gluten 1/8 inch thick, about 16 slices per baby loaf. Put each steak into boiling broth one at a time in a large saucepan. Simmer for a minimum of 1 hour.

Dip steak into egg and flour or cracker crumbs and fry until crispy in butter or oil. Serve gravy over top just at serving time.

CHICKEN FRIED STEAK

Slice 18 slices of gluten from a baby loaf. Place in pan; add water mixture (below) and put on low boil for at least an hour. Be careful not to burn.

Dip steak into egg and flour or cracker crumbs and fry in 1/4 cup butter until golden brown, about 2 minutes on each side. Serve hot.

WATER MIXTURE

4 C water
2 Tbsp chicken soup mix or chicken bouillon
1/4 tsp poultry seasoning

Mix all ingredients and heat to boiling.

LOW FAT

SPAGHETTI SAUCE

1/2 lb ground beef
1 baby loaf gluten ground
1 8-oz cans tomato sauce
1 6-oz can tomato paste
2 3/4 C tomato juice or water
1 pkg spaghetti seasoning mix

Brown meat; add ground gluten and all the remaining ingredients. Simmer for about 15 minutes. Serve warm over spaghetti noodles.

BROTH FOR BEEF

6 C water
1 pkg onion soup mix
2 Tbsp beef bouillon
1 tsp garlic salt

Mix all ingredients and heat to boiling.

BROWN SUGAR TOPPING

2 C ground gluten
1 C coconut (optional)
1/2 C brown sugar
1 tsp vanilla
1/4 C soft butter

Mix all ingredients together, making sure butter is thoroughly mixed in. Spread thin on lightly greased baking sheet. Bake at 350° for 8 to 10 minutes. Stir twice. Do not let get too brown.

CINNAMON TOPPING

2 C ground gluten
1/4 C soft butter
1/2 C brown sugar
2 tsp cinnamon
1/2 tsp cloves
1/2 tsp vanilla

Follow directions for Brown Sugar Topping (above).

COCOA TOPPING

2 C ground gluten
1/4 C soft butter
1/2 C brown sugar
2 Tbsp cocoa
1 tsp vanilla

Follow directions for Brown Sugar Topping (above).

EZEKIEL FLOUR

EZEKIEL FORMULA
Ezekiel 4:9

1 cup red wheat
1 cup barley
1 cup beans
1 cup lentils
1 cup millet
1 cup white wheat

Mix together and grind to fine flour just before using.

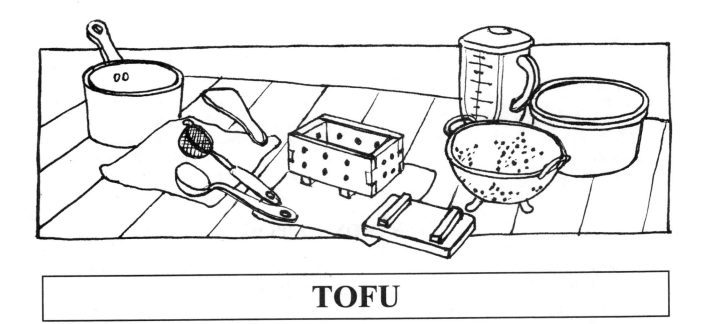

TOFU

Called by its other names, bean curd and soy cheese, this bland, custard-like soybean product hardly sounds appetizing. In reality, tofu is not only extremely tasty, quickly taking on the flavor of the foods it's mixed with, but it is also one of the most nutritious sources of protein available. An 8-ounce portion, for example, provides 45 percent of recommended daily protein, has no cholesterol and has only 160 calories. In contrast, a similar portion of ground beef may contain twice the protein value, but is laden with 20 percent fat and 490 calories, plus cholesterol. Little wonder the Asians have utilized tofu as their main protein source for centuries. And dieters in the West are now discovering its virtues.

The soy bean, by the way, is the only legume containing all eight essential amino acids, necessary to sustain life. And in tofu form, it is highly digestible with a digestion rate of 95 percent (certainly an excellent food for babies, elderly folks and others with digestion disorders).

What really makes tofu so appealing is its adaptability: it can replace eggs, cream cheese, sour cream and mayonnaise in most dishes. It is also the ideal substitute for ricotta in lasagna. And although tofu lacks its own taste, it develops a meat-like flavor when broiled. Use it instead of meats, fish, and poultry in just about any recipe.

HOMEMADE TOFU IN 10 STEPS

1. <u>Soak soybeans.</u> (1 lb of whole dry soybeans equals about 2-1/2 cups) Soak the soybeans for 8 to 10 hours, or overnight, in enough water to cover about an inch.

2. <u>Drain soybeans.</u> Drain the soaked soybeans, discarding the water, and rinse them thoroughly under running water.

3. <u>Measure water.</u> **(a) For blenders or food processors:** measure 7 cups of water into a gallon-sized pot, and in another pot, place 8 cups water. Bring both to a boil, then turn to very low heat. **(b) For meat grinders, grist mills or Champion juicers:** measure 15 cups of water into a gallon-sized pot and bring to a boil, then turn to very low heat.

4. <u>Puree soybeans.</u> **(a) If using a blender or food processor:** blend 1 cup soybeans with 1-1/2 cups boiling water from the smaller pot for 1-1/2 to 2 minutes. Add the soybean slurry to the water in the gallon pot. Repeat until all beans are ground. Rinse utensils with last of hot water and add to larger pot. **(b) If using meat grinder, grist mill, or Champion juicer** (have homogenizer plate in place): grind the beans very fine and add to the 15 cups of boiling water in the gallon pot.

5. <u>Strain soymilk.</u> To separate the soymilk from the okra (soybean residue), moisten a sack (tofu press sack, linen sack, jelly bag, or 3 layers of cheese cloth) and use it to line a colander which has been placed inside a heavy pot. Carefully pour into it the hot soybean/water mixture. Twist the sack or cheese cloth closed, and press with a jar or potato masher. Continue to squeeze and press until okra is as dry as possible. Remove the okra sack. (The okra can be used for other recipes in this book.)

6. <u>Cook soymilk.</u> Bring soymilk to near-boil (very steamy), then reduce heat to simmer, stirring continuously to prevent scorching. Cook 7 minutes. Remove from heat.

7. <u>Prepare coagulant.</u> Into one cup of water, stir 1 tsp natural nigari or 2 tsp terra alba (domestic calcium sulfate) until dissolved. (To order, see address below.)

8. <u>Curdle soymilk.</u> While stirring the still hot soymilk, slowly add about 1/3 cup of coagulant solution. Stop stirring and sprinkle another 1/3 cup over the surface. Cover the pot and wait 2 to 3 minutes. Gently stir the mixture (curds will form) and sprinkle the remaining coagulant solution over any remaining milky areas. Cover pot; wait 3 minutes. Curds should now be distinct with no milky areas. (If milky spots remain, make a little more solution, stir it gently into those areas, cover and wait another 3 minutes.)

9. <u>Ladling and pressing curds.</u> Moisten a 12" x 12" square of fine mesh or cheese cloth and spread it in a tofu press (either a commercial variety or colander or old bread pan with holes drilled in it.) Ladle the larger curds gently into it. Then pour the whey slowly down one side

to retrieve the very small curds. Fold the edges of the cloth over the top and place on the lid (a small plate or another bread pan).

Now add a 3-5 pound weight on top. Press for about 15-30 minutes. Less pressing will give a more delicate tofu for eating chilled or in dips or salad dressings. Longer pressing will give a firmer tofu for slicing or frying.

10. <u>Remove tofu.</u> Place tofu press in a sink of cold water to chill. After about 5 minutes, unfold the cloth and gently lift out your finished cake of tofu. Serve immediately for best flavor or store in refrigerator in a tub of cold water. It is important that you change the water daily to keep the tofu fresh.

To order coagulant, write:
 Gem Cultures
 30301 Sherwood Road
 Fort Bragg, CA 95437

Diagram for construction of Tofu Box

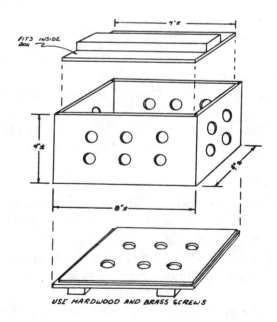

USE HARDWOOD AND BRASS SCREWS

SOYBEAN MILK

2 C dried soybeans
6 C water for soaking
12 C water
Honey
Vanilla
Nutmeg

Rinse soybeans well. Place in a large bowl with 6 cups water. Soak 8 hours or overnight. Drain well and discard water. Place half the beans in a blender with 3 cups water. Blend to a fine paste. Empty blender. Repeat with remaining soybeans; adding 3 more cups of water.

Spread 3 layers of cheese cloth over a large saucepan. Pour soybean paste into cheese cloth. Bring corners together and twist, squeezing milk from soybean paste. Add remaining 6 cups water to paste; stir and squeeze cheesecloth, again adding it to soybean milk in large saucepan. Discard paste. Bring soymilk to boil and simmer 6 min. Remove from heat. Serve hot or cold. Add honey, vanilla and nutmeg to taste.

TOFU LASAGNA

1 14-oz pkg tofu, soft
3/4 C parmesan cheese
1 1/2 C sour cream
1 tsp pwd chicken bouillon
1 26-oz can spaghetti sauce
1 pkg large flour tortilla shells
2 C grated cheese

In a large bowl, combine tofu, parmesan cheese, sour cream and bouillon; set aside.

In a 9x13 pan, make layers of spaghetti sauce, tortilla shells, and 1/3 of the tofu mixture. Sprinkle top with cheese. Continue layering until all the ingredients are used. Cover with foil. Bake at 350° for 1 hour.

MA PO TOFU

2 to 3 slices bacon, chopped
2 Tbsp minced fresh garlic
1 lb tofu (1 container)
1 qt canned tomatoes (drained)
2 dashes salt
Pepper to taste
3 to 4 green onions, chopped
2 Tbsp soy sauce
1 tsp chili with salted black
    bean*
3 large eggs, slightly beaten

Fry bacon, remove, leaving grease. Add garlic, cook few seconds then add tofu which has been chopped into small pieces. Add drained tomatoes, chop somewhat. Add salt and pepper; bring to boil. Add reserved bacon, soy sauce and bean paste. Stir well and add eggs. Simmer gently until thickened. Just before serving add the chopped green onions. Serve over rice. Makes 4-6 servings.

*The chili with salted black bean can be purchased at most oriental food stores.

SWEET AND SOUR VEGETABLES WITH TOFU

2 Tbsp cornstarch
1/2 C vinegar
1/2 C brown sugar
2 Tbsp Soy sauce, low sodium
1/4 tsp ginger
1 16-oz can crushed pineapple, undrained
1 Tbsp oil
1-2 cloves garlic, crushed
1 onion, chopped
1 large green pepper, sliced
6 large mushrooms, sliced
1 8-oz can sliced water chestnuts, drained
1 pkg frozen pea pods **or** 1 pkg frozen
    mixed vegetables
1 pkg (14 oz) firm tofu, cubed

Prepare sauce by making a paste of cornstarch and vinegar. Cook over med. heat, adding next 4 ingredients. Simmer until thick; set aside.

Heat oil and garlic in fry pan. Stir in next 5 ingredients and cook until done. Gently stir in cubed tofu and prepared sauce. Heat until warmed through. Serve over rice. Makes 6 servings.

SOY PASTA

LOW FAT

1 C soy flour
1 C all purpose flour
2 large eggs
6-8 Tbsp cold water
Flour

In a large bowl or on a work surface, combine flours into a mound. Make a well in center. Break eggs into well; add 2 Tbsp water. With a fork, beat eggs with circular motion, gradually drawing in the flour from sides of well. Add water, 1 Tbsp at a time while continuing to mix.
When dough becomes stiff, knead for 10-15 min. (This is important so noodles will be tender.) Let rest for 30 min.

With pasta machine, roll 1/4 of dough at a time to desired thickness (may use setting 5). If rolling by hand, roll as thin as possible and cut as directed on pg. 135.

SOY PASTA IN WHITE CLAM SAUCE

LOW FAT

1 10-oz can baby clams, whole
1 medium onion, chopped
1 garlic clove, minced
2 springs parsley, chopped
1/4 tsp oregano, dried
Salt to taste
Soy pasta (recipe is in this book)

Rinse baby clams, and reserve broth in can. Saute onion and garlic in few tablespoons of clam broth until softened. Add parsley, oregano, and salt. Stir well; add clams along with 1/4 cup of reserved clam broth. Simmer until heated through. Serve with soy pasta. Makes 6 servings.

LEMON AND CREAM SAUCE FOR PASTA

EXCELLENT!

1 recipe soy or all-purpose pasta
Boiling salted water
1 12-oz can evaporated milk
2 Tbsp chopped parsley
2 tsp grated lemon peel
Dash of salt
2 Tbsp butter
2 Tbsp grated Parmesan cheese

Cut fresh pasta into med-wide noodles, 10" long; cook in boiling water until done. Drain. Place evaporated milk in large fry pan over med-high heat and cook until bubbling; add parsley, lemon peel and salt; cook 1 min. Add hot noodles to cream mixture; reduce heat to low and toss gently; add butter and cheese. Toss and coat evenly. Serves 4.

TOFU SPAGHETTI SAUCE

2 Tbsp olive oil
2 cloves garlic
2 onions, diced
2 green peppers, chopped
1/2 carrot, grated
4 mushrooms, thinly sliced
2 C cooked tomatoes
2 C water
1 bay leaf
2 pkgs (24 oz) tofu, crumbled
1/2 C ketchup
3 Tbsp butter
3/4 tsp salt **or** 2-1/2 Tbsp
    soysauce
Dash of pepper
Spaghetti
1/2 C grated Parmesan cheese

In large heavy pot, heat oil; add garlic and onions. Saute 3-4 min. Add next 3 ingredients; cook 4 more min. Add tomatoes, water and bay leaf; bring to boil; simmer 15 min. Add next 5 ingredients; simmer 1 hour, stirring occasionally.

Serve over cooked spaghetti topped with Parmesan cheese.

TOFU TACOS

1 pkg (14 oz) tofu
2/3 C brown rice
1/4 C peanuts
1/2 green pepper, diced
2 cloves garlic, crushed
1/4 tsp chili powder
1/4 C ketchup
1/2 tsp salt **or** 1 Tbsp red miso
2-3 Tbsp olive oil
6 tortilla shells

Garnishes:
Chopped tomato
Minced onion
Shredded lettuce
Grated cheese

Combine first 8 ingredients in a large bowl; mash thoroughly. Heat oil in skillet and fry the tortillas. While still hot, top each cooked tortilla with cheese. Spoon on the tofu mixture and garnishes. Serve with taco sauce.

TOFU ENCHILADAS

4 tsp olive oil
2 cloves garlic, minced
1 onion, minced
1 Tbsp whole wheat flour
1-1/2 Tbsp red miso **or** 1 Tbsp shoyu
1 C water
Dash tabasco sauce
Dash white pepper
1/4 tsp oregano
2 Tbsp ketchup
6 Tbsp Parmesan cheese
1 green pepper, minced
8 oz tofu
1/2 C chopped olives
5 tortilla shells (5" round)

Heat skillet and coat with 1 tsp oil; add garlic and saute 1 min. Add 1/2 of the onion; saute 3 min. Mix in flour; stir 30 seconds, then add 1 Tbsp miso and saute 15 seconds more. Add water a little at a time, stirring constantly until smooth. Mix in next 4 ingredients and 2 Tbsp Parmesan cheese. Cover and simmer 15 min. Remove from heat and allow to cool, then mix in 2 Tbsp minced raw onion.

While sauce is cooling, heat skillet and add 1 tsp oil, green pepper and remaining onion; saute for 3 min. Stir in remaining 1-1/2 tsp miso and white pepper. Remove from heat. Combine with tofu and 2 Tbsp Parmesan cheese; mix well.

Heat oven to 350°. Pour half the sauce in small casserole dish. Dip one surface of a tortilla shell into remaining sauce, then, holding this side upward, spread with 1/5 of tofu mixture. Roll tortilla loosely and place in casserole dish. Repeat with remaining tortillas and tofu. Pour remaining sauce over tortillas and sprinkle 2 Tbsp Parmesan cheese on top. Bake 15 to 20 minutes. Makes 3 servings.

CHINESE-STYLE TOFU

4 Tbsp oil
2 tsp grated ginger root
2 tsp minced garlic
3-4 red chiles, minced
10 mushrooms, thinly sliced
6 green onions, whites thinly sliced and greens cut into 2" lengths
24 oz. firm tofu
4 Tbsp red miso mixed with 1/2 C water
2 Tbsp soy sauce
2 Tbsp honey
2 Tbsp sesame butter **or** cashew butter
1 tsp vinegar
2 tsp cornstarch dissolved in 2 Tbsp water

Heat oil in skillet; add ginger root, garlic and red chiles. Saute 2-3 min. Add mushrooms and whites of onions; saute 2-3 min. Add greens of onions and tofu cubes and saute for 1 min.

Combine miso, soy sauce, honey, cashew or sesame butter, and vinegar; mix well. Stir into above mixture and simmer for 1 min.

Stir in dissolved cornstarch and simmer for about 1 min, or until thickened. Makes 6 servings.

SESAME TOFU CASSEROLE

2 onions, diced
10 mushrooms, thinly sliced
1 large tomato, cut into thin wedges
1 tsp oil
2 C yogurt or sour cream
2 oz dried onion soup or mushroom soup
24 oz tofu cut into small cubes
2 Tbsp roasted sesame seeds

Combine first 3 ingredients; mix lightly. Layer 1/2 of mixture on bottom of lightly oiled casserole dish. Combine yogurt and dried onion soup in a bowl, mixing well. Pour 1/4 of this mixture over vegetables in casserole dish. Top with a layer of 1/2 tofu and 1 Tbsp sesame seeds. Then pour another 1/4 of yogurt mixture over tofu. Repeat layers. Bake at 350° for 30 minutes. Makes 4 servings.

WALDORF SALAD WITH TOFU

6 oz firm tofu
1 C grated carrots
1/2 C diced celery
1 C apples, diced
1/2 C raisins
1/2 C walnuts, diced
1-1/2 Tbsp Hatcho miso
1 tsp honey
1 tsp white wine
2 Tbsp sesame butter

Combine all ingredients, mixing well. Makes 4 servings.

CURRIED TOFU AND RICE SALAD

14 oz firm tofu
2 1/2 C cooked brown rice (cooled)
3 Tbsp minced green onion
2 Tbsp minced parsley
1 green pepper, chopped

Dressing:
6 Tbsp oil
1/3 C rice vinegar
1 Tbsp lemon juice
1 tsp curry powder
1/4 tsp 7-spice chili powder
1 clove garlic, crushed
3/4 tsp salt
Dash pepper
Lettuce leaves
Tomato wedges

Combine first 5 ingredients, mixing gently.

Prepare dressing by combining all ingredients. Mix lightly with the above mixture and allow to stand for several hours to mingle flavors.

Serve on lettuce leaves garnished with tomato wedges. Makes 6 servings.

TOSSED SALAD WITH TOFU

8 lettuce leaves
1 tomato cut into thin wedges
2 fresh mushrooms, thinly sliced
1 large cucumber, sliced
1 green pepper, thinly sliced
1 hard boiled egg
1/4 C French dressing
6 oz tofu, cut into small
    cubes
1/2 tsp salt
1/4 C sunflower seeds (optional)

Tear lettuce leaves into bite-sized pieces. Combine with next 5 ingredients. Add dressing and toss lightly. Add tofu cubes and season with salt; toss again. Top with sunflower seeds (if desired).
Makes 4 servings.

TOFU WITH CHICKEN

1 lb tofu
1 tsp tamari sauce
1 chicken breast, skinned and boned
1/2 C onions, chopped
1/2 C mushrooms, sliced
2 Tbsp tamari sauce

Slice tofu into 1/2" slices and place in one layer on plate. Cover tofu with another plate and weigh down with a 2-lb weight. Let stand for 30 min. and drain. Sprinkle with 1 tsp tamari sauce.

Heat a lightly oiled pan; add tofu and cook until lightly browned, about 5 min. Set aside on serving platter and keep warm. Slice chicken breasts into thin pieces and cook in lightly oiled pan until they stiffen up and lose their pink color. Add the onions and cook until onions soften. Add mushrooms and heat through. Add tamari sauce and simmer 5 min. Pour mixture over tofu slices and serve hot.
Makes 4 servings.

TOFU MEATLOAF

1 lb ground beef
2 C tofu, mashed
1 onion, minced
1/2 C celery, minced
2 Tbsp parsley, minced
1/4 tsp nutmeg
2 egg whites
1/2 C wheat germ
2 Tbsp tamari sauce

Preheat oven to 350°. Combine all ingredients; mix well and spoon into loaf pan. Bake at 350° for 1 hour. Makes 10 servings.

TOFU TUNA BAKE

1-1/4 C tofu, drained and cubed
1 7-oz can tuna, water packed, drained
3/4 C mayonnaise
2 Tbsp onion, minced
2 Tbsp lemon juice, fresh
1/2 C Cheddar cheese, grated
3 Tbsp wheat germ

Combine tuna, mayonnaise, onion, lemon juice and Cheddar cheese. Fold in tofu and place in lightly oiled casserole dish. Sprinkle with wheat germ. Bake at 350° for 45 minutes. Makes 4 servings.

CREAMY TOMATO SOUP WITH TOFU

1 C cooked brown rice
1-1/4 C milk (soy or dairy)
3/4 C water
1/2 onion, diced
2 large tomatoes, diced (can use canned tomatoes)
4 tsp shoyu **or** 1 tsp salt
Dash pepper
1/2 tsp honey
Dash of basil **or** oregano
3/4 C grated cheese
12 oz tofu, diced

Combine first 9 ingredients in a blender and puree until smooth. Transfer to a heavy pot and bring to boil; cover and simmer for 15 min, stirring occasionally. Mix in cheese and tofu; return just to a boil. Remove and serve. Makes 5 servings.

SOYBEAN SOUP

2 C dried soybeans
1 large can V-8 juice
1 small onion, chopped
1 garlic clove, mashed
2 celery stalks, chopped
2 Tbsp brewer's yeast
1/2 C Cheddar cheese, grated

Soak soybeans in 1 cup water for 1-2 hrs. Place in flat dish and freeze overnight. Drop beans into 1-1/2 cups boiling water. Cover and simmer 4 hrs. Mash soybeans with the V-8 juice (or blend in blender). Set aside. Water saute onion, garlic, and celery. Add to soup along with the brewer's yeast and cheese. Simmer 30 min. Makes 8 servings.

SOYBEAN SOUP

1 med onion, chopped
2 stalks celery, chopped
1/4 tsp garlic powder
1 C whole wheat macaroni, uncooked
4 C broth (chicken or beef)
2 C lima beans, cooked
3 Tbsp tomato paste
1 carrot, chopped
1 C soybeans, cooked
4 mushrooms, sliced
1/2 tsp salt (optional)
1/2 tsp oregano
1/4 tsp basil
3 Tbsp Parmesan cheese, grated

Saute onion and celery in few Tbsp water. Add garlic powder. Cook macaroni and set aside. Combine vegetables with broth, lima beans, and tomato paste. Simmer slowly. In blender, combine carrot, 1 cup soybeans, and broth. Blend until coarsely chopped. Add to vegetable mixture. Add mushrooms, seasonings and reserved macaroni. Heat through. Serve hot, topped with Parmesan cheese. Makes 6 servings.

CURRIED TOFU IN PITA OR POCKET BREAD

(To make bread, see recipe for Pocket Bread)

Filling:
2 Tbsp oil
2 C sliced mushrooms
2 C sliced onions
1/2 C grated carrots
2 C shredded cabbage
14 oz firm tofu, mashed (2 C)
2-1/2 Tbsp butter or margarine
2 Tbsp whole wheat flour
1 C water
1 tsp curry powder
1 tsp salt
6 pita breads (wheat or white), cut in halves

In fry pan, saute mushrooms in the oil for 2 min. Add onions and carrots and saute 2 more min. Add cabbage; saute 2 more min. Remove from heat.

Melt 2-1/2 Tbsp butter in skillet. Add flour and saute 30 seconds. Mix in curry powder and salt. Add water slowly, stirring constantly. Cook, stirring 1 min more. Combine tofu, curry mixture and fried vegetable mixture in large bowl, mix well. Heat pita bread in oven for few min. Stuff with mixture. Serve hot or cold.

HIGH PROTEIN SOY AND WHEAT BREAD

2 C soybeans
4 C lukewarm water
2 Tbsp yeast
1/2 C honey
12 C whole wheat flour
1/4 C oil
2-1/2 Tbsp salt

Soak soybeans overnight, drain and rinse. Combine half the beans and 2 cups of water in a blender; puree for about 3 min., or until smooth. Pour the puree into a large mixing bowl. Puree the remaining beans in the same way and add to the bowl together with honey, yeast, and 4 cups of flour. Using a large wooden spoon, mix for about 5 min. to form a smooth sponge. Cover bowl with moist towel and allow to stand about 40 min. in a warm place until sponge doubles in volume. Add oil and salt. Fold in about 2 cups of wheat flour at a time to form a smooth firm dough. Turn dough onto a well-floured board and knead in remaining flour. Knead 10 min. or until light and smooth. Place in large lightly oiled bowl; cover and allow to double. Punch down and rise again.

Preheat oven to 350°. On lightly-floured board, divide dough into 6 equal portions. Shape into loaves and place in greased loaf pans. Rise 10 to 15 min. Bake 40 to 50 minutes.

TOFU APPLESAUCE GRANOLA

6 oz tofu, chilled
1/4 tsp salt
1 C applesauce, chilled
1/2 C raisins
Dash of cinnamon
1/4 C crunchy granola

Mash together the tofu and salt. Mix in applesauce and raisins. Serve topped with cinnamon and granola.

JAPANESE TOFU AND EGGS

1 Tbsp oil
1 small onion, thinly sliced
1 egg, lightly beaten
6 oz tofu, thinly sliced
2 tsp shoyu (soy sauce)
1 tsp honey

Heat the oil in a skillet; add onion and saute for 3-4 min, or until transparent. Stir in remaining ingredients, cover and cook for 2-3 min. or until eggs are firm. If desired, top with grated cheese.

SCRAMBLED EGGS AND TOFU

1 Tbsp butter
6 oz firm tofu
2 eggs, lightly beaten
Salt and pepper

Melt butter in skillet; add tofu. Mash well and saute over medium heat until lightly browned. Add eggs and scramble until firm; season with salt and pepper.

If desired, saute any of the following together with the tofu: chives, alfalfa sprouts, mushrooms, green onions, green peppers, and/or season with 1/2 to 1 tsp shoyu.

TOFU TARTAR SAUCE

1 C dill pickles
8 oz tofu
4 Tbsp lemon juice
1 tsp salt
1/2 tsp hot mustard
2 hard boiled eggs
2 Tbsp diced onions
2 Tbsp minced parsley
2 Tbsp chopped green olives (optional)

Combine 1/4 cup minced pickles with next 5 ingredients and puree in a blender until smooth. Combine with remaining pickles and other ingredients. Mix well. Serve with deep fried tofu or fish.
Makes 2-1/2 cups sauce.

TOFU SESAME SHOYU DRESSING

12 oz tofu
2 Tbsp shoyu
2 tsp sesame oil
1/2 tsp honey
1-2 Tbsp green onion **or** parsley

Combine all ingredients, mashing well. Serve on tomatoes and cucumber slices.
Makes 1-1/2 cups dressing

CREAMY TOFU DIP OR DRESSING

6 oz firm tofu (2/3 C)
1-1/2 to 2 Tbsp lemon juice **or** vinegar
2-1/2 Tbsp oil
1/4 tsp salt
1 tsp shoyu **or** 1-1/2 tsp red miso

Combine all ingredients in a blender for 20 seconds. Let stand for 1/2 hour.
Season with choice of:
Avocado - Add 1 avocado mashed with few drops tabasco sauce and 2 Tbsp minced onion
Herb - Add 1/2 tsp fresh or dried herbs (oregano, marjoram, basil, etc.)
Garlic & Dill - Add 1/2 to 1 clove of garlic and 1/4 tsp dill weed
Cheese & Garlic - Add 1/4 C Parmesan or grated cheese and 1/2 clove garlic, minced.
Blue Cheese - Add 1-1/2 Tbsp lemon juice, 3 Tbsp oil, 1 Tbsp blue cheese, 1/2 clove garlic, minced, 1/2 tsp salt and 1/4 tsp fresh mustard.

TOFU MAYONNAISE

6 oz firm tofu
1-1/2-2 Tbsp lemon juice **or** vinegar
2 Tbsp oil
1/2 tsp salt

Combine all ingredients in blender and puree for 20 seconds or until smooth.

TOFU EGG SALAD

14 oz firm tofu
1/2 C celery, finely chopped
1 green onion, chopped
1/4 tsp garlic powder
1/4 C chopped red bell pepper
4 Tbsp mayonnaise (can use less)
1 Tbsp (scant) Dijon mustard
2 Tbsp brewer's yeast
1-1/2 tsp Spike seasoning (a must)

Rinse, strain and mash tofu. Add the remaining ingredients. Chill.

Can use to stuff tomatoes or avocados.
Can use as a sandwich spread.
Can add alfalfa sprouts.

LOW FAT

FRIED RICE WITH TOFU

2 cloves garlic, minced (optional)
4 Tbsp olive oil
3 eggs, beaten
14 oz tofu
1 C sliced mushrooms
1 stalk celery, chopped
1/2 C alfalfa sprouts, (optional)
4 green onions, chopped
1 green pepper, chopped
1 C peas or mixed vegetables
4 C cooked brown rice
4 Tbsp soy sauce
Pinch white pepper

In wok or large skillet, heat 2 Tbsp oil until hot. Add garlic and cook until lightly browned; reduce heat to medium. Add eggs and tofu; stir lightly until eggs are almost set. Remove from pan and set aside.

In the same pan, heat the remaining oil. Add all vegetables and stir fry about 3 min. Continue stirring while adding the egg mixture. Gradually add the soy sauce and pepper, and serve immediately.
Makes 6 servings.

Pattern for Brown Sugar Cookies

I recommend using a gallon jar
lid for the cookie cutter.

MENU PLANNING

MONTH _____ YEAR _____

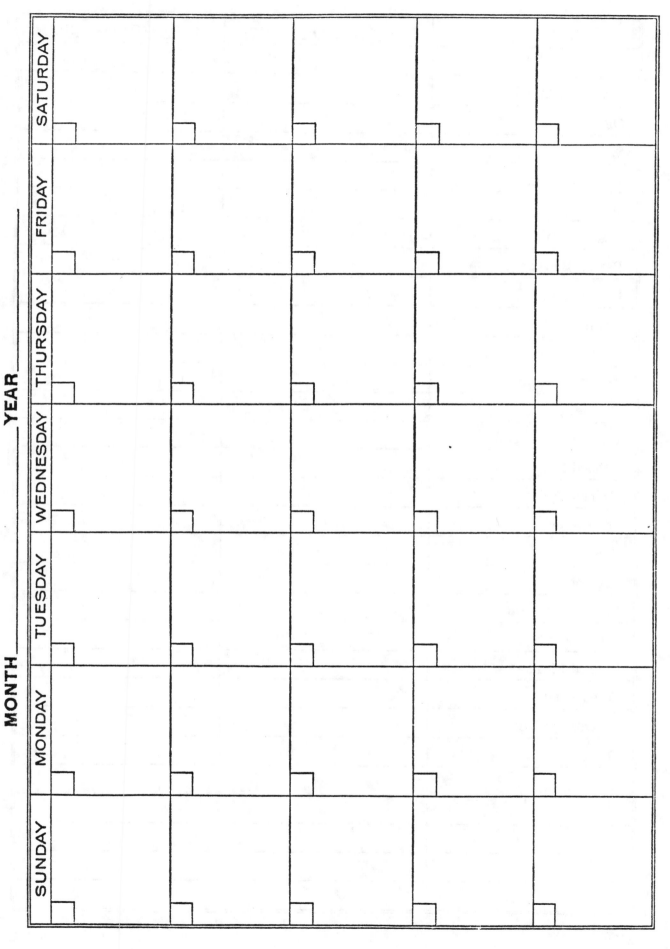

SUNDAY	MONDAY	TUESDAY	WEDNESDAY	THURSDAY	FRIDAY	SATURDAY

ITEM	STANDARD QUANTITY	DURATION/SVG SIZE
Wheat		
Powdered Milk		
Oil		
Salt		
Honey or Sugar		
Water		
Yeast		
Baking Powder		
Baking Soda		
Powdered Eggs		
Butter, powder		
Tomatoe, powder		
Cheese, powder		
Unflavored Gelatin		
Canned Milk		
Canned Fruits		
Soup Base		
Rice		
Legumes		
Beef/Chicken Broth		
Seeds (alfalfa,etc)		
Canned Meats		
Dried Potatoes		
Dehydrated Veggies		
Other:		

INDEX

A

ALFALFA
    Alfalfa Omelet (41)
    Quick Alfalfa Drink (21)
ALL PURPOSE PASTA (136)
ALL AMERICAN MOUSSE (59)
ALMOND PASTE BARS (206)
ALMOND PASTE FILLING (146)
ALMOND PASTE FRUIT ROUNDS (204)
ALMOND PEACH PIE CUSTARD (171)
ALMOND SPROUT MILK (221)
ALMONDS
    Almond Paste, How to Make (146)
    Almond Peach Pie Custard (171)
    Barley and Almond Casserole (116)
    Cheese Cake Almond Topping (182)
    Julie's Almond Chocolate Cake (174)
    Marlene's Almond Paste Sweetbread (145)
    Spiced Rice with Almonds (122)
ANCHOVY AND BEAN SALAD (49)
APPETIZERS
    Cheese Ball (110)
    Marinated Raw Mushrooms (50)
    Salmon Log (93)
APPLE FILLING (219)
APPLES
    Apple Filling For Crepes (37)
    Applesauce Custard Pie (190)
    Applesauce Mousse (60)
    Dried Apple Pie (171)
    Margaret's Applesauce Cake (185)
    Wheat Berry and Apple Salad (54)
APRICOT FRUIT COCKTAIL JELLO SALAD (57)
AVOCADO SALMON SALAD (43)

B

BABY FOODS
    Almond Milk (221)
    Baby Formula (226)
    Bread Pudding (167)
    Graham Crackers (160)
    Rice Pudding (165)
    Whole Wheat Cereal (226)
BAKED NAVY BEANS (132)
BARBECUE SAUCE (109)
BARLEY
    Baked barley (116)
    Barley and Almond Casserole (116)
    Chicken and Barley Soup (76)
    Mushroom Barley Pilaf (117)
    Pearls O'Barley Salad (54)
BASIC MIX
    Creamy Soup Base Mix (65)
    Mexican Spice Mix (125)
BASIC QUICHE (39)
BASIC YULE LOG (187)
BEAN AND CHEESE SALAD (50)
BEAN BURRITOS (127)
BEAN PIZZA (126)
BEAN SPROUT SALAD (63)
BEAN STROGANOFF (132)
BEANS
    Anchovy and Bean Salad (49)
    Bean and Cheese Salad (50)
    Bean Pizza (126)
    Complete Protein Bean and Corn Salad (51)
    Bean and Sprout Salad (63)

    Crock Pot Beans (123)
    Guadalajara Bean Soup (81)
    Irene's Wonderful Baked Beans (127)
    Marinated Bean Salad (51)
    Marlene's Favorite Chili Beans (125)
    Mixed Bean Soup With Kielbasa Sausage (79)
    Netherlands Bean and Vegetable Soup (80)
    Spam and Bean Salad (50)
    Spicy Bean Muffins (150)
    White Beans and Chicken Chili (90)
BEANS AND CASHEW SALAD (48)
BEANS, Black
    Black Beans and Rice (122), (131)

BEANS, Lima
    Ham and Lima (79)
    Lima Bean Sausage Casserole (130)
    Lima Beans and Rice (133)
    Sour Cream Limas (131)
    Wintertime Limas (134)
BEANS, Navy
    Baked Navy Beans (132)
    Crock Pot Beans (123)
    Navy Beans with Sausage (130)
BEANS, Pinto
    Bean Burritos (127)
    Bean Pizza (126)
    Bean Stroganoff (132)
    Beef and Bean Enchiladas (134)
    Chili Beans (124)
    Crock Pot Chalupa (123)
    Crock Pot Chili (124)
    Mexican Refried Beans (126)
    Pinto Bean Pecan Pie (169)
    Quick Refried Beans (125)
    Refried Beans (125)
BEANS, Soy
    Cream of Soybean (74), (81)
    Soybeans and Carrot Loaf (128)
    Soy Milk (233)
    Soybeans and Corn (128)
    Soybean Minestrone (69)
    Soybean Pasta (137), (235)
    Soybean Pie (168)
    Soybean Salad (44)
    Soybeans for Sandwiches (129)
    Soybean Sausage Patties (133)
    Soybean Souffle (133)
    Soybean and Vegetable Soup (81)
BEAR CLAWS (162)
BEEF AND BEAN ENCHILADAS (134)
BEEF, Corned
    Corned Beef Casserole (99), (107)
    Corned Beef Turnovers (98)
BEEF, Ground
    Deluxe Tamale Pie (102)
    Ground Beef Cracked Wheat Casserole (89)
    Ground Turkey and Hamburger Mixture (87)
    Hamburger and Wheat Casserole (85)
    Impossible Cheeseburger Pie (110)
    Impossible Taco Pie (109)
    Meat Turnovers (104)
    Mock Tamale Casserole (110)
    Taco Beef Soup (66)
    Tamale Pie (102)
    Tamale Pie Casserole (103)
BEEF STROGANOFF WITH NOODLES (138)

BING CHERRY AND PINEAPPLE MOLD (56)
BISCUIT MIX (212)
BLUE CHEESE YOGURT DRESSING* (62)
BLUEBERRY CRISP (190)
BLUEBERRY PUMPKIN MUFFINS (32)
BOSTON BAKED WHEAT (88)
BOSTON CLAM CHOWDER (66)
BRAN
    Maple Bran Muffins (33)
    Quick And Easy Bran Muffins (40)
    Bran English Muffins (149)
    Bran Flakes (27)
BREAD PUDDING (167)
BREADS
    100% Whole Wheat (153)
    Bread Pudding (167)
    Corn (155)
    Dilly Casserole (148)
    Ezekiel Bread (142)
    Flour Tortillas (151)
    Glazed Potato Doughnuts (147)
    High Protein Soy and Wheat (244)
    Jan's Dinner Rolls (159)
    Marlene's Never-Fail Bread (144)
    Orange Rolls (157)
    Pocket (152)
    Polish Rye (154)
    Pumpernickel (156)
    Quick Lemon Nut (156)
    Sky High Biscuits (148)
    Sourdough Rye (155)
    Sweet Rye (148)
    Wendy's Sourdough White (164)
    Zucchini (177)
BREADS, sweet
    Julie's Danish Pastries (161)
    Marlene's Almond Paste Sweet Bread (145)
    Orange Rolls (157)
BREAKFAST
    Breakfast Rice (41)
    Breakfast Treat (41)
    Homemade Cold Cereal (26)
    Sunday Breakfast (42)
BREAKFAST RICE (41)
BREAKFAST TREAT (41)
BROCCOLI
    Broccoli Soup (72)
    Broccoli Buttermilk Soup (73)
    Brown Rice with Broccoli (120)
    Meatless Rice and Broccoli Casserole (120)
    Tuna and Broccoli (95)
BROWN RICE AND SAUSAGE CASSEROLE (121)
BROWN SUGAR COOKIES (201)
BROWN SUGAR FROSTING (185)
BROWN SUGAR TOPPING (229)
BULGUR
    Bulgur Wheat (83)
    Tomato Bulgur Salad (56)
BUTTER HORNS (162)
BUTTER TARTS (173)
BUTTERMILK (220)

C
CAKES
    Basic Yule Log (187)
    Blueberry Crisp (190)
    Caramel Frosted Filbert Roll (189)
    Cheese Cake (182)

    Christmas Yule Log (188)
    Eggless Chocolate Cake (175)

    Ezekiel Applesauce Cake (142)
    Ezekiel Pound Cake (142)
    Fruit Cocktail Cake (183)
    German Plum Cake (182)
    Honey Cake (180)
    Honey Crumb Cake (35)
    Jar Fruit Cake (192)
    Julie's Almond Chocolate Cake (174)
    Lemon Yogurt Cake (186)
    Linzertorte (175)
    Madge's Oatmeal Cake (185)
    Margaret's Applesauce Cake (185)
    Margaret's Carrot Cake (183)
    Margaret's Chocolate Chiffon Cake (179)
    Marlene's Fruit Cake (184)
    Pan Honey Cake (198)
    Poppy Seed Cake (177)
    Sour Cream Chocolate Bundt Cake (182)
    Toffee Squares (202), (207)
    Warm Golden Pineapple Cheese Cake (178)
    Wheat Carrot Cake (181)
    Whole Wheat Chiffon Cake (176)
    Yogurt Breakfast Cake (35)
    Zucchini Cake (177)

CANDY
    Caramel Popcorn Balls (193)
    Christmas Fudge (194)
    Honey Candy (193)
    Honey Taffy (194)
    Peanut Butter Kisses (194)
    Sesame Bars (194)
    Sprouted Wheat (193)
    Whole Wheat Candy (192)
CANNED TOMATO COCKTAIL (216)
CARAMEL FROSTED FILBERT ROLL (189)
CARAMEL FROSTING (193)
CARAMEL POPCORN BALLS (193)
CARAWAY DRESSING (54)
CARROTS
    Creamy Carrot Soup (72)
    Copper Pennies (47)
    Curried Carrot Bisque (73)
    Curried Rice and Carrots (118)
    Margaret's Carrot Cake (183)
    Soybean and Carrot Loaf (128)
CAULIFLOWER
    Cream of Cauliflower Soup (70)
CEREAL
    Bran Flakes (27)
    Breakfast Rice (41)
    Breakfast Treat (41)
    Cooked Whole Wheat (25)
    Cracked Wheat Cereal (25)
    Granola (27)
    Granola Variety (27)
    Grape Nuts (26)
    Homemade Cold Cereal (26)
    Package Cereal (26)
    Sunday Breakfast (42)
    Wheat Pudding (28)
    Whole Wheat Cereal for Babies (226)
CHEESE
    Cheese (224)
    Cheese Ball (110)
    Cottage Cheese (214)
    Cream Cheese or Riccota (222)
    Farmer's Cheese (226)
    Mock Enchilada (111)
    Quick Soft Pressed (224)
    Yellow Cheddar (224)

CHEESE CAKE (182)
CHEESE CAKE ALMOND TOPPING (182)
CHEESE FILLING (162)
CHICKEN
  Chicken and Barley Soup (76)
  Chicken Casserole (85)
  Chicken Enchilada (90)
  Chicken Filling (99)
  Chicken Fried Steak (228)
  Chicken or Turkey Filling (97)
  Chicken Pilaf (113)
  Chicken Pot Pie (100)
  Chicken Sauce (105)
  Chicken with Rice and Raisins (114)
  Spinach Chicken with Rice (113)
  Tofu With Chicken (240)
  White Beans and Chicken Chili (90)
CHIFFON CAKE (176)
CHILI
  Chili Beans (124)
  Chili Corn Chowder (75)
  Chili Sauce (218)
  Cracked Wheat Chili (88)
  Crock Pot Chili (124)
  Marlene's Favorite Chili (124)
  White Beans and Chicken Chili (90)
CHIVE-CORN MUFFIN (42)
CHOCOLATE
  3-Layered Chocolate Bars (207)
  Chocolate Chiffon Pie (191)
  Christmas Yule Log (188)
  Delicious Best Brownies (208)
  Eggless Chocolate Cake (175)
  Miniature Chocolate Pecan Tarts (208)
  Sour Cream Chocolate Bundt Cake (181)
  Whole Wheat Brownie Mix (199)
CINNAMON TOPPING (229)
CLEAR LEMON FILLING (187)
COCOA TOPPING (229)
COLE SLAW (44)
COMPLETE PROTEIN BEAN AND CORN SALAD (51)
COOKED WHOLE WHEAT (25)
COOKED YOGURT DRESSING* (62)
COOKIES
  3-Layered Chocolate Bars (207)
  Almond Paste Bars (206)
  Almond Paste Fruit Rounds (204)
  Brown Sugar (201)
  Christmas Butter (205)
  Delicious Best Brownies (208)
  Filled Raisin (206)
  Fragile Hazelnut (203)
  Honey (196)
  Honey Wheat Peanut Butter (197)
  Iris's Ginger Snaps (198)
  Kiflings (205)
  Lebkuchen (203)
  Marshmallow and Nut Brownies (209)
  Oat and Wheat Jam Squares (199)
  Oatmeal (199)
  Orange Oatmeal (200)
  Partridge and Pears (205)
  Peanut Butter Crisscross (197)
  Pistachio Fingers (195)
  Ranger Cookies (196)
  Raspberry Hazelnut Schnitten (210)
  Raspberry Jam Circles (201)
  Snickerdoodles (200)
  Sour Cream (202)
  Springerle (209)
  Sunflower Seed (186)

Toffee Squares (202), (207)
Whole Wheat Brownie Mix (199)
Whole Wheat Peanut Butter (197)
COPPER PENNIES (47)
CORN
  Bread (155)
  Chili Corn Chowder (75)
  Chive-Corn Muffin (42)
  Corn Chowder (72)
  Shrimp and Corn Chowder (78)
  Soybeans and Corn (128)
  Spicy Corn Crisps (157)
CORNED BEEF CASSEROLE (99), (107)
CORNED BEEF TURNOVERS (98)
COTTAGE CHEESE (214)
CRAB
  Crab a la King (107)
  Crab and Artichoke Casserole (96)
  Crab and Shrimp Filling (98)
  Crab and Shrimp over English Muffins (96)
  Crab Salad in Aspic Rings (48)
  Crab Spaghetti Casserole (139)
CRACKED WHEAT CEREAL (25)
CRACKED WHEAT CHILI (88)
CRACKER
  Cracker Pie (191)
  Graham (160)
  Oat Bran Squares (159)
  Oatmeal Butter Crackers (158)
  Spicy Corn Crisps (157)
  Wheat Thins (160)
CRANBERRY
  Cranberry Dessert (176)
  Cranberry Mincemeat Pie (170)
  Cranberry Frozen Salad (57)
  Cranberry Orange Muffins (34)
CREAM CHEESE (OR RICOTTA) (222)
CREAM OF CAULIFLOWER SOUP (70)
CREAM OF SOYBEAN SOUP (74), (81)
CREAM PUFF FILLING (166)
CREAM SAUCE (212)
CREAM SOUP (211)
CREAM SOUP MIX (211)
CREAMY BROWN RICE SALAD (53)
CREAMY CARROT SOUP (72)
CREAMY DILL SAUCE (93)
CREAMY POTATO BISQUE (77)
CREAMY SOUP BASE MIX (65)
CREPE BATTER (36)
CREPES
  Apple Filling For Crepes (37)
  Basic Crepes (38)
  Chicken Filling (99)
  Crepe Batter (36)
  Salmon Souffle Crepes (39)
  Whole Wheat Crepe Batter (37)
CROCK POT BEANS (123)
CROCK POT CHALUPA (123)
CROCK POT CHICKEN (99)
CROCK POT CHILI (124)
CROCK POT CRACKED WHEAT AND LENTILS (87)
CROCK POT LENTIL SOUP (80)
CRUNCHY SALAD (63)
CRUNCHY SALMON SALAD (45)
CRUST
  Never Fail Pie (168)
  Pizza (158)
  Whole Wheat Pie (168)
CRUSTY LEMON PIE (172)
CURRIED BROWN RICE (116)
CURRIED CARROT BISQUE (73)

CURRIED CREAM OF CORN SOUP (66)
CURRIED RICE AND CARROTS (118)
CUSTARDS
        Almond Peach Pie Custard (171)

D
DELI RYE BREAD (155)
DELUXE TAMALE PIE (102)
DIET LEMON SNOW (190)
DILL PICKLES (218)
DILL SALMON SAUCE (214)
DILLY CASSEROLE BREAD (148)
DOUBLE DECKER SALMON LOAF (45)
DOUGHNUT GLAZE (147)
DRIED APPLE PIE (171)
DRESSINGS, See Salad Dressings

E
EASY SALSA (131)
EASY SWEET PICKLES (218)
EGG SUBSTITUTE (213)
EGGLESS CHOCOLATE CAKE (175)
ELEGANT CREAMY CLAM CHOWDER (67)
ENCHILADA, MOCK (111)
ENGLISH MUFFINS (31), (149)
ERWIN'S SALMON LOAF (105)
EZEKIEL BREAD (142)
EZEKIEL FLOUR (229)
EZEKIEL PANCAKES AND WAFFLES (25)
EZEKIEL POUND CAKE (142)

F
FARMER'S CHEESE (226)
FIGURE EIGHTS (162)
FILLINGS
        Almond Paste Filling (146)
        Apple Filling (219)
        Apple Filling for Crepes (37)
        Cheese Filling (162)
        Chicken Filling (99)
        Chicken or Turkey Filling (97)
        Clear Lemon Filling (187)
        Cream Puff Filling (166)
        Pineapple Filling (187)
        Raisin Filling (200)
        Sesame Sandwich Filling (153)
        Raspberry Filling (187)
FILLED NUTMEG COOKIES (206)
FLOUR TORTILLAS (151)
FOUR-GRAIN ENGLISH MUFFINS (150)
FRAGILE HAZELNUT COOKIE SANDWICHES (203)
FRENCH ONION SOUP (70)
FRESH FROZEN STRAWBERRY JAM (219)
FROSTINGS (Toppings and Glazes)
        Brown Sugar Frosting (185)
        Brown Sugar Topping (227)
        Caramel Frosting (193)
        Cheese Cake Almond Topping (182)
        Cinnamon Topping (229)
        Cocoa Topping (229)
        Glaze (33)
        Glaze, Lemon (177)
        Glaze, Doughnut (147)
        Glaze, Sugar (146)
        Honey Syrup (28)
        Marlene's Favorite Chocolate Frosting (175)
        Mocha Buttercream Frosting (188)
        Parmesan Herb Topping (147)
        Streusel (32)
        Whipped Topping (213)

FROZEN BING CHERRY SALAD (57)
FRUIT COCKTAIL CAKE (183)
FRUIT LEATHER (216)

G
GERMAN PANCAKES (29)
GERMAN PLUM CAKE (182)
GERMAN POTATO SALAD (43)
GERMAN SALAD DRESSING (61)
GLAZE (33)
GLAZED POTATO DOUGHNUTS (147)
GLUTEN (227)
GRAHAM CRACKERS (160)
GRANOLA (27)
GRANOLA, VARIETY (27)
GRAPE AND CHEESE MOLD (55)
GRAPE NUTS (26)
GREEN BEAN AND SAUSAGE SOUP (80)
GREEN CHILI PASTA (141)
GROUND TURKEY AND HAMBURGER MIXTURE (87)
GUACAMOLE (126)
GUADALAJARA BEAN SOUP (81)

H
HAM
        Ham Strata (36)
        Ham and Baby Lima Bean Soup (79)
        Ham and Fried Rice (117)
        Ham and Potato Casserole (101)
        Ham Strata (36)
        Turkey and Ham Casserole (86)
HAMBURGER AND WHEAT CASSEROLE (85)
HAMBURGER CRACKED WHEAT CASSEROLE (89)
HEALTH DRINKS
        Pineapple Juice Drink (40)
        Quick Alfalfa Drink (21)
HEARTY SPLIT PEA SOUP (79)
HINTS FOR BETTER BREAD (143)
HOMEMADE COLD CEREAL (26)
HOMEMADE PECTIN (215)
HONEY
        Honey Crumb Cake (35)
        Honey Syrup (28)
        Honey Cake (180)
        Honey Candy (193)
        Honey Crumb Cake (35)
        Honey Rice Pudding (167)
        Honey Syrup (28)
        Honey Taffy (194)
        Honey Wheat Peanut Butter Cookies (197)
        Pan Honey Cookies (198)
HOT FUDGE SAUCE (166)

I
IMPERIAL MOUSSE (171)
IMPOSSIBLE CHEESEBURGER PIE (110)
IMPOSSIBLE TACO PIE (109)
INDIAN CURRY DISH (119)
IRIS'S GINGER SNAPS (198)

J
JELLO, See Salads, Gelatin
JAM
        Fresh Frozen Strawberry (219)
JAR OF FRUIT CAKE (192)
JULIE'S ALMOND CHOCOLATE CAKE (174)
JULIE'S DANISH PASTRIES (160)

K

KAREN'S IMPOSSIBLE SALMON PIE (106)
KIFLINGS (205)
KULEBIAKU (91)

L

LEBKUCHEN (203)
LEMON GLAZE (177)
LEMON-AVOCADO DRESSING (63)
LEMON-YOGURT CAKE (186)
LENTIL
      Lentil and Brown Rice (82)
      Crock Pot Cracked Wheat and Lentils (87)
      Crock Pot Lentil Soup (80)
      Lentil Soup (70)
      Lentils over Rice (115)
      Meatless Burritos (113)
LIMA BEAN SAUSAGE CASSEROLE (130)
LIMA BEAN SOUP (69)
LIMA BEANS AND RICE (133)
LINZERTORTE (175)
LOW FAT COTTAGE CHEESE SALAD (64)

M

MACARONI AND SAUSAGE BAKE (104), (140)
MACARONI SALAD (52)
MACARONI SALMON SALAD (46)
MACARONI SHRIMP SALAD (52)
MADGE'S OATMEAL CAKE (185)
MAPLE BRAN MUFFINS (33)
MARINATED RAW MUSHROOMS (50)
MARINATED BEAN SALAD (51)
MARLENE'S ALMOND PASTE SWEET BREAD (145)
MARLENE'S FRUIT CAKE (184)
MARLENE'S NEVER-FAIL WHEAT BREAD (144)
MAYONNAISE (212)
MEAT TURNOVERS (104)
MEATLESS POTATO CASSEROLE (108)
MEATLESS RICE AND BROCCOLI CASSEROLE (120)
MEXICALI DRESSING (51)
MEXICAN REFRIED BEANS (126)
MEXICAN SPICE MIX (125)
MILK
      Almond Sprout (221)
      Baby Formula (226)
      Buttermilk (220)
      Sour (221)
      Soybean (223)
      Sweetened Condensed (220)
      Whole (220)
MILLET
      Spanish Millet Loaf (89)
MINESTRONE (68)
MIXED BEAN SOUP WITH KIELBASA SAUSAGE (79)
MOCHA BUTTER CREAM (188)
MOCK ENCHILADA (111)
MOCK PUFF PASTRY (100)
MOCK TAMALE CASSEROLE (110)
MOUSSE
      All American Mousse (59)
      Applesauce Mousse (60)
      Imperial Mousse (171)
      Wedding Coconut Lemon Mousse (58)
MUFFINS
      Apple Banana Muffins (32)
      Blueberry Pumpkin Muffins (32)
      Bran English Muffins (149)
      Chive-Corn Muffins (42)
      Cranberry Orange Muffins (34)
      English Muffins (31)

      Four Grain English Muffins (150)
      Maple Bran Muffins (33)
      Oatmeal Apple Muffins (33)
      Popovers (29)
      Poppy Seed Muffins (34)
      Quick And Easy Bran Muffins (40)
      Spicy Bean Muffins (150)
      Super-Healthy Carrot Bran Muffins (31)
MULLIGATAWNY (75)
MUSHROOMS
      Marinated Raw Mushrooms (50)
      Mushroom Barley Pilaf (117)

N

NAVY BEANS WITH SAUSAGE (130)
NECTARINE CREAM MOLD (58)
NETHERLANDS BEAN AND VEGETABLE SOUP (80)
NEVER FAIL PIE CRUST (168)

O

OATS
      Madge's Oatmeal Cake (185)
      Oat and Wheat Jam Squares (199)
      Oat Bran Squares (159)
      Oatmeal Apple Muffins (33)
      Oatmeal Butter Crackers (158)
      Oatmeal Cookies (199)
      Orange Oatmeal Cookies (200)
OMELETS
      Alfalfa Omelet (41)
ORANGE DRESSING (60)
ORANGE OATMEAL COOKIES (200)
ORANGE ROLLS (157) .
OYSTER STEW (77)

P

PACKAGE CEREAL (26)
PAN HONEY CAKE (198)
PANCAKES
      Ezekiel Pancakes (25)
      German Pancakes (29)
      Pfannkuchen (30)
      Whole Wheat Buttermilk Pancakes (28)
PARMESAN HERB TOPPING (147)
PARTRIDGE AND PEARS (205)
PASTA
      All Purpose Pasta (136)
      Beef Stroganoff with Noodles (138)
      Crab Spaghetti Casserole (139)
      Green Chili Pasta (141)
      Rye Noodle Reuben (137)
      Rye Pasta (136)
      Soy Pasta (137)
      Spam and Mushroom Spaghetti (141)
      Spinach Pasta (136)
      Triple Egg Pasta (135)
      Tuna Spaghetti Pie (139)
      Turkey Tetrazzini (140)
      Whole Wheat Pasta (136)
PASTRIES (97)
PEANUT BUTTER CRISSCROSS COOKIES (197)
PEANUT BUTTER KISSES (194)
PEAR-ADISE SALMON SALAD (48)
PEARLS O' BARLEY SALAD (54)
PFANNKÜCHEN (30)
PICKLED BEETS (219)
PICKLES
      Dill (218)
      Sweet (218)

PIES
Almond Peach Pie Custard (171)
Applesauce Custard (190)
Butter Tarts (173)
Chocolate Chiffon (191)
Cracker (191)
Cranberry Mincemeat (170)
Crusty Lemon (172)
Dried Apple (171)
Pecan Tarts (172)
Pinto Bean Pecan (169)
Pumpkin (169)
Pumpkin Pecan (170)
Soybean (168)
PILAF WITH CURRANT AND PINE NUTS (121)
PINEAPPLE FILLING (176), (187)
PINEAPPLE JUICE DRINK (40)
PINEAPPLE PECAN JELLO SALAD (58)
PINTO BEAN PECAN PIE (169)
PIZZA CRUST (158)
POCKET BREAD (152)
POLISH RYE (154)
POPOVERS (29)
POPPY SEED CAKE (177)
POPPY SEED DRESSING (61)
POPPY SEED MUFFINS (34)
PUDDINGS
Bread Pudding (167)
Easy Christmas Pudding (167)
Honey Rice Pudding (167)
Rice Pudding (165)
Rum Raisin Rice Pudding (192)
Wheat Pudding (165)
PUMPERNICKEL BREAD (156)
PUMPKIN
Blueberry Pumpkin Muffins (32)
PUMPKIN PECAN PIE (170)
PUMPKIN PIE (169)

Q
QUICHES
Basic Quiche (39)
Ham Strata (36)
Quiche Lorraine (30)
Quick Quiche Combinations (40)
QUICK ALFALFA PICKUP (21)
QUICK AND EASY BRAN MUFFINS (40)
QUICK LEMON NUT BREAD (156)
QUICK QUICHE COMBINATIONS (40)
QUICK REFRIED BEANS (125)
QUICK STEAK (225)
QUICK TUNA ANCHOVY SPREAD (153)

R
RAISIN FILLING (200)
RAISIN-FILLED HONEY COOKIES (196)
RANCH STYLE SALAD DRESSING (61)
RASPBERRY FILLING (187)
RASPBERRY JAM CIRCLES (201)
REFRIED BEANS (125)
RICE, White
Black Beans and Rice (122)
Breakfast Rice (41)
Chicken with Rice and Raisins (114)
Curried Rice and Carrots (118)
Fried Rice with Tofu (247)
Ham and Fried Rice (117)
Honey Rice Pudding (167)
Indian Curry Dish (119)
Lentils over Rice (115)
Lima Beans and Rice (133)

Meatless Burritos (113)
Meatless Rice and Broccoli Casserole (120)
Pilaf with Currant and Pine Nuts (121)
Pudding (165)
Rice and Wheat Pilaf (121)
Rice with Canned Shrimp (115)
Rum Raisin Rice Pudding (192)
Salmon and Rice (114)
Spanish Rice (12)
Spiced Rice with Almonds (122)
Spinach and Rice Casserole (119)
Spinach Chicken with Rice (113)
Shrimp, Rice, and Wheat Salad (49)
Vegetable Rice (118)
Wheat and Rice Casserole (88)
Wheat, Rice, and Tuna Salad (46)
RICE, Brown
Brown Rice and Sausage Casserole (121)
Brown Rice with Broccoli (120)
Creamy Brown Rice Salad (53)
Curried Brown Rice (116)
Lentil and Brown Rice Soup (82)
RICOTTA (ITALIAN COTTAGE CHEESE) (222)
RUM RAISIN RICE PUDDING (192)
RUSSIAN SALMON SOUP (76)
RYE NOODLE REUBEN (137)
RYE PASTA (136)

S
SALAD DRESSINGS
Blue Cheese Dressing (62)
Blue Cheese Yogurt (62)
Caraway Dressing (62)
Cooked Yogurt Dressing (62)
Creamy Tofu Dip/Dressing (246)
Curried Chicken Salad (55)
German Salad Dressing (61)
Lemon-Avocado Dressing (63)
Mexicali (51)
Orange (60)
Poppy Seed (61)
Ranch Style (61)
Salmon Louis (45)
Simple Yogurt (62)
Sweet French (60)
Vinaigrette (53)
Tofu Sesame Shoyu (246)
SALADS
Anchovy and Bean (49)
Avocado Salmon (43)
Bean and Cheese (50)
bean Sprout (63)
Beans and Cashew (48)
Cole Slaw (44)
Complete Protein Bean and Corn (51)
Copper Pennies (47)
Crab Salad in Aspic Rings (48)
Creamy Brown Rice (53)
Crunchy Salad (63)
Crunchy Salmon (45)
Curried Tofu and Rice Salad (239)
Curried Chicken Salad (55)
German Potato (43)
Low Fat Cottage Cheese (64)
Macaroni Salmon (46)
Macaroni Shrimp (52)
Marinated Bean (51)
Pear-Adise Salmon (48)
Pearls O' Barley (54)
Sesame Salad (64)
Shrimp, Rice, and Wheat (49)

Soybean (44)
Spam and Bean (50)
Tabouli (44)
Tofu Egg (247)
Tomato Bulgur (56)
Tomato Shrimp (52)
Tossed Salad with Tofu (240)
Tuna, Banana, Pineapple (49)
Waldorf Salad with Tofu (239)
Wheat Berry and Apple (54)
Wheat Berry and Mushroom (53)
Wheat, Rice, and Tuna (46)
Whole Meal (47)
SALADS, Gelatin
All American Mousse (59)
Applesauce Mousse (60)
Apricot Fruit Cocktail Jello (57)
Bing Cherry and Pineapple Mold (56)
Cranberry Frozen (57)
Double Decker Salmon Loaf (45)
Frozen Bing Cherry Salad (57)
Grape and Cheese Mold (55)
Nectarine Cream Mold (58)
Pineapple Pecan Jello (58)
Summer Tuna Mold (47)
Tomato Shrimp (52)
Wedding Coconut Lemon Mousse (58)
SALMON
Avocado Salmon Salad (43)
Double Decker Salmon Loaf (45)
Erwin's Salmon Loaf (105)
Karen's Impossible Salmon Pie (106)
Kulebiaku (91)
Macaroni Salmon (46)
Pear-Adise Salmon Salad (48)
Russian Salmon Soup (76)
Salmon Souffle Crepes (39)
Salmon and Rice (114)
Salmon Log (93)
Salmon Louis Dressing (45)
Salmon Mountain Strata (106)
Salmon Pie with Dill Sauce (94)
Salmon Souffle Crepes (39)
SALSA
Salsa, Wonderful (217)
SAUCES
BBQ Sauce (109)
Caramel Sauce (215)
Danish Cream Sauce (223)
Chicken Sauce (105)
Chili Sauce (218)
Creamy Dill (93)
Hot Fudge Sauce (166)
Dill Salmon Sauce (214)
Spaghetti Sauce (216), (228)
Strawberry Sauce (60)
Tartar Sauce (95), (214)
White Clam Sauce (235)
SAUERKRAUT AND RIB SOUP (67)
SAUERKRAUT SOUP (67)
SAVORY BAKED NOODLES (137)
SESAME BARS (194)
SESAME SALAD (64)
SESAME SANDWICH FILLING (153)
SHRIMP AND CORN CHOWDER (78)
SHRIMP AND CRAB CASSEROLE (93)
SHRIMP COCKTAIL SAUCE (215)
SHRIMP JAMBALAYA (86)
SHRIMP, RICE, AND WHEAT SALAD (49)
SIMPLE YOGURT DRESSING* (62)
SKY HIGH BISCUITS (148)

SNICKERDOODLES (200)
SOFT ICE CREAM (226)
SOUPS
Boston Clam Chowder (66)
Broccoli Buttermilk (73)
Broccoli (72)
Chicken and Barley (76)
Chili Corn Chowder (75)
Corn Chowder (72)
Cream (211)
Cream of Cauliflower (70)
Cream of Soybean (74)
Cream Soup Mix (211)
Creamy Carrot (72)
Creamy Potato Bisque (77)
Creamy Soup Base Mix (65)
Creamy Tomato with Tofu (241)
Crock Pot Lentil (80)
Curried carrot Bisque (73)
Curried Cream of Corn (66)
Elegant Creamy Clam Chowder (67)
French Onion (70)
Green Bean and Sausage (80)
Guadalajara Bean (81)
Ham and Baby Lima Bean (79)
Hearty Split Pea (79)
Lentil and Brown Rice (82)
Lentil (70)
Lima Bean (69)
Minestrone (68)
Mixed Bean Soup with Kielbasa Sausage (79)
Mulligatawny (75)
Netherlands Bean and Vegetable (80)
Oyster Stew* (77)
Russian Salmon (76)
Sauerkraut and Rib (67)
Sauerkraut (68)
Shrimp and Corn Chowder (78)
Soybean and Vegetable (81)
Soybean Minestrone (69)
Spinach (71)
Taco Beef (66)
Turkey (71)
Vegetarian Clam Chowder (78)
SOUR CREAM (222)
SOUR CREAM CHOCOLATE BUNDT CAKE (181)
SOUR CREAM COOKIES (202)
SOUR CREAM LIMAS (131)
SOUR MILK (221)
SOURDOUGH STARTER (213)
SOY MILK (233)
SOY PASTA (235)
SOYBEAN AND CARROT LOAF (128)
SOYBEAN AND VEGETABLE SOUP (81)
SOYBEAN MINESTRONE (69)
SOYBEAN PIE (168)
SOYBEAN SALAD (44)
SOYBEAN SAUSAGE PATTIES (133)
SOYBEAN SOUFFLE (132)
SOYBEANS AND CORN (128)
SOYBEANS FOR SANDWICHES (129)
SPAGHETTI SAUCE (216), (226)
SPAM AND BEAN SALAD (50)
SPAM AND MUSHROOM SPAGHETTI (141)
SPAM CASSEROLE (105)
SPANISH RICE (120)
SPANISH WHEAT (84)
SPICED RICE WITH ALMONDS (122)
SPICY BEAN CAKE (179)
SPICY BEAN MUFFIN (150)
SPICY CORN CRISPS (157)

Index 258

SPICY TOMATO CATSUP (217)
SPINACH AND RICE CASSEROLE (119)
SPINACH PASTA (136)
SPINACH SOUP (71)
SPRINGLES (209)
SPROUTED WHEAT CANDY (193)
SPROUTED WHEAT CHILI (90)
STRAWBERRY SAUCE (60)
SUGAR GLAZE (146)
SUMMER TUNA MOLD (47)
SUNDAY BREAKFAST (42)
SUPER-HEALTHY CARROT BRAN MUFFINS (31)
SWEET AND SOUR VEGETABLES WITH TOFU (101)
SWEET FRENCH DRESSING (60)
SWEET RYE BREAD (148)
SWEETENED CONDENSED MILK (220)

T

TABOULI SALAD (44)
TACO BEEF SOUP (66)
TAMALE PIE (102)
TAMALE PIE CASSEROLE (103)
TAMALE TOPPING (103)
TARTAR SAUCE (214)
TARTAR SAUCE (95)
TOFFEE SQUARES (202), (207)
TOFU
    Applesauce Granola (244)
    Chicken (240)
    Chinese-Style (238)
    Creamy Dip or Dressing (246)
    Creamy Tomato Soup (241)
    Curried in Pita or Pocket Bread (243)
    Curried Tofu and Rice Salad (239)
    Egg Salad (247)
    Enchiladas (237)
    Fried Rice with Tofu (247)
    Japanese Tofu and Eggs (245)
    Ma Po Tofu (234)
    Mayonnaise (246)
    Meat Loaf (241)
    Scrambled Eggs and Tofu (245)
    Sesame Shoyu Dressing (246)
    Sesame Tofu Casserole (238)
    Soft (226)
    Soy Pasta (235)
    Spaghetti Sauce (236)
    Sweet and Sour Vegetables (234)
    Tacos (236)
    Tartar Sauce (245)
    Tofu Lasagna (233)
    Tofu (soy cheese) (224)
    Tossed Salad with Tofu (240)
    Tuna Bake (241)
    Waldorf Salad (239)
TOMATO BULGUR SALAD (56)
TOMATO SHRIMP SALAD (52)
TOPPINGS, See Frostings
TORTILLA, Flour (151)
TRIPLE EGG PASTA (135)
TUNA AND BROCCOLI (95)
TUNA CASSEROLE (95)
TUNA OR SALMON PATTIES (94)
TUNA SPAGHETTI PIE (139)
TUNA, BANANA, PINEAPPLE SALAD (49)
TURKEY AND HAM CASSEROLE (86)
TURKEY SOUP (71)
TURKEY TETRAZZINI (140)

V

VEGETABLE RICE (118)
VEGETARIAN CHOWDER (78)

VINAIGRETTE DRESSING (53)

W

WAFFLES (29)
    Waffles (29)
    Ezekiel Waffles (25)
WARM GOLDEN PINEAPPLE CHEESE CAKE (178)
WEDDING COCONUT LEMON MOUSSE (58)
WHEAT
    Boston Baked Wheat (88)
    Bulgur Wheat (83)
    Cooked Whole Wheat (25)
    Cracked Wheat Cereal (25)
    Ground Beef Cracked Wheat Casserole (89)
    Spanish Wheat (84)
    Wheat and Rice Casserole (88)
    Wheat Berry and Apple Salad (54)
    Wheat Berry and Mushroom Salad (53)
    Wheat Carrot Cake (181)
    Wheat Chili, Cracked (88)
    Wheat Pudding (165)
    Wheat, Rice and Tuna Salad (46)
    Wheat Sprout Patties (89)
    Wheat Thins (160)
    Whole Wheat Buttermilk Pancakes (28)
    Whole Wheat Crepe Batter (37)
WHIPPED TOPPING (213)
WHITE BEANS AND CHICKEN CHILI (90)
WHITE SAUCE (211)
WHITE SAUCE MIX (211)
WHOLE MEAL SALAD (47)
WHOLE MILK (220)
WHOLE WHEAT BREAD (153)
WHOLE WHEAT BROWNIE MIX (199)
WHOLE WHEAT BUTTERMILK PANCAKES (28)
WHOLE WHEAT CANDY (192)
WHOLE WHEAT CEREAL FOR BABIES (224)
WHOLE WHEAT CHEESE BAKE (85)
WHOLE WHEAT CHIFFON CAKE (176)
WHOLE WHEAT, Cooked (25)
WHOLE WHEAT CREAM PUFFS (166)
WHOLE WHEAT CREPE BATTER (37)
WHOLE WHEAT PASTA (136)
WHOLE WHEAT PEANUT BUTTER COOKIES (197)
WHOLE WHEAT PIE CRUST (168)
WINTERTIME LIMAS (134)
WONDERFUL SALSA (217)

Y

YOGURT (221)
    Yogurt Breakfast Cake (35)
YOGURT BREAKFAST CAKE (35)

Z

ZUCCHINI CAKE (177)

For information regarding this book, its recipes, or
large group demonstrations and lectures
please visit our website:

www.MarlenesMagic.com